Q-SHIPS VERSUS U-BOATS

Q-SHIPS
VERSUS
U-BOATS
America's Secret Project

Kenneth M. Beyer

NAVAL INSTITUTE PRESS
ANNAPOLIS, MARYLAND

Library of Congress Cataloging-in-Publication Data
Beyer, Kenneth M., 1920–
    Q-ships versus U-boats : American's secret project / Kenneth M.
Beyer.
      p. cm.
    Includes bibliographical references (p. 229) and index.
    ISBN 1-55750-044-4 (alk. paper)
    1. Atik (Q-ship) 2. Asterion (Q-ship) 3. World War, 1939–1945—
Naval operations, American. 4. Q-ships. 5. World War, 1939–1945—
Naval operations—Submarine. 6. World War, 1939–1945—Naval
operations, German.   I. Title.
D783.B49 1999
940.4'51373—dc21   98-53195

Printed in the United States of America on acid-free paper ∞
06 05 04 03 02 01 00 99 9 8 7 6 5 4 3 2
First printing

Frontispiece: top, USS *Asterion,* photographed 12 May 1942 by a
U.S. Navy blimp in the Straits of Florida (U.S. Coast Guard); *bottom,*
U-123, photographed on or about 12 May 1942 in Kiel, Germany
(Reinhard Hardegen/Sharkhunters International, Inc.).

To Rear Admiral Edward Flood Beyer, USNR, Retired
My father, a master of ships and seas

Edward Flood Beyer Jr.
His son and my brother, an inspiration

Captain Kirk Crothers Miller Jr., USN, Retired
A destroyer man; true blue and gold

The officers and men of USS *Atik*/SS *Carolyn*
All killed in action

My shipmates in USS *Asterion*/SS *Evelyn*
They carried on

Fähnrich zur See Rudolf Holzer, Kriegsmarine, U-123
Killed in action

Contents

Foreword, by Dean C. Allard   *ix*

Preface   *xiii*

Acknowledgments   *xv*

Introduction   *xix*

1
Looking toward the Unknown   *1*

2
America's Awakening: Project LQ   *10*

3
Operation Drumbeat   *19*

4
Carolyn and *Evelyn:* The Ships and the Men   *37*

5
Getting Under Way   *58*

6
Advancing toward Destiny   *70*

7
The Mystery of the Mystery Ship   *82*

8
The Search for the Unknown   *114*

9

Confrontation   *133*

10

The Game Is Over   *178*

Appendix 1

Ship's Roster (Enlisted Men), USS *Atik*/SS *Carolyn*   *207*

Appendix 2

Precommissioning Detail (Key Petty Officers),
USS *Atik* (AK101)   *209*

Appendix 3

Ship's Roster (Enlisted Men), USS *Asterion*/SS *Evelyn*   *211*

Appendix 4

Precommissioning Detail (Officers and Key Petty Officers),
USS *Asterion* (AK100)   *215*

Notes   *217*

Bibliography   *229*

Index   *233*

Foreword

Q-Ships versus U-Boats describes a desperate attempt by the U.S. Navy
to counter the blitz waged by German U-boats off the Eastern American
Seaboard in World War II. One response to this threat was the decision by
American naval officials in January 1942 to convert and deploy vessels
known as Q-ships. More than two decades earlier, Britain's Royal Navy
created these "mystery" ships as part of its effort to defeat the German
submarine assault on Allied mercantile fleets during the First World War.
Q-ships were small but well-armed warships disguised as merchantmen.
Naval leaders hoped that these apparently inconsequential units would
entice an enemy submarine to surface and come close alongside its prey.
At that point Q-ship crews planned to expose their armament and, if all
went well, destroy a surprised U-boat.

The American Q-ships discussed in this book are USS *Atik* (formerly
the merchantman *Carolyn*) and USS *Asterion* (the former SS *Evelyn*).
The author, Kenneth Beyer, was the supply officer in the latter vessel.
Since both mystery ships were converted simultaneously in the Navy Yard
at Portsmouth, New Hampshire, their crews came to know each other.
Atik and *Asterion* departed from Portsmouth on the same winter day in
March 1942. As they undertook their hazardous efforts to attract German
submarines, the Q-ships did not operate within visual range of each other.
Nevertheless, Captain Beyer's account of the operations of both *Atik* and
Asterion has an authenticity deriving from his personal experience on
board one of those ships. The vividness of the author's account is rein-
forced by his deep understanding of the sea and of the U.S. Navy gained
as a member of a seagoing family and later as a career naval officer.

Over and above his personal testimony, Kenneth Beyer's book is based on meticulous research in the records, books, and other sources relating to his subject. Despite the secrecy surrounding the Q-ship project, the author located many pertinent documents in the U.S. Navy's official files. These sources are supplemented by personal interviews and by correspondence with participants or with members of their families that bring to life many individual players in this drama. Moreover, Captain Beyer made extensive use of German records, notably the logs of individual U-boats. The author gives an especially full account of U-123 and its commander, Reinhard Hardegen, whom the author interviewed many years later in Germany. The mutual respect that developed between Beyer and Hardegen, despite the deadly game they played in 1942, is an example of the sense of brotherhood that opposing warriors can develop for each other.

A highlight of this book is a discussion of the tragic fate of USS *Atik*, which went down with all hands only a few days into her first war cruise. Since there were no survivors, we will never know exactly what happened on board *Atik*. But Captain Beyer is in an excellent position to speculate on the events that engulfed the ship's crew as their ship was sunk. He also makes ingenious use of German sources to give a historical picture of events on the enemy's side. The author's argument that both U-123 and U-105 participated in the destruction of *Atik* is a new and fascinating contribution to our knowledge about the probable fate of that vessel.

Americans sometimes have a tendency to make their enemies ten feet tall. That inclination is evident in much of the literature describing the German submarine campaign off the East Coast during the first half of 1942. Captain Beyer acknowledges that German submarines wrought great destruction. But he also observes that some German torpedoes were defective, that submarine crews made navigational errors, and that there were marked variations in the ability of individual commanders. Captain Beyer notes that the wary Reinhard Hardegen stands out among the German commanders because of his effectiveness. Hardegen's U-123 was one of the few submarines sinking enough tonnage to justify Germany's hope of seizing victory by denying to the Allies the vital seaborne logistics they required.

Above all, this history is a tribute to the brave men who gave up their lives in *Atik*. Captain Beyer also credits the valor of all the other individuals associated with the Q-ship effort. The author's admirable loyalty to the victims and survivors of that campaign is demonstrated by the years of effort he invested in researching and writing *Q-Ships versus U-Boats*. Q-ship families can now join with naval veterans, historians, and everyone else interested in the history of the great sea war of 1939–45 in thanking Kenneth M. Beyer for his outstanding contribution.

Dean C. Allard
Former director of naval history, U.S. Navy

Preface

THE REAL WAR WILL NEVER GET INTO THE BOOKS.

Walt Whitman, "The Real War"

This story is about ships—the mystery ships USS *Atik* and USS *Asterion*, the secret Q-ships of the U.S. Navy; the intrusive U-boats, the deadly submarines of Hitler's navy; and the attacks that took place along the U.S. Atlantic Coast in the early months after the United States entered World War II—and about the people who, in the line of duty, lived and died aboard those ships.

It is a story that must be told. Why? Because it happened, and because 140 brave men gave their lives in the performance of this historical drama. But this is not the story of what actually happened, for exactly what happened is not known—will never be known. It is the story of what probably happened. It is not, however, fiction. It is based on actual events. Reasonable conjecture, plus my firsthand knowledge of USS *Atik*/SS *Carolyn* and the men who served aboard her, formed the foundation for my conclusions.

This is the story of Project LQ, implemented in the Office of the Chief of Naval Operations, Washington, D.C. It is about two mystery ships—the Q-ships USS *Asterion* and USS *Atik*—employed as decoys in the battle against the German submarines, the U-boats, in the early months of 1942. The project was directed by President Franklin D. Roosevelt. It was classified Secret. The ships involved were manned by volunteers of the U.S. Navy and the U.S. Naval Reserve.

The narrative is also about the enemy, the German U-boat command and the U-boats, especially U-123, U-105, and U-552, that menaced Allied shipping along the East Coast of the United States shortly after war was declared by Hitler's Germany. Careful translation of logbooks and numerous discussions with former U-boat commanders have provided the details for this segment of the story.

Project LQ was real. The enemy was real. The heroism of the players in this drama was real, especially the valor of those Americans and Germans who, in the line of duty, gave their lives. My primary objective in writing this work is to recognize the courage of the volunteers who went to sea when duty called. Many never returned.

Acknowledgments

Astounding to me were the number of persons contributing to the writing of this book. While I put pen to paper and fingertips to keyboard, many others responded to my needs. I am eager to recognize them, for I could not have completed this work without their help. For that and their friendship I am sincerely grateful.

My brother, Edward F. Beyer Jr., prodded me over the years to write the first draft of "LQ." I regret that he did not live to see the finished work. Dr. Michael Gannon, professor of history at the University of Florida and author of *Operation Drumbeat*, provided me with material from his files and introduced me to Reinhard Hardegen, the commander of U-123. Reinhard Hardegen, as a Kapitänleutnant in 1942 and commander of U-123, plays a significant role in this story. His friendship, correspondence, and interviews permitted me to recognize the high character and integrity of this former adversary. Horst v. Schroeter, Vizeadmiral A.D., Bundesmarine (FGN Retired), through his generous correspondence offered information on the attack by U-123 on *Carolyn/Atik*. Mr. Fred N. Geils, now deceased, former U-boater, painstakingly sat with me and translated numerous pages of German documents. Dr. Hans-Georg Hess, former commander of U-995, now a prominent lawyer, walked me through his boat, which is on display at Laboe, near Kiel, Germany. His wife, Heilwig, graciously played hostess during my visit to Hannover and Idensen, Germany.

Cdr. Roger C. Metz, U.S. Navy (Retired), now deceased, shared with me his recollections of life aboard *Evelyn/Asterion*. Mrs. Kathleen Lloyd and Mr. Bernard F. Cavalcante at the Naval Historical Center,

Washington, D.C., were most considerate and accommodating. Dr. Jürgen Rohwer at the Library of Contemporary History, Stuttgart, provided pertinent data for which I am grateful. Capt. Robert W. Landfair, SC, USN (Retired), and his wife, Patricia, were my "sounding board" throughout this work. Horst Bredow of the U-Boot Archiv, Stiftung Traditionsarchiv Underseeboote, in Cuxhaven-Altenbruch, Germany, was most helpful in providing photographs and information. Ms. Yvonne Parker at the U.S. Naval Academy Alumni Association assisted me in obtaining photographs of the academy graduates. Dr. Stephen E. Ambrose, professor of history and author, offered reassuring comments and encouragement. Dr. Damon B. Delston, son of Lt. Daniel Deckelman who was lost in USS *Atik*, shared his recollections of what it was like to grow up with little knowledge of his father. Ms. Dolores M. Ouellette, niece of Armand Ouellette, forwarded to me copies of pertinent correspondence concerning her uncle. Col. Gary L. Kosmider, U.S. Army (Retired), USMA, 1958, son of Chief Yeoman Daniel Kosmider, kindly offered me personal papers regarding his father. Dr. R. M. Browning Jr., historian, U.S. Coast Guard, Washington, D.C., obtained for me the only photograph taken of USS *Asterion* in her SS *Evelyn* Q-ship camouflage. He also researched and provided me with data on SS *San Jose* and SS *Brazos*. *Semper paratus.* Mrs. Betsy Miles at the Naval Surface Weapons Center, Dahlgren, assisted me in locating technical data on depth charges.

Others who played a significant role in producing this work were Dr. Dean E. Allard, the former director of naval history, U.S. Navy Department, whose gentle persuasion encouraged me to record the details of Project LQ; Ms. Ann Happ clarified the intricacies of computer documentation; Mr. Paul Wilderson, executive editor, Naval Institute Press, patiently directed me through the preparation and publication phases of the book. And lastly, I must turn to my family. Son, Kevin, an avid and enthusiastic reader, was most helpful with his reviews and comments. His critiques were useful. Daughter, Lisa, bent on psychology, provided her evaluations of my analysis of the principal characters in the story. Wife, Bobbie (Barbara), who was suspicious of my assignment during our periodic courting days in 1942, shared my strong desire to tell this story. She

Acknowledgments

was the confrere for serious deliberations. She always used sound and considerate judgment during my periods of intense writing when solitude was paramount. She tolerated my idiosyncrasies. I am eternally grateful to all.

Introduction

The notion of using submarine decoy ships, or Q-ships, during World
War II is attributed to President Franklin D. Roosevelt. However, the concept originated in England in World War I when Winston Churchill was
first lord of the admiralty. Early in 1915 the unrestricted sinking of British
and French merchant ships by German submarines began. By the end
of March, some 45 ships totaling 130,000 tons had been sunk. On 7 May
1915 *Lusitania* was attacked by U-20 (commanded by Walter Schwieger).
The monthly sinkings increased astoundingly, peaking in April 1917 at
413 ships and 860,000 tons. The arming of merchant ships and coastal
craft was the first defensive step taken to counter the U-boat menace.

Queenstown, renamed Cobh in 1922, became the admiralty's central
point of antisubmarine operations. Merchant ships were armed. Yachts,
trawlers, coastal steamers, and sailing vessels were armed, some with navy
gun crews, and sent on patrol. From this auxiliary patrol the idea of the
"mystery ship," or "decoy ship," evolved. The steamship SS *Antwerp* was
fitted out with concealed weapons and commissioned as a decoy ship
with Cdr. G. Herbert, DSO, RN, in command. *Antwerp* had all the outward appearance of a merchantman. She flew the flag and displayed the
markings of a neutral country. The objective was to lure the unsuspect-
ing submarine to the surface and destroy it at close range with superior
firepower. Additional decoy ships were commissioned, and a number,
with a Q prefix for Queenstown, was assigned to each.

The degree of success of the Q-ship as an antisubmarine weapon in
World War I is difficult to measure. British and German records differ.
V. E. Tarrant, in his book *The U-Boat Offensive, 1914–1945*, writing about
Q-ships in World War I, states, "More than 180 ships were so fitted

throughout the course of the war and they accounted for eleven U-boats in all, but at the disproportionate cost of 27 of their own number." Contrasting data are provided by E. Keble Chatterton in his book *Q-Ships and Their Story*. Chatterton reports nineteen U-boats were sunk by Q-ships, and "there were close upon eighty steamers and sailing craft either being fitted out as decoys or already thus employed." More information on the history of Q-ships can be found in the article "U.S. Navy Mystery Ships" by Edward F. Beyer and Kenneth M. Beyer.

Q-SHIPS VERSUS U-BOATS

1

Looking toward the Unknown

THIS ASSIGNMENT IS CONSIDERED HAZARDOUS
SEA DUTY. YOU ARE ASKED TO VOLUNTEER.

> Cdr. William J. Carter, Office of the Chief
> of the Bureau of Supplies and Accounts,
> Navy Department, Washington, D.C.,
> February 1942

"MR. BEYER, SIR, Commander Clark would like to see you in his office."
That simple request actively involved me in the story being told. Cdr. A. B.
Clark was the supply officer of the new battleship USS *North Carolina*
(BB55). I was a naval reserve ensign on duty in the ship for training. *North
Carolina* on that day, 4 February 1942, had returned to the Brooklyn
Navy Yard from a very successful battle practice with her sister ship, USS
Washington (BB56). These two fast battleships were America's first mod-
ern big-gun platforms since *West Virginia* was laid down in 1920. Presi-
dent Roosevelt had promised Prime Minister Churchill that he would
deploy *North Carolina* and *Washington* to the eastern Atlantic to augment
the British home fleet for a period of time before sending them to the
Pacific. Indeed, these two ships were valuable assets to the Allied war
effort. Deployment was imminent.[1]

I acknowledged the summons and proceeded to Commander Clark's
office, which was in the adjoining compartment. "You wish to see me,
Commander?" His response was right to the point: "Yes, Kenneth, I have

a set of orders for you. I don't know why the urgency, but you are to be in Washington today. It's eleven o'clock, you don't have much time. I know you must be as surprised as I am." Indeed, I was surprised and said so. Clark continued, "Well, you have done a fine job here. We shall all miss you. You had better hurry along and get packed." I thanked the commander and told him how much I appreciated what he and Lieutenant Watts had done to train me to be a naval officer.[2]

Lt. (jg) William Parks Watts, a graduate of the naval academy, class of 1938, was my division officer, my mentor, and my good friend. He guided me through my first active duty tour on the newest and "hottest" capital ship in the U.S. Navy, the "Showboat": spit and polish, spotless uniforms, shining gold braid, tradition and regulation, gloves and swords, social and military etiquette, calls made and returned, calling cards, and performance short of excellence unacceptable. Indeed, the term "officer and gentleman" was personified in the officers of USS *North Carolina*. I was so pleased and proud to become one of them. Bill taught me the drills and guided me through navy regulations, the Uniform Code of Military Justice, the many manuals and instructions pertaining to the logistics and financial business of naval ships, and naval etiquette and tradition. I became a part of it. He even introduced me to the young lady I hoped to marry someday. It was not easy to say good-bye to Bill.

Nor was it easy to say good-bye to "Carie," as the ship was affectionately called by those who knew her. At 1515 hours, with orders in my pocket, my personal gear waiting near the taxi on the dock at the foot of the forward gangway, and a tear in each eye, I saluted the officer-of-the-deck: "I have been detached and am carrying out my orders, sir." "Good luck and fair sailing, Ensign Beyer" were the OD's parting words as he, Commander Clark, and Lieutenant Watts all returned my salute. I faced aft from the quarter deck, saluted the colors, and bid farewell to "Carie."

My orders, dated 2 February 1942, were brief: "You are hereby detached from duty on board the USS *North Carolina* and from such other duty as may have been assigned you; you will proceed to Washington, D.C., and not later than February 4, 1942, report to the Chief of the Bureau of Supplies and Accounts, Navy Department, for duty." As I rode from the Brooklyn Navy Yard to Manhattan and Pennsylvania Station, I tried not to look back to where I had been but to look forward to the unknown, to whatever the navy had in mind for me. I certainly had no idea, and trying to second-guess the navy was a futile exercise. It was a long and anxious ride on the Pennsylvania Railroad to Union Station in Washington. It was 2030 when I reported to the Navy Department duty officer at Main Navy on Constitution Avenue. He date-stamped my orders and kept a copy. He advised me to return the next day at 0800 and gave me directions to the office of Admiral Spear, located in a temporary building across the Reflecting Pool and at the corner of 17th Street and Independence Avenue. By luck I found sleeping accommodations at the Army-Navy Club on 17th Street at Farragut Square. I rested in the welcome solitude of my room and mulled over the events of the day. I fell asleep wondering, what in the world am I doing here in Washington?[3]

Thursday, 5 February 1942, determined the course of future events, favorable for one, unfavorable for another. A few minutes before 0800 that morning I presented myself and my orders to a lieutenant seated in the outer office of Adm. Ray Spear. He invited me to sit in a reception area across from his desk. With my orders in his hand, he vanished into the inner sanctum of the admiral's suite of offices. At about that time, another lieutenant entered the office from the main corridor, looked around, and proceeded to take off his gloves and overcoat. I stood up, introduced myself, and told him a lieutenant should return soon to take his orders. We shook hands and he said his name was Ed Joyce. As we sat, he said he knew a Captain Beyer with the United Fruit Steamship Company and asked if we were related. I said, yes, that was my father. Then I asked him if he was related to Doctor Joyce, the senior medical officer of the Fruit Company. He said, yes, he was Doctor Joyce's son. The lieutenant returned and Joyce handed him his orders. The lieutenant said we were expected and that Lieutenant Commander Honaker would take us both in tow.

Salty language, I thought, for a bureaucrat, but it was encouraging to know we were expected. Ed Joyce and I continued our conversation as we waited. Ed said he had been a ship's officer with United Fruit Company for six years until called to active duty in the navy. At the time he received orders to Washington, he was at the Brooklyn Navy Yard. He had been married for a year and didn't know what to tell his bride about whether to stay in New York or accompany him to Washington. I told Ed that I, too, had been with the company, but only for a year when called to active duty. Our oral résumés were cut short when Lieutenant Commander Honaker entered, introduced himself, and ushered us into a nearby conference room. There we met Cdr. W. J. Carter. We were served coffee and invited to a seat at the conference table. My first thought was that if this was the way navy ensigns were treated, it had to be a great navy. The euphoria did not last long.

Commander Carter was quick to tell us why we were there. The navy had undertaken a program that by its very nature was highly sensitive and for security purposes, classified Secret. Within the Navy Department, the program had been termed Project LQ, and it was known to only those personnel directly involved. He paused and then said we were both selected because of our background and character. Then he added that the assignment was considered hazardous sea duty and we were asked to volunteer. He said that if we declined the assignment, there would be no mention of the meeting in our official record. He requested that as he explained the details, Ed or I stop him if either one of us decided not to participate.

There were neither threats nor coercion in Carter's remarks. While he offered no encomium for the project, he emphasized its importance to the immediate war effort, the involvement of the president, and the need for such officers as ourselves to manage the unusual logistics necessary to obscure the true mission of the operation. The commander continued his explanation, providing more specifics as to the tasks intended for us: "There will be two heavily armed merchant-type ships. They will be freighter configuration and have sizable navy crews. All personnel will be specially selected. The ships will operate as disguised merchantmen, U-boat decoys, or Q-ships as the British called them. You will be responsible for the logistics and finances for the ship to which assigned and, of course, any other duties assigned by your commanding officer."

At this point Commander Carter paused. As neither Joyce nor I reacted negatively, he continued his briefing in more detail:

The officers and crew will wear civilian clothes at all times, merchant marine type. You, no doubt, will have to buy the clothing with your ship's funds. Each of you will be designated "treasurer" of a bogus company and will have a revolving account at Riggs National Bank here in Washington. Accounting for all funds will be simple, but important. You will have written procedures to guide you. Both ships are being converted and outfitted at the Navy Yard in Portsmouth, New Hampshire. One ship is named USS *Asterion* (AK100) and the other USS *Atik* (AK101). *Asterion* is scheduled to deploy a week before *Atik*. That is a brief outline of the program. You may decline at this point.

Both Joyce and I agreed to the assignment. We asked a few questions regarding the selection of the commanding officers and the other line officers, and if the ports we would enter for fueling and other logistics would be only U.S. ports. Lieutenant Commander Honaker replied that we would have an opportunity later in the day to discuss such matters and to review the written procedures. He said he would take us to Riggs Bank to meet its president and to arrange for our accounts.

Commander Carter asked Lieutenant (jg) Joyce, the senior of us, if he had a choice of ship. Ed said he really didn't care but would take the first to leave Portsmouth. I, intending to be considerate rather than gallant, challenged Joyce's statement: "Commander, Lieutenant Joyce has been married only a year. I am single. I believe it both fair and reasonable that I take the first ship." Honaker ended the debate before it progressed further: "Beyer goes to *Asterion*; Joyce to *Atik*."

As if on cue, Rear Admiral Spear entered the room and we were introduced. He was a tall, thin man, with a rather stern face but a most pleasant personality. He remained standing, as we did, and addressed Joyce and me: "Have you gentlemen been briefed on this project and have you accepted the assignment? I assure you both there will be no demerits in your record if you decline. This is a most important and unusual task, and it is not without its dangers." Commander Carter answered the admiral's question. Spear's face softened as he continued his remarks: "You officers are special. I have personally discussed the project and the selection of officers with Admiral Horne, the vice chief of naval operations. He assured me that all personnel have been very carefully picked. Now, if there is anything you need, just ask for it. If I were a young man, I would gladly take your place. Good luck, gentlemen." As the admiral departed, I thought to myself—Admiral, there is no age limit to this duty that I know of.

Honaker, Joyce, and I walked the short distance to 15th Street and Pennsylvania Avenue to Riggs Bank. Robert V. Fleming, the bank president, a short, stocky, and amiable man, greeted us warmly. Fleming said he would set up two accounts and have checkbooks prepared: Asterion Shipping Company, K. M. Beyer, treasurer; Atik Shipping Company, E. T. Joyce, treasurer. We signed signature specimen cards, and our work at Riggs was completed. Honaker mentioned that it would be a week before a treasury check would be delivered for deposit in the project's master account under the names of Horne and Farber, Vice Adm. Frederick Horne and his assistant, Rear Adm. William S. Farber. At that time one hundred thousand dollars would be transferred to each of the two company accounts. Our tasks for this day were done. Honaker asked us to return to his office at 1000 the next day to receive our written instructions for conducting the financial affairs of the "company."

Friday, 6 February, was a bright but cold day in Washington. Commanders Carter and Honaker once again met with Joyce and me. We were given three typewritten pages of procedures. The sheets were onion skin copies, no letterhead, no watermark, and no signature. The instructions were simple and succinct. In essence there were no navy forms and none of the specified reports required by navy ships in commission. We would maintain a simple ledger, pay invoices by check, and make a monthly financial summary report in code to Honaker's office. "Well, gentlemen," Honaker said, "you can now throw your navy regulations and your supply manuals over the side." I did just that, literally, some two months later.

Clearly, the instructions were intended to give Ed Joyce and me complete flexibility. There were no restrictions. Concurrence by our respective commanding officer was the only authorization needed for the expenditure of funds. It was apparent, too, that these ships and their operations would be completely divorced from traditional naval operations. This point became abundantly clear during Honaker's final remarks: "For

Q-SHIPS VERSUS U-BOATS

the purpose of communicating with family and friends, you have been assigned to these navy cargo ships; but remember, their true mission is classified Secret and shall not be discussed with anyone not officially involved in the project and then only on a need-to-know basis. You must be very careful, and I urge you both while on this assignment to limit your contacts with inquisitive friends both inside and outside the navy."

Later, as I thought about Honaker's admonition, I began to realize some of the peculiarities of this assignment. I had to change my customary mode of conduct from a proud young naval officer aboard a mighty man-o'-war, the battleship USS *North Carolina*, to a proud young officer aboard a navy cargo ship. And even then, I would have to concoct or fabricate a contrived mission for this cargo ship that wasn't a cargo ship at all. Did this mean I would have to learn to lie with a straight face? The nuns in parochial school and my mother had taught me differently! The image of being an "officer and a gentleman" was beginning to erode with this new assignment. C'est la guerre.

My visit to Washington was nearly over. The meetings, the instructions, and the commitment were completed. But my written, official orders that would send me to Portsmouth and USS *Asterion* would not be ready until the next day, Saturday morning. Ed's orders were available and he departed, first for New York and a visit with his bride, and then to Portsmouth. I was not unaware of the perilous nature of the mission or even the uncertainty of survival. I needed a mental diversion. The young lady to whom Bill Watts had introduced me attended school in Washington. By chance, I had her telephone number in my little black book. I called Abbott's Art School on Connecticut Avenue and talked with Miss Barbara Hemphill. She happened to be available for lunch, a movie matinee, dinner, and the theater. It was a most enjoyable diversion. I kept my secret and concluded that duty in Washington was just grand.

Saturday was a busy day. I picked up my orders, phoned my mother at home on Shore Road in Brooklyn, advised her of my change of duty, and said I would be there midafternoon. I boarded a Pennsylvania "clocker" once again and arrived home on schedule. Here I was put to the test of my "fabricated" mission. This would be the true inquisition.

Mine was a family that loved the sea, ships, and the navy. Our top-floor apartment in Bay Ridge overlooked the Narrows and was across from the quarantine station on Staten Island. In 1938 and 1939 it was not unusual to see such superliners as *America, Queen Mary, Rex, Bremen, Europa, Normandie,* and others pass below our apartment windows. My father, a naval reserve commander and senior master with the United Fruit Steamship Company, was called to active duty on 23 January 1942, along with his ship, SS *Pastores,* and its entire crew. She became USS *Pastores* (AF16) when commissioned. He later commanded an APA and retired after the war with the rank of rear admiral, USNR. My mother was the beacon that summoned us all home. She chased the ships; established our homes, New Orleans, San Francisco, and New York; raised three children; and was loved by all. My brother, Ed, three years my senior, draft deferred because of an old injury, was a graduate of Leland Stanford University and a manager with Sperry Gyroscope Company. He wanted a navy commission and would negotiate, unsuccessfully, with 90 Church Street each month. This only intensified his interest in his father's and brother's activities. My sister, five years my junior, was still in school, but later would conscript a husband from the naval academy. Their interest in my new orders was intense.

The imagined demotion from ensign in a battleship to ensign in a cargo ship was the topic of much discussion in the family. My sister concentrated on the lack of glamour. My brother was a bit more reasonable. He conceded that being a head of department in a cargo ship was more responsibility than a junior officer in a battleship. Therefore, he considered it a promotion. My mother reasoned that going to war in a noncombatant auxiliary was much less dangerous for her little boy than in a battleship. She accepted my strong concurrence. I endured the interrogation successfully until my brother drove me to Grand Central Station at midnight, Sunday. The family was a bit suspicious when I left my sword and several suits of blues and whites at home. I am not sure my brother accepted my explanation: "We don't dress up on board a navy cargo ship."

At five o'clock in the morning Boston was dark and cold. I transferred to the Boston and Maine Railroad for the sixty-mile run to Portsmouth. The B and M did not depart until ten. At half past eleven that morning, the train deposited me safely at my destination. Excitement within me intensified. Soon I would meet my shipmates and see *Asterion*. I began to consider with some anxiety not the mission, but the unknown. There was much to consider, including how Project LQ came into being and what was the U-boat threat that had caused the U.S. Navy to take such immediate and covert action.[4]

2

America's Awakening: Project LQ

ALWAYS MYSTIFY, MISLEAD, AND SURPRISE THE ENEMY.

Lt. Gen. Thomas J. "Stonewall" Jackson,
Confederate States of America

The Oval Office, Washington, D.C.,
1400 Eastern War Time, 19 January 1942

THE NAVAL AIDE to the president, Capt. John L. McCrea, USN, announced to President Roosevelt the arrival of Admiral King for the prearranged meeting. Roosevelt spoke first, greeting the admiral in a tone of genuine pleasure that matched the smile on his face. He extended his hand from his seated position behind the presidential desk. King responded with a Good afternoon, Mr. President.[1]

Both men had strong hands, and the handshake reflected their friendly independence, their singular determination, and their mutual respect. King was well aware that Roosevelt had been the assistant secretary of the navy throughout World War I and had a deep affection for and interest in the naval service. The president knew King and respected him as a tough, sea-going admiral, and a grim realist. For that reason he had recently promoted him to the newly established position of commander in chief, U.S. Fleet. Roosevelt came right to the point.[2]

After thanking the admiral for coming to the White House, he launched into the matter of the merchant ship sinkings along the coast. As King accepted the gesture to be seated but declined the coffee, Roosevelt expressed his concern about German U-boats running loose along the Atlantic coast and sinking allied ships, especially the tankers, without some kind of response from the navy. The president shared with King the opinion of Churchill that the Americans were not doing enough to protect the North Atlantic convoys and that there had been terrible losses south and east of Greenland. Roosevelt reminded King that the admiralty had warned the Americans about Dönitz sending U-boats over to U.S. waters, and now Churchill would complain about Allied ships getting no protection over here. Roosevelt confided that Churchill would probably write another confidential and personal "From the Former Naval Person" note and politely solicit more help. Roosevelt, no doubt, apologized for preaching, but that was his way of soliciting thoughts from the outspoken admiral.[3]

King was no stranger to the president. He knew he could speak his mind. King's strong arguments had convinced Roosevelt to make Argentia, Newfoundland, and Reykjavik, Iceland, the bases for destroyer pools for escorting the Atlantic convoys. Others, including Adm. Harold R. Stark, the chief of naval operations, favored the Portuguese Azores. Roosevelt, too, was keenly aware of King's disagreement with Churchill's "grand strategy of dispersion," locating British fleet units all around the world rather than concentrating his forces in one location at a time to battle the enemy. King, as commander in chief, Atlantic Fleet, had been vocal in his criticism of the British admiralty's inability to track Germany's capital ships, especially in reference to the hunt for *Bismarck* in May 1941. However, it was the Argentia (Newfoundland) Conference in August 1941 that confirmed in Roosevelt's mind that King was his "navy operations admiral" rather than Stark. This meeting was attended by Churchill and Adm. Sir Dudley Pound, first sea lord (the British counterpart to the U.S. chief of naval operations), Roosevelt, and Admiral

Stark. King organized and orchestrated these proceedings. In time, the president would make the change. In the interim, Roosevelt made King commander in chief, U.S. Fleet, and gave him operational command of all U.S. naval forces.[4]

Both Roosevelt and King knew about *Cyclops* and *Frisco* and *Norness* and U-boat attacks on other ships, including five during the preceding twenty-four hours off the North Carolina coast. Roosevelt conceded that the lack of adequate destroyers and other antisubmarine ships could be attributed, in part, to the isolationists in Congress. But the president wanted to know if the navy was doing all it could do to meet this new phase of the war.

King responded with the most current details of ship availability and deployment, as follows: Fourteen destroyers were on the East Coast; seven were escorting the two new battleships, *North Carolina* and *Washington,* and the carrier *Hornet* on day-and-night battle practice and air defense exercises; and seven were on various other assignments. These battleships and crews were being prepared for deadly action, first against the German capital ships and later against the Japanese. That was one of King's top priorities. When ready, these two fast battleships were scheduled to go to England and help the British seek out and engage *Tirpitz,* the smaller battleships *Gneisenau* and *Scharnhorst,* and the cruiser *Prinz Eugen.* The admiral emphasized that these were Hitler's best and most dangerous surface ships and that damage at this time to *North Carolina* and *Washington* could not be risked. Logistics and repairs, he reported, kept at least three destroyers in port. The remaining four were assigned among Eastern Sea Frontier, the new sonar school in Key West, and the Gulf Sea Frontier. There were no other suitable ships for antisubmarine work here on the coast. Roosevelt listened as King's accounting continued: No fewer than thirty-five destroyers plus three of the large Coast Guard cutters were assigned to the Mid-Ocean Escort Group. Those ships and crews took a terrible beating from the weather and from continuous operations in the Iceland and Greenland area.[5]

King offered his opinion that the fleet posture in the Pacific theater was precarious and the Japanese posed a greater threat to the overall situation than the Germans. The admiral, as expected, had done his home-

Q-SHIPS VERSUS U-BOATS

work. He had drafted a strategy for containing the Japanese advance, which his command staff under Capt. Francis Low had prepared. He reported that Admirals Fletcher in *Yorktown*, Wilson Brown in *Lexington*, and Spruance in the heavy cruiser *Northampton*, with Halsey in *Enterprise*, were running all over the Pacific to make the Japanese think the U.S. Navy had more firepower out there than it actually did. Nimitz had been in the CinCPac seat only two weeks; he would be asking for more ships. King left no doubt that he would not pull ships from the Pacific Fleet to defend merchantmen in the western Atlantic. He had too much at stake in the Pacific.[6]

The president fully understood King's summary and obvious determination. He asked about the use of Q-ships on the Atlantic coast and offered the opinion that the decoy concept, while an old tactic, should be new to the young U-boat captains. He thought the ruse might work for a while. King knew about submarine decoy ships. It was a matter of World War I British naval history. He had not given any thought to employing them. He knew it was a very dangerous game, that it took very special officers and men to fight those ships, and that at best the British had had only marginal success. Roosevelt suggested that the tactic should be tried, which King took to be a directive from his commander in chief. He would have a few merchant ships converted and placed in service until something better was available to send after the U-boats. This was a risky course of action, a dubious scheme, but one he would initiate without delay.[7]

King was off to his office in Main Navy, oblivious of the scenery on 17th Street, the Corcoran Gallery of Art, Constitution Hall, and the Pan American Union. His mind was focused on his new task. He appreciated the need for quick action. He knew there would be more sinkings along the East Coast. Each day he scanned the secret reports from the British admiralty on U-boat locations and movements in the central and western Atlantic. He was well aware of the movement of U-boats westward. He also knew he had no resources to effectively counter the threat.

The British admiralty, early in 1939, had established a Submarine Tracking Room. Here, under Fleet Paymaster E. W. C. Thring and later Cdr. Rodger Winn, RNVR, intelligence data, battle reports, U-boat sightings and attacks, and U-boat wireless transmissions as detected by direction findings were plotted and analyzed to determine known and suspected enemy locations and movements. Commander Winn's efforts in the tracking room provided some meaningful plots but often too late to successfully divert convoys. Nonetheless, the information gained in terms of U-boat locations, concentrations, and movements was a valuable element of anti-U-boat strategy and tactics.[8]

Wireless or radio communication within the U-boat service was a normal and routine procedure. Wireless signals between operating U-boats and BdU (U-boat headquarters) in Paris and later at Kernevel near Lorient, France, were encoded in a secret cipher system called Hydra. Although the code system was designated Heimisch Gewässer (for ships in home waters), it was used extensively within the U-boat service. The equipment for encoding and decoding in the Hydra system was called Enigma, which was an electromechanical device, a Schlüssel M, that utilized a series of rotor wheels to mechanically convert plain language to code and vice versa. An accompanying document, also highly classified, contained the daily selection and arrangements of the rotors. As in all naval ships, the utmost care had to be taken to ensure that coding information and equipment never fell into the hands of the enemy. Accordingly, the protection and even destruction of Enigma and the Hydra documentation if capture was imminent was a prime responsibility of every U-boat and surface ship commander.[9]

By mid-1941 the admiralty made a significant breakthrough in naval intelligence gathering that would greatly improve the U-boat tracking operation. Through the efforts of a dedicated assemblage of brainpower at Station X, the Government Code and Cypher School located at Bletchley Park, a Victorian mansion in Buckinghamshire, the German naval code used by the U-boat service was broken. Many factors contributed to breaking the German code. First, the brilliance of the Cambridge mathematicians, especially Alan Turing, the cryptanalyst at the Code and Cypher School. Second, the possession of a Polish coding machine known as Rejewski's Bombe, which operated on the same mechanical principle as the German machine Enigma. Third, the German code books, sets of rotors, and an Enigma with the Hydra settings, were captured during various raids and ship sinkings in 1940 and 1941.[10]

The most dramatic of these acquisitions occurred during the attack on U-110 east of Cape Farewell, the southern tip of Greenland. U-110, under the command of Kapitänleutnant Fritz-Julius Lemp, on 8 May 1941, was depth charged by the British corvette HMS *Aubrietia*. The heavily damaged submarine was forced to surface. Lemp gave orders to abandon ship as gas fumes filled the boat. The destroyer HMS *Bulldog* came alongside and dispatched a boarding party. Lemp was shot and killed in his attempt to reboard his U-boat to hasten the scuttling and to destroy the classified material. The doomed U-110 provided the British with complete documentation on Hydra and the Enigma coding machine.[11]

Rodger Winn now had the capability to read all U-boat radio communications. With decrypted German radio signals being provided by Alan Turing, Winn was able to maintain a clear picture of U-boat movements throughout the Atlantic operational area. Despite brief periods of interruptions or signal blackouts, the Submarine Tracking Room established itself as an indispensable part of operational intelligence. However, in late November 1941, Dönitz suspected a breach in security because his U-boats were having little success in locating trans-Atlantic convoys. As a result, on 1 February 1942 a fourth rotor was added to the Enigma machine. This greatly curtailed the information flowing into the Tracking Room and the efforts of Winn and his deputy, Patrick Beesley. Without these daily reports the Tracking Room was limited to data collected by their old devices plus the indispensable and intimate knowledge gained from having read over a period of months the classified wireless traffic between the individual U-boat commanders and U-boat headquarters. Winn and Beesley, by now, were well acquainted with many U-boats and their commanders. They knew the tonnage and endurance of each, the longer-range Type IXB 1,000-tonners and the smaller Type VIIC 750-ton shorter-legged boats. They had also become familiar with the individual U-boat commanders, their backgrounds, their tactics, even their idiosyncrasies. This intelligence was especially useful in developing tactics for the British and Canadian units defending the North Atlantic convoys.[12]

U-boat operational data of interest to the U.S. Navy were shared routinely with Washington. However, U-boat activity in the western Atlantic before January 1942 was nonexistent. Therefore, this information was of little importance to Eastern Sea Frontier on the Atlantic coast and Gulf Sea Frontier concerned with operations in the Florida Straits and Gulf of Mexico. Even when on 12 January the admiralty advised U.S. Naval Operations in Washington of the probable U-boat advances to positions southwest of Cape Cod, little effort was made to establish a defense force. Until 14 January, the focus had been on mobilization and on protecting the North Atlantic convoys. With the sinking of *Norness*, a new dimension to the Atlantic battle was established.[13]

Admiral King had his orders from the commander in chief. It was an urgent command, and his response was quick. Now he had tangible evidence of a U-boat attack southwest of Cape Cod: *Norness*. *Cyclops* and *Frisco* were further to the north and east, but close enough to note. He realized that with the sinking of *Norness* only fifty-three nautical miles south of Martha's Vineyard, Massachusetts, the seriousness of the U-boat campaign had advanced a full order of magnitude. But even with this attack, Admiral King apparently reasoned that the probability of finding a U-boat in the thousands of square miles of the Atlantic south and east of Cape Cod with so few resources, meaning his limited destroyer force, would be an exercise in futility. King's concern remained the sparsity of resources and the establishment of priorities. He must employ his fleet units judiciously.

As the admiral continued his transit to Constitution Avenue and Main Navy, his thoughts raced on. Uppermost in his mind was the fact that the enemy had approached near the coastline of the United States. King realized that this had not happened since 1918 when three U-boats attempted to blockade the U.S. East Coast. Although the blockade met with very limited success, King knew that an effective U-boat campaign in U.S. waters with more modern German submarines was possible and, indeed, probable. King must have regretted his past inattention to the efforts of Rodger Winn and Patrick Beesley. Ironically, shortly afterward, when King needed all the U-boat operational intelligence obtainable to conduct his defense, U-boat command discontinued using Hydra, substituting a new code system, Triton, and a new Enigma machine.[14]

What Admiral King needed were more fast ships with antisubmarine capabilities. He knew he could not defeat the U-boat assault without the proper tools: aircraft carriers, aircraft, pilots, and destroyers or destroyer escorts all trained in antisubmarine warfare strategy, tactics, and operations. These assets would not be forthcoming for many months. In the meantime, the president had requested Q-ships, and Q-ships he would get. King had at his side one of the best "know how to do it and get it done" administrators in the Navy Department: Vice Adm. Frederick J. Horne. This would be his project.

By 1530 that day, King had assembled in his conference room on the second floor and contiguous to his office overlooking Constitution Avenue three senior officers: Vice Admiral Horne, Rear Adm. W. S. Farber, both from the office of the chief of naval operations, and Rear Adm. Ray Spear, chief of the navy's Bureau of Supplies and Accounts and head of the navy's supply-logistics system. His declaration was brief: He had just returned from a meeting with President Roosevelt. At his behest the navy would procure, convert, and operate two or more Q-ships. These decoy ships would be employed to counter the U-boat attacks on merchant ships along the East Coast. The project would begin now. The ships should be ready for sea in the minimum amount of time. By the very nature of the project, secrecy was of the utmost importance. There would be no delays. He tasked Admiral Horne to administer the project and asked for a plan of action in forty-eight hours and periodic verbal progress reports.[15]

King left the conference room and entered the adjoining office of Adm. Harold R. Stark, chief of naval operations (CNO). Admiral Stark, under the secretary of the navy, Frank Knox, was responsible for strategic planning, administration, shipbuilding, and organization of the naval establishment. Stark had held the position of CNO since 1939, when Hitler attacked Poland, and was well respected by Roosevelt and King as a planner and diplomat. However, he was not considered a "fighting" admiral. King briefed the CNO, emphasizing that he had assigned the task to Admiral Horne, subject to his approval. Stark had no objections and told

King to use any of his staff that were required and to keep him informed. For the moment, King's task relative to the Q-ship project was done.

Only minutes before, when King had tasked the three admirals, Horne made notes on a yellow, lined, legal-size pad. He had written such words as secrecy, expedite, merchant hulls, conversion, armaments, selected crews (hazardous duty volunteers), funding, operation orders/operations command. These elements became the agenda items of the meeting that continued after King left. Admirals Horne, Farber, and Spear had worked together on other programs. Following some limited discussion, Horne assigned action items and classified the project Secret. It was agreed that correspondence would be kept to a minimum. A central file would be maintained only in Horne's private office, the office of the vice chief of naval operations. The meeting adjourned until 1400 the next day, 20 January. The file and the decoy ship venture thereafter were known as Project LQ.[16]

While the plan for U-boat countermeasures was in its embryonic state at Main Navy, Adm. Karl Dönitz, commander, U-boats, had already made his presence known with Paukenschlag: Operation Drumbeat. The first two U-boats to disturb the heretofore tranquil U.S. waters had attacked several merchantmen only a few miles off the coast of New Jersey, Virginia, and North Carolina. Dönitz's drumbeat was clearly heard in the Oval Office and in Main Navy.

3

Operation Drumbeat

ANGREIFEN! RAN! VERSENKEN!
(ATTACK! ADVANCE! SINK!)
U-Boat Motto

AFTER ALL, WE ARE AT WAR.
SACRIFICES MIGHT HAVE TO BE MADE.

Cdr. Thomas J. Ryan, USN, Navy Department,
Washington, D.C., January 1942

ON 13 JANUARY 1942 Adm. Karl Dönitz, commander, U-boats, executed Operation Drumbeat (Paukenschlag), his "surprise" attack on Allied merchantmen in U.S. coastal waters. As early as September 1941, the admiral had developed a plan whereby twelve Type IXc boats would be positioned along the American Atlantic coast between Newfoundland and Cape Hatteras. These long-range boats would be on station ready to strike when the United States was drawn into the war. The Japanese attack on Pearl Harbor advanced the German High Command's schedule for removing restrictions on U-boat operations against U.S. ships. Six U-boats were allocated to Operation Paukenschlag, but by late December only five boats were ready to deploy. Once in U.S. waters, these boats would be ready to attack upon receipt of a radio signal from the admiral.[1]

Admiral Dönitz and U-boat command regarded the plan with confidence and great expectations. The objective of the operation was three-fold: (1) take full advantage of the element of surprise by striking an extremely heavy blow on merchantmen while antisubmarine defenses were weak; (2) restrict attacks to "really worthwhile targets—ships of 10,000 tons and more"; and (3) sink as much shipping as possible in the most economical manner. Dönitz stated in his memoirs, "We could not afford to launch an attack that might end in failure, but in the virgin waters of the American theater we expected success on a scale that would repay the long voyages involved." By mid-January Dönitz's five boats were in Canadian and U.S. waters.[2] The admiral's Group Paukenschlag consisted of five experienced U-boat commanders: Fregattenkapitän Richard Zapp, U-66; Kapitänleutnant Heinrich Bleichrodt, U-109; Kapitänleutnant Reinhard Hardegen, U-123; Kapitänleutnant Ulrich Folkers, U-125; and Fregattenkapitän Ernst Kals, U-130. On 9 January Dönitz transmitted by encrypted message his order to commence attacks on the thirteenth. His wireless transmission, Offizier 1058/9/1/42, assigned an attack area to each of the five U-boats.[3]

Marine quadrant, literally naval square, was a highly classified grid system, utilizing the Mercator projection superimposed on a standard German naval chart. It covered all ocean and coastal surfaces, world-wide. It was used for communicating U-boat locations by radio to and from German naval headquarters and for security reasons replaced the more traditional latitude-longitude system. The basic grid arrangement utilized an alphanumeric method such as CA5327 for citing locations. The grid chart was essential to utilizing the code. By 15 January all boats were on station: U-123 in CA, the coast of New York and New Jersey; U-125 in CA, the open Atlantic east of U-123; U-66 south of U-123, along the coast of Delaware, Virginia, and North Carolina; U-130 in Quadrant BB south of Cape Breton Island; and U-109, also in BB, west of U-130 and southeast of Halifax, Nova Scotia.[4]

Reinhard Hardegen in U-123 was the first to strike. In the early morning of 12 January, one day before Dönitz's attack date and far from his assigned area, Hardegen sank the 9,000-ton British freighter *Cyclops*. On the next day, Ernst Kals in U-130 successfully attacked the tankers *Frisco* and *Friar Rock*. Hardegen struck again on 14 and 15 January sinking the 10,000-ton *Norness* and the smaller tanker *Coimbra*. Both attacks occurred in the approaches to New York harbor: *Norness* some fifty miles

Q-SHIPS VERSUS U-BOATS

south of Martha's Vineyard and *Coimbra* thirty miles south of Shinnecock Inlet, Long Island, and sixty-five miles east of Ambrose light.[5] Before leaving the New York area, Hardegen claimed to have seen the lights of Coney Island. No doubt a gratifying experience but hardly a productive tactical maneuver. His next credible attack was on 19 January in the Cape Hatteras area. Had Hardegen found meaningful targets in the immediate Ambrose light area, his feat might have rivaled that of Kapitänleutnant Günther Prien who in October 1939 entered Scapa Flow and sank the battleship HMS *Royal Oak*. Prien thereafter became known as "the Bull of Scapa Flow." Would Reinhard Hardegen have become "the Bull of the Bronx"?[6]

By 17 January the Paukenschlag boats had attacked a total of six merchantmen, of which only two were between 8,000 and 10,000 tons. Furthermore, Hardegen claimed four sinkings, although one victim has never been identified. Kals, in U-130, was the only other commander to report successful attacks. With an average of only one successful attack per day, Operation Drumbeat was not going well.[7]

On 17 January Dönitz released all boats from their assigned attack area.[8] Kals, Bleichrodt, and Folkers proceeded south and westward toward the coast. Hardegen also decided to run south toward Cape Hatteras, a pivotal point for coastal traffic. Zapp was already approaching the cape, but well off the coast. He was the next to find a target. On 18 January he sank the U.S. tanker SS *Allan Jackson*. Folkers, in U-125, experienced repeated torpedo problems. He, too, remained well off the coast. He was given credit for sinking only one ship, SS *West Ivis*, on 26 January some eighty miles southwest of Hatteras. Between 18 and 27 January the five boats claimed a total of twenty attacks, a two-per-day average. On 27 January all five boats were en route home to the Bay of Biscay. Their attacks, including *Cyclops* on 12 January, for the entire period of their patrols totaled twenty-nine ships. Hardegen was credited with ten attacks, including the unconfirmed freighter and the 8,000-ton tanker *Malay*, which was only damaged. His accomplishments were recognized by the German naval command, and Grand Adm. Eric Raeder awarded him the Knight's Cross.

Dönitz claimed that the "success achieved by the five boats of the first

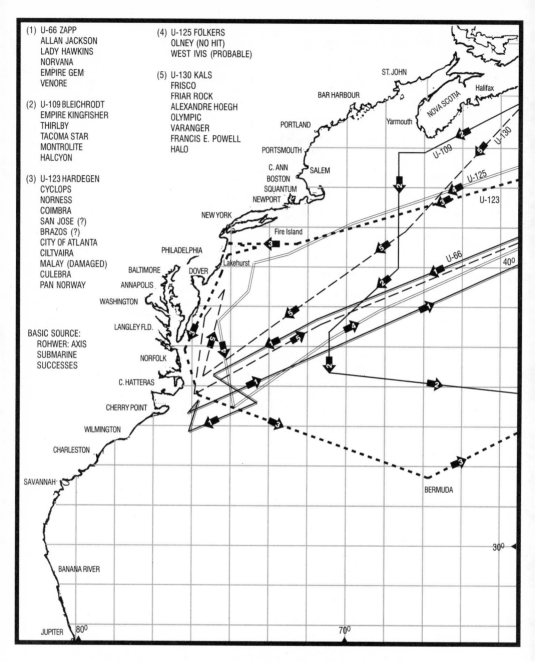

(1) U-66 ZAPP
    ALLAN JACKSON
    LADY HAWKINS
    NORVANA
    EMPIRE GEM
    VENORE

(2) U-109 BLEICHRODT
    EMPIRE KINGFISHER
    THIRLBY
    TACOMA STAR
    MONTROLITE
    HALCYON

(3) U-123 HARDEGEN
    CYCLOPS
    NORNESS
    COIMBRA
    SAN JOSE (?)
    BRAZOS (?)
    CITY OF ATLANTA
    CILTVAIRA
    MALAY (DAMAGED)
    CULEBRA
    PAN NORWAY

(4) U-125 FOLKERS
    OLNEY (NO HIT)
    WEST IVIS (PROBABLE)

(5) U-130 KALS
    FRISCO
    FRIAR ROCK
    ALEXANDRE HOEGH
    OLYMPIC
    VARANGER
    FRANCIS E. POWELL
    HALO

BASIC SOURCE:
ROHWER: AXIS
SUBMARINE
SUCCESSES

Paukenschlag, 13 January–6 February 1942, allied ships attacked. U-boat commanders could not always identify the target by name at the time of the attack. The author believes Hardegan actually sank two ships other than *San Jose* and *Brazos*, probably *Olympic* and *Norvana*. Zapp and Kals must have attacked two other unidentified ships.

'Operation Drumbeat' was great." This assertion by the admiral appears to be based more on wishful thinking than on fact. He recorded a more realistic statement in his war diary: "From the commanding officer's report [Hardegen] it is perfectly clear that 'Drumbeat' could have achieved far greater success had it been possible to make available the twelve boats for which U-boat Command asked. . . . Good use, it is true, was made of this unique opportunity, and the successes achieved have been very gratifying; we were, however, not able to develop to the full the chances offered us."[9]

The accomplishments of Operation Drumbeat as presented to the German naval High Command gained for Dönitz a vote of confidence from none other than Hitler. The Naval High Command War Diary stated the following: "On the afternoon of January 23, 1942, Captain von Puttkamer telephoned to say that the Führer had noted with great satisfaction the rising figures of sinkings off the American coast." This accolade apparently won for Dönitz a greater degree of freedom for the allocation of his U-boats. He directed other long-range boats to the western Atlantic: U-106 (Rasch); U-103 (Winter); and U-107 (Gelhaus). To further exploit the favorable operating conditions along the U.S. coast, the admiral decided to deploy the smaller VIIC boats to the area. His decision was based on the fact that "their radius of action was found in practice to be considerably greater than our theoretical calculations and previous experience had led us to assume." The VIIC boats would soon be on the scene: U-552 (Topp), U-203 (Mützelburg), U-754 (Oestermann), U-432 (Schultze), and U-578 (Rehwinkel).[10]

Although Operation Paukenschlag had ended, the battle of the American coastal area had just begun. By 23 January Project LQ had moved quickly and secretly forward within the U.S. Navy Department. Only senior officers were involved in planning the details and executing the approved plan. Admiral Stark had designated Cdr. Thomas J. Ryan Jr., USN, from the Fleet Maintenance Division in the Office of the Chief of Naval Operations (OPNAV) to be the sole contact with the Personnel Bureau for crew selection and with the Maritime Commission for acquiring the merchant hulls.[11] Commander Ryan was an ideal choice; he had had destroyer duty and staff duty, had a law degree, and was trained in

NAVY DEPARTMENT

Op-23E-RSM   OFFICE OF THE CHIEF OF NAVAL OPERATIONS

WASHINGTON

23 January, 1942

MEMORANDUM

To: Bureau Chiefs and Heads of Offices of the Navy Department.
     Commandants of Naval Districts.
     Commandants of Navy Yards.

1. The bearer, Commander T. J. Ryan, Jr., U.S.N., who must show you satisfactory identification, has authority to represent me in all matters concerning a special project.

2. I would appreciate it if you will regard his requests concerning this project as emanating from me, and I request that you act upon them accordingly.

H. R. Stark

---

ship maintenance. Ryan briefed Adm. Randall Jacobs, chief of naval personnel, who designated Cdr. Joseph W. McColl Jr. and Cdr. Samuel W. DuBois as the contact officers within personnel. Officer and crew selection and detailing began as soon as specific requirements were determined. The ships' manning plan would be influenced by the type and size of the hulls selected. This was Ryan's next task.[12]

Ryan proceeded to the office of Adm. Emory S. Land, head of the Maritime Commission. The objective of Project LQ was discussed with the admiral. Land summoned Huntington T. Morse and S. H. Helmbold to his office, introduced them to Ryan, and directed them to fulfill the navy's requirements. Morse and Helmbold provided data on the availability of existing hulls and new construction. They discouraged the use of tankers, because they were in great demand. Ryan, whose "professional and private" evaluation of the project was that the ships, once deployed, would have a life expectancy of not more than thirty days, was satisfied with two old steamships that had seen better days. These two ships, SS *Evelyn* and SS *Carolyn*, were built in 1912 by Newport News Shipbuilding and Dry Dock Company. They were 3,200 tons each, with a speed of ten to eleven knots, and were owned and operated by the A. H. Bull Steamship Company. They could be made available on short notice. With drawings from the commission under his arm, he returned to Main Navy and received approval for using the two "old ladies."[13]

At 0900, 20 January 1942, Commander Ryan convened a meeting at OPNAV to determine the conversion, armament, and manning of the two ships. Commanders McColl and DuBois from personnel were there, plus a naval architect from the Bureau of Ships. The ships' drawings were reviewed, sketches were made of the locations of the guns and depth charge launchers, and a rough design was agreed to for living spaces for the expanded crew. It was determined that a crew of 135 enlisted personnel, mostly petty officers, and 6 officers could adequately fight the ship and provide the high degree of damage control that might be needed to keep the ship afloat after sustaining one or more torpedo hits.[14] Because of the secrecy of the project, it was proposed that the small, somewhat isolated Naval Ship Yard at Portsmouth, New Hampshire, do the conversions. The meeting concluded with Ryan advising the attendees to proceed with tentative plans, as discussed, subject to confirmation within twenty-four hours.

While Ryan was meeting with his group, Admiral Horne met with Admiral King. Horne proposed commander, Eastern Sea Frontier, Rear Adm. Adolphus Andrews as the operational commander for the Q-ships. King agreed and directed Horne to send a priority message to Andrews asking for his comments on the employment of Q-ships. King's final comment was to advise Horne that Captain McCrea at the White House had sent word that the president would finance the project from his National Defense Emergency Fund. Horne passed the word regarding funding to Admiral Spear who would establish the appropriate accounting procedures for controlling the money. He then set about the task of sending a classified message to Andrews, asking for his comments on the use of "Queen Ships."[15]

At 1400 Admirals Farber and Spear and Commander Ryan met with Admiral Horne. Ryan presented a summary of his actions. He proposed a third ship, a Grand Banks fishing trawler, that could operate with the fishing fleet close to the shipping lanes used by the North Atlantic convoys. His proposal was approved, as was the procurement of the two Bull Line ships, *Evelyn* and *Carolyn*. Two hours later, Horne entered King's office and gave a verbal account of the launching of Project LQ. King was satisfied. With the general plan approved, implementation began.

Early on Wednesday morning, 21 January, Ryan was on his way to Boston. He had talked by telephone to Capt. John S. Barleon, chief of staff to the commandant, First Naval District (COM1), and arranged for a meeting with a select number of staff members. Ryan needed a trawler and he had learned that COM1 had one available. At the COM1 meeting Ryan was told that a trawler-type diesel vessel of 520 tons, a speed of ten to eleven knots, and a cruising radius of 4,488 miles had been purchased by the navy and was being converted into a minesweeper at the Boston Navy Yard. When commissioned it would be named USS *Eagle* (AM132). Barleon indicated that if directed by CNO, *Eagle* could be reassigned and outfitted as a Q-ship. Ryan asked that the proceedings of the meeting be summarized immediately in a classified secret document and that it include his direction as the representative of CNO to convert the minesweeper into a Q-ship without delay. He signed the minutes of the meeting and returned to his JO2 Lockheed utility aircraft, which was standing by. The commander's next stop was Portsmouth, New Hampshire, about sixty miles north of Boston.[16]

The Portsmouth Navy Yard was primarily a submarine construction and overhaul yard but on occasion would do repair work on surface ships, especially auxiliaries. There was no doubt in Ryan's mind that the yard was capable of doing the work; the question was a matter of scheduling and maintaining security. But as Ryan had reasoned, this would be a problem no matter where the work was done. In a one-hour meeting with the assistant captain of the yard, Cdr. Charles F. M. S. Quinby, and the construction officer, the groundwork was laid for the two freighters to be converted without delay. Detailed information would be provided within seventy-two hours by classified mail or courier. Ryan returned to Washington.

Meanwhile, in Main Navy on Wednesday, Admiral Spear met with his two action officers, Cdr. W. J. "Nick" Carter and Lt. Cdr. W. W. "Walt" Honaker, to discuss and resolve the problem of handling and accounting for the funds authorized by the president, logistics support of the ships, and the selection and detailing of a logistics or supply officer for both freighters. Key to the logistics support of the Q-ships operating as merchantmen rather than naval ships was the disbursement of funds in payment for services and stores purchased and received. Surely, U.S. Treasury checks could not be used. The navy had no experience in such matters. With Farber's concurrence, Spear sent Carter to the White House to meet with McCrea. McCrea's advice was, "Let's call the experts."

Captain McCrea phoned F. J. Lawton, whom he knew in the Office of the Director, Bureau of the Budget. A general discussion on the handling of funds for confidential purposes ensued. Lawton outlined the procedure. This included a letter from the president to the secretary of the treasury stating that the president allocated the funds in a specified amount to an expending agency for confidential purposes. That agent could then expend the funds and, if necessary, place the funds in a bank account. McCrea agreed to draft an appropriate letter. He would contact Admiral Horne to obtain the name of the "agent." McCrea also suggested to Carter that Riggs Bank be used since its president, Robert V. Fleming, was personally cleared to handle official government matters up to the security classification of Secret. "Nick" Carter now had in mind a scheme for financing the clandestine operations of the ships. He reviewed his general plan with Admiral Spear and obtained approval from Admiral Horne. With the concurrence of Horne, Spear called on Robert Fleming at Riggs and apprised him of the proposed financial stratagem. Fleming pledged his full and secret support.[17]

Project LQ was gaining momentum. Commander Ryan, for the Navy Department, and Morse and Helmbold, on behalf of the Maritime

Commission, signed an agreement for the loan of the steamers *Evelyn* and *Carolyn* to the navy. The Portsmouth Navy Yard took action to procure the armament, equipment, and material to effect the conversion of the two ships. Adm. Randall Jacobs, at the Personnel Bureau, began screening officers for the three ships, with personal attention given to finding the commanding officers and the executive officers, but with no less interest in the candidates to fill the remaining billets for each ship: gunnery officer, supply officer, engineering officer, and communications officer. Admiral Jacobs left to Admiral Spear the task of selecting the two supply officers, as ships' logistics and financial management were the specialty of Spear's bureau. Qualifications and availability were the primary considerations; however, Admiral Horne insisted that personnel be assigned only on a volunteer basis.

Decoy ship disguise applied to the ship's name as well as her outward appearances. While the two freighters would operate as merchantmen and retain their original names, SS *Evelyn* and SS *Carolyn*, a U.S. ship (USS) name had to be assigned for naval personnel records, official duty station identification, and a post office address. The trawler had already been named USS *Eagle* as a minesweeper and, for the time being, would retain her name. At the request of Commander Ryan the Naval History Office offered two names for the AK (cargo) type ships: USS *Asterion* (AK100) for *Evelyn* and USS *Atik* (AK101) for *Carolyn*. Ryan then called on Commander Carter to inform him of the ships' names.

During that meeting Carter outlined the funding plan to Ryan. The sum of five hundred thousand dollars from the president's emergency fund would be put in a joint account in the name of F. J. Horne and/or W. S. Farber. Three additional accounts would be opened in the name of three bogus or sham companies: Asterion Shipping Company, Atik Shipping Company, and Eagle Fishing Company. A disbursing officer aboard each ship would be designated "treasurer" and authorized to write checks on his "revolving fund" account. As expenditures were made, each account would be reimbursed by transfer from the Horne-Farber account. The funding and financial accounting jigsaw puzzle was now beginning to fit together; only one major section was yet to be completed, naming the treasurers. Carter and Admiral Spear would select the treasurers. On 19 February, after McCrea had provided the president's funding authorization, Honaker was sent to Riggs with the five-hundred-thousand-dollar treasurer's check in hand.[18]

Cdr. Tom Ryan was the catalyst for Project LQ, the person who initiated and coordinated the various tasks in a timely sequence. His enterprising nature, initiative, logic, and perspicacity were instrumental in rushing Project LQ through the halls of Main Navy. Ryan easily adapted to wearing the rank of Admiral Horne or even Admiral King when necessary to move past some perfunctory chief of staff, flag lieutenant, or aide. He was a man of action. It had won him the Medal of Honor in 1923 while attached to the American Embassy, Tokyo. He was in Japan during the earthquake of 1923 and was honored for his heroic rescue action following that earthquake and the fire that occurred in Yokohama on 1 September of that year. Ryan was skilled in engineering and command, and he had earned a law degree. His southern charm and New Orleans mannerisms also served him well.

Although he had some reservations about Project LQ, he had no acceptable alternatives. He sensed that Admiral King was not overly enthusiastic about the task. Admirals Horne, Farber, and Spear were not asked to give an evaluation of the project, and they offered none. Admiral Andrews and his operations people appeared eager to support the project. Ryan understood their reaction: They were without adequate forces to meet the U-boat assault; they would accept anything.

Ryan would play a key role in selecting the officers to man these U-boat traps. He did not expect these ships to survive but one encounter with a U-boat, although he would have them loaded with logs or empty steel barrels to help keep them afloat after one or two torpedo hits. If they survived to that point, they would engage in an artillery duel at close range, probably in the darkness of night, with a small target. The U-boat, on the other hand, would have a large, dead-in-the-water, flaming hulk to attack at point-blank range. The project would require officers with special characteristics, officers who, knowing the odds, would, when asked, volunteer for this "adventure." Tom Ryan immersed himself in his task: "After all, we are at war. Sacrifices might have to be made. And the more skilled and resourceful the command, the fewer the casualties, hopefully."

Ryan sat at a table in the conference room of the chief of naval personnel, Adm. Randall Jacobs. Across the table were Commanders McColl and DuBois. On the table were some twenty to twenty-five folders: Officers' Records. DuBois had listed six commanding officer candidates in order of overall qualifications. Ryan had the list in hand. Two names were prominent at the top of the short list: Lt. Cdr. Harry L. Hicks, USN, and Lt. Cdr. Glenn W. Legwen Jr., USN. Both officers were naval academy graduates, class of 1927; they were thirty-seven years old, and their jackets indicated good experience and outstanding performance.[19]

Lieutenant Commander Hicks had been born in South Carolina and entered the naval academy from Rome, Georgia. After graduation he served in USS *Tennessee* for three years in the gunnery department, then two years on the staff of Destroyer Squadron Five in USS *Pillsbury*, a year on Yangtze Patrol in China in USS *Tutuila*, and then back to the academy for postgraduate work in ordnance and communications. He returned to sea duty in the cruiser *Vincennes* and the destroyer *Hamilton*. At the time of the review by Ryan, Hicks was commanding officer, USS *Sylph* (PY12), a converted 800-ton, 200-foot yacht fitted out with sound gear and depth charges. *Sylph* was assigned to the Third Naval District (Admiral Andrews) for offshore U-boat patrol in the New York–Long Island area. Ryan and DuBois both considered him "technically" qualified for command.

Ryan's attention turned to Lieutenant Commander Legwen. Legwen entered the academy from Augusta, Georgia. After graduation he had considerable sea duty as a junior officer. In addition, he had advanced training in torpedoes and underwater sound. In November 1941 he completed the Command and Staff Course at the Naval War College, and was currently on duty in the Office of the Chief of Naval Operations. Legwen, too, was considered a strong candidate to devise and master the unorthodox "rules of engagement" for Q-ship tactics.

It's one thing to know the tools of the trade, but it's another matter to have the cunning and will to use them. What about the temperament of these two officers? Ryan turned to the file of performance evaluations, or fitness reports, on each candidate. He looked for such words as "temerity," "audacity," and "recklessness," and found none. He did not expect to see such adjectives as "courageous," "valiant," or "audacious" for they are used only in extraordinary circumstances. Ryan was looking for practical men and such phrases as "uses good judgment," "conducts himself well under stress," "performed exceptionally well during battle practice," "a strong leader," and words such as "reliable," "tenacious," and "determined." He was looking for brave and daring men capable of valor, gallantry, and boldness. However, he did not want reckless men. After a cursory review of the remaining records of commanding officer candidates, Ryan agreed to the selection of Hicks and Legwen.

Of almost equal importance was the selection of executive officers—the next senior officer in the chain of command of each ship. McColl passed two jackets to Ryan. One was the file on Lt. Leonard Vincent Duffy, USNA, class of 1929, and the other on Lt. Lawrence Robert Neville, class of 1933. Duffy, age thirty-five, was aboard the new battleship USS *Washington*, completing shakedown before her imminent departure for England. He had had destroyer and cruiser duties and commanded USS *Napa* (AT32) in the Asiatic Fleet. He had also had six months under instruction at the Naval Torpedo Station, Newport, Rhode Island. Neville, age thirty, had had duty in USS *Asheville* (PG21), a coastal gunboat on China Station, and in the gunnery division in USS *Arkansas* (BB33) in North Atlantic waters. Both officers had progressive careers and outstanding fitness evaluations.

Ryan was pleased with McColl's selections and asked to see the records of the three remaining line officers for each ship. Lieutenants Henry Carl Schwaner Jr., naval academy class of 1936, and Daniel Bernard Deckelman, class of 1937, were the nominees for gunnery officers. Both had ordnance training and served in the gunnery departments aboard heavy cruisers. Each had top 10 percent fitness reports and commendations for excellence in ordnance studies, gunnery exercises, and seamanship. Both officers were twenty-eight years old and married.

McColl had searched for engineering officers who could operate the old triple expansion steam engines and the boilers, and who could keep all the other old equipment maintained. These were technologically simple systems but they were old and worn. There were two sources for officers with these qualifications: "mustangs" and the Merchant Marine Reserve Corps. Mustangs were chosen for promotion from the ranks of the enlisted or noncommissioned petty officers. Guy Brown Ray was such an officer. He was selected from the ranks of machinist mates and warrant officers and commissioned ensign in November 1941. Previously, he had seen duty at the Naval Ship Yard at Portsmouth. McColl told Ryan he thought this would be an advantage since the ships had to be modified, and Ray would know his way around and could expedite the work. He currently was on duty at the naval shipyard at Brooklyn, New York. The other officer was Lt. Harold James Beckett, USNR, an engineering officer in the Merchant Marine Reserve who had been on active duty since July 1940 and was currently with Hicks in *Sylph*. Both Ray and Beckett were in their mid-forties and married.

Ensigns John Lukowich and Edwin Madison Leonard were naval reserve officers on active duty. Lukowich graduated from City College of New York. Leonard earned a bachelor's degree from the University of South Carolina and a law degree from the University of Virginia. Both ensigns attended the U.S. Naval Reserve Midshipman School, New York, also known as USS *Prairie State*, and received further training in communications. Lukowich then saw duty in the Office of the Commandant, Third Naval District (COM3), 90 Church Street, New York City, while Leonard was detailed to USS *Washington* for communications duty. Lukowich was twenty-four and Leonard twenty-three years old. Ryan noted that the day before had been Leonard's birthday and reflected "hopefully, he will see his twenty-fourth." Both were bachelors and should be available for immediate transfer to Portsmouth and the two ships. It was agreed, tentatively, that *Eagle* would keep her present crew.

Ryan seemed pleased with the candidates and asked McColl if he had aligned the officers by ship, that is, those for *Asterion* and those for *Atik*. McColl had done this, except for the two supply-logistics officers. He proposed Hicks, commanding; Duffy, executive; Deckelman, gunnery; Beckett, engineering; and Leonard, communications for *Atik*. Hicks and Beckett were together in *Sylph*, and Duffy and Leonard may have known each other in *Washington*, so McColl kept these officers together.

Legwen, Neville, Schwaner, Ray, and Lukowich were proposed for *Asterion*. Ryan agreed and asked McColl to go forward with the detailing, subject to possible last-minute change. Before releasing the orders, Ryan wanted to interview Legwen and Hicks.

It was approaching noon, Thursday, 22 January. Ryan returned to his office, where he telephoned Eastern Sea Frontier in New York to speak to the chief of staff. He spoke with Cdr. Sydney S. Bunting, the assistant chief of staff and flag secretary, and asked if it was possible to have Lt. Cdr. Harry Hicks in *Sylph* come to Washington for a one-day meeting. Bunting checked *Sylph*'s operating schedule and indicated it would be arranged. The meeting was set for 1300 the next day, Friday, 23 January.

Ryan then turned within OPNAV to find Legwen. A few telephone calls would accomplish this task. At 1330 Commander Ryan was in Admiral Farber's office, giving him a five-minute status report on Project LQ. Farber indicated that he would brief Admiral Horne at the first opportunity and told Ryan to "carry on." At 1500 Lt. Cdr. Glenn Legwen entered the conference room. Ryan had been to the security office, seen a photograph of Legwen, and verified his top secret security clearance. Legwen, even some nine years later, recalled vividly his first meeting with Ryan and his introduction to Project LQ. Ryan began the conversation by telling Legwen he had been selected as the prospective commanding officer of a ship that would be engaged in a secret operation. However, Ryan continued, the assignment would not be final until Legwen accepted and Admiral Horne approved his selection. Ryan explained the mission of the project and the ship, emphasizing that the entire matter, including the present meeting, was classified Secret.[20]

Legwen recalled that he sat silently, listening attentively to each word. Ryan stated that the duty was considered hazardous and that Legwen was being asked to volunteer. Ryan paused, then proceeded to outline the plan to operate several submarine decoy ships, Q-ships—armed merchant hulls, disguised, no armament showing outwardly, equipped with 4-inch cannons, depth charges and throwers, and sonar. Ryan again paused to give his associate an opportunity to react. Legwen had some questions. How big is this ship? How fast is she? Will she be well manned? Will she have torpedoes and launchers? Ryan responded: 3,600 tons; 11

knots; adequately manned with qualified officers and men; and no tor-pedo tubes. Legwen asked if he would have a free hand in fighting the ship, since Q-ship tactics were not taught at the naval academy or the War College. Ryan responded that fighting the ship was the command-ing officer's prerogative. Legwen remained silent for several moments then replied, "Yes, how can I, once selected, not accept." Then Legwen asked, "What is the life expectancy of this command?"

Ryan hesitated, wondering how to respond. "In all candor, if you are lucky, thirty days. If you are both successful and lucky, perhaps longer." Ryan searched for some positive aspects. "The ship will be loaded with pulp wood logs or empty steel drums for buoyancy after a torpedo hit. In theory, the ship is a platform for attacking with guns should the U-boat surface. Night attacks, darkness, visibility are all variables." Ryan con-cluded, "If in your judgment you are in a position to locate a submerged U-boat with your sonar and attack with depth charges, that would be your decision." Legwen was asked to return on Saturday for further dis-cussion and confirmation. He would have a day or two to sort things out.

The next day, Friday, 23 January, at 1300, Lt. Cdr. Harry Lynwood Hicks and Commander Ryan met in the admiral's conference room. Ryan used the same approach he had taken with Legwen. Hicks, too, was curi-ous about the configuration of the ship and the tactics to be employed. He volunteered for the assignment, almost nonchalantly. He was pleased to have Beckett as his engineer. Then he asked a question that Ryan could not answer. After being told that the officers and crew would be wearing civilian or merchant marine clothing and the ship would be identified by her nonmilitary name, *Carolyn*, Hicks asked, "What if by chance we are captured by a German armed raider, are we covered by the Geneva Convention and do we become prisoners of war? Or are we placed in jeopardy because we are military personnel and subject to treatment as enemy agents or spies?" Ryan was apparently caught off guard but recovered by agreeing to find the answer to Hicks's question. He thought capture was possible, but not probable. There was a pause. Hicks concluded: "I guess the only practical answer is—don't get cap-tured!" Both officers smiled. Ryan apprised Hicks of more details and said he could expect orders within a week.

Saturday morning at 1000 Legwen arrived at Horne's office and met Ryan. The meeting was short. Legwen agreed to the assignment. Ryan advised him of his academy classmate's selection and reviewed some of the points brought up by Hicks. Ryan said he would continue to investigate the question concerning the crews' status if they were captured, which meant appropriate action would be taken when and if such an event occurred. Legwen was advised that orders would be issued within a week and that he and Hicks would be processed through OPNAV and Eastern Sea Frontier together.[21]

Meanwhile, in a temporary wartime building across the Reflecting Pool from Main Navy, Commander Carter, in supplies and accounts, was presenting to Admiral Spear the names of his two candidates to fill the shipboard financial accounting and supply billets. One was Lt. (jg) Edgar Thomas Joyce, SC-M, USNR, and the other, Ens. Kenneth M. Beyer, SC-M, USNR. Carter provided a brief résumé of the two officers. He explained that both officers were selected because they were Merchant Marine Reserve currently on active duty. Carter reasoned that since both officers had had merchant marine experience, they would be familiar with operating in accordance with Maritime Commission and private steamship company procedures, and therefore, an asset to the project. Spear agreed and told Carter to bring them to Washington. Carter walked over to Ryan's office and gave him the names of the two officers. Ryan had all the officers selected. McColl and DuBois were identifying and locating the 135 petty officers and seamen for each ship. Project LQ was moving ahead at flank speed.

Rear Adm. Adolphus Andrews, commander, Eastern Sea Frontier, responded to Admiral King's dispatch about the "Queen Ships." His four-page letter dated 29 January 1942 was classified Secret. Andrews referred to the U-boat attacks on *Norness*, *City of Atlanta*, *Coimbra*, *Malay*, *Varanger*, and *Halo*. What he did not refer to, if he knew, was that by 29 January, nine more ships had been attacked along the East Coast. Andrews's letter spoke of "Queen Ship" strategy, armament, and operating procedures. In essence, the letter emphasized that U-boat attacks along the coast were at night, on the surface, and at close range; that the Q-ships should have significant reserve buoyancy in order to remain afloat after being torpedoed; that the Q-ship should have a "relatively insignificant appearance [so] that upon sighting it a submarine would not submerge"; that two battery-control officers should be provided should one or the other be knocked out; and that the Q-ship project was worth trying. Most of the details Commander Ryan had already considered.[22]

Andrews indicated his willingness to undertake the operational control of the Q-ships. As early as 12 January Eastern Sea Frontier had been advised of the movement of U-boats to the Canadian and U.S. East Coast. Andrews was willing to accept almost any reasonable help. Admiral Horne was pleased and reported the fact to Admiral King. Both admirals were well aware that Project LQ was not the final answer to this new U-boat offensive. But for now it was an expediency, a measure they hoped would alleviate a desperate situation.[23]

By 1 February Commander Ryan's efforts during the previous two weeks began to materialize. SS *Carolyn* and SS *Evelyn* were en route to the Portsmouth Navy Yard; orders to all officers were in process; and designated enlisted personnel were beginning to enter the pipeline leading to New Hampshire. Lieutenant Commanders Hicks and Legwen were brought together officially on Wednesday, 4 February, in Washington. Ryan had arranged for them to meet with Admirals Horne and Farber in OPNAV and with Commanders McColl and DuBois in naval personnel. Horne warmly welcomed the two officers. He explained the urgency of their mission and how ill prepared the Atlantic Fleet was to meet the growing menace of U-boat attacks occurring along the Atlantic coast. It was apparent the two admirals did not wish for further discussion. They congratulated the two officers on their selection and wished them good hunting. With orders in hand, the two prospective commanding officers concluded their briefings in Washington and departed.[24] They would see Ryan again on 9 February at 90 Church Street in New York.

This photo of U-123 was taken in Kiel, Germany, on or about 12 May 1942. She was leaving the shipyards after undergoing repair and refit incident to battle damage received from *Atik* and USS *Dahlgren*.
(Reinhard Hardegen/Sharkhunters International, Inc.)

KL Reinhard Hardegen
(Horst Bredow, U-Boot Archiv)

U-123 gun crew at
10.5-cm battery
(Horst Bredow)

Adm. Karl Dönitz and KL Hardegen
(Horst Bredow, U-Boot Archiv)

The Q-ship USS *Asterion*/SS *Evelyn* was photographed by a U.S. Navy blimp on 12 May 1942. *Asterion* was located in the Straits of Florida on a southerly course. Apparently the airship's crew did not detect the two 4-inch guns mounted forward of the smokestack or the depth charges and projectors located aft of the deckhouse.
(U.S. Coast Guard)

Glenn W. Legwen,
USNA, 1927
(USNA Alumni Association)

Lawrence R. Neville,
USNA, 1933
(USNA Alumni Association)

Henry C. Schwaner Jr.,
USNA, 1936
(USNA Alumni Association)

The author, Ens., SC,
USNR
(U.S. Navy photo)

Harry L. Hicks, USNA,
1927
(USNA Alumni Association)

Harry L. Hicks, Lt. Cdr.,
USN
(U.S. Navy photo)

Leonard V. Duffy, USNA,
1929
(USNA Alumni Association)

Daniel B. Deckelman,
USNA, 1937
(USNA Alumni Association)

Harold J. Beckett, Lt.,
USNR
(U.S. Navy photo)

Edwin M. Leonard, Ens.,
USNR
(U.S. Navy photo)

Thomas J. Ryan Jr., USN (Rear Adm., Retired), an official of the United
Fruit Company, Edward F. Beyer, USNR (Rear Adm., Retired)

4

Carolyn and *Evelyn:* The Ships and the Men

The commissionings are not a matter of
record in the Navy Department.

> Vice Adm. Frederick J. Horne,
> USN, Vice Chief of Naval Operations,
> Washington, D.C., March 1942

The city of Portsmouth, on the Piscataqua River, is the only commercial port on the New Hampshire coast. The river at this point separates the states of New Hampshire and Maine. The Naval Shipyard, Portsmouth, New Hampshire, is actually located on Seavey Island on the north, or Maine, side of the river, contiguous to Kittery, Maine. Politically, Maine claims the shipyard; geographically, the question is still unresolved. As long as the Boston and Maine Railroad knew where Portsmouth was, the local confusion was no concern of mine. I had other matters on my mind. Who were the officers and men who would be my comrades-in-arms? What was the appearance and configuration of the ship *Evelyn*, which would be my platform for facing the enemy?

Travel from the railroad station in Portsmouth, New Hampshire, to the Portsmouth Naval Shipyard in Maine, was much easier than I had expected. Travel time was compressed by a most interesting history lesson offered by the taxi driver. I listened intently as he gave his lecture: John Paul Jones lived here in 1777 while fitting-out *Ranger*. Daniel

Webster practiced law here from 1807 to 1813. Adm. David Glasgow "Damn the Torpedoes" Farragut died in Portsmouth on 14 August 1870. On 5 September 1905 the Treaty of Portsmouth, ending the Russo-Japanese war, was signed in the naval shipyard. In 1914 the naval shipyard began specializing in the design and construction of submarines. And one final item, at that time, 9 February 1942, a dinner of two 1½-pound Maine lobsters cost as little as $3.50. As the taxi driver expounded, we crossed the river to Kittery and then onto a fixed bridge spanning Back Channel to Seavey Island and the main gate of the shipyard. The marine sentry checked my identification card, saluted, and passed us through to the commandant's office.

A lieutenant in the commandant's office took a copy of my orders and then directed me to a Commander Quinby. I found the commander, introduced myself, and surrendered my orders. Quinby greeted me warmly and stated that he would arrange for the processing and billeting of the officers and crew until the two ships were placed in commission. He was dutiful, but not officious. He provided a chart of the shipyard, with the key buildings named and numbered. He also handed me the listing of the names of the ships' officers and their bachelor officers quarters (BOQ) room assignments. He mentioned that Lieutenant Neville, the prospective executive officer of *Asterion,* had left a few minutes earlier to check into the BOQ. Quinby suggested I proceed to the BOQ and meet with him. I did as he suggested.[1]

The weather was cold, very cold, and clear; a typical sunny February day for Maine. My dress blue uniform and heavy bridge coat gave me ample warmth. The BOQ was only three hundred yards away. The walk with my two suitcases was invigorating. The patches of snow here and there on the sidewalk made a crunching sound under my shoes. A more than ample ration of steam heat welcomed me to the BOQ. The building was an old wooden structure dating back to World War I, if not the Russo-Japanese Peace Treaty signing. It appeared neat, clean, and well furnished. It would be my home for the next several weeks.

A personal scrutiny and appraisal of Lt. Lawrence Neville was my main interest at this time. As the executive officer, he would be second in command and a key player in fighting the ship and staying alive. The "exec" is the executive administrator and coordinator of the daily shipboard routine. He takes direction only from the captain, and he orchestrates the activities of the several departments of the ship organization. The degree of formality in such matters depends on the personality and policy of the captain and the exec. With only six officers on board, each would play a key role, and the unusual mission of the Q-ship might well dictate a deviation from the ordinary U.S. Navy ship organizational structure. This matter would soon be resolved: As head of the Supply Department, I, as well as all other heads of department (gunnery, first lieutenant, navigation, engineering, communications), would have direct access to the captain. However, this is the exception rather than the rule.

Lieutenant Neville was in his quarters unpacking his gear when I knocked on his door. I introduced myself, and he invited me into his sitting room. In his blue uniform and his neatly trimmed mustache, he presented a striking appearance. He was slender and stood about six feet tall, a handsome man. He smoked cigarettes in a carved ivory holder. A gentleman, indeed, in speech and mannerism. I asked if I should leave so he could continue his unpacking, but he said, no, he would like to chat and then have lunch together if I was available. I told him I was eager to see the ship and would like to do that after lunch. He said he, too, wanted to see *Evelyn* and we might do that together in the early afternoon.

We walked back to Commander Quinby's office. Neville was anxious for details. Quinby mentioned that all officers were to arrive at the shipyard that day, 9 February 1942, except Legwen and Hicks. The two prospective commanding officers were in New York for discussions with commander, Eastern Sea Frontier staff people and, unless delayed, would report the next day. I asked Commander Quinby if he had available any information on the ship's characteristics. He said he did and pulled from a folder a copy of a paper that had a listing of such data. It was not classified, and as he handed it to me he said we could keep it. I thanked him and said I would share it with Lieutenant Neville. Neville, the polished gentleman, invited the commander to join us at lunch. He declined saying he suspected the two of us had much to talk about. We departed for lunch at the Officers Club, a short distance across MacDonough Avenue from where we were.[2]

The O-Club was on the upper deck of one of the old, permanent buildings. I wondered if John Paul Jones had had his fill of cod, lobster, haddock, and rum there. The decor represented more the colonial navy than the submarine service, although pictures of submarines were displayed in one corner, boats built at the shipyard dating back to 1923. I noted *Squalus*, renamed *Sailfish* after she foundered off Portsmouth in May 1939 and was later salvaged. But the primary motif in the main dining area was the colonial era: obsolete cutlasses and reproductions of paintings of U.S. warships active in the late eighteenth and early nineteenth century. While I found the references to early American history interesting, especially since I was present on land where events of historical importance had happened, the display of the submarine photos was more intriguing. As I studied the picture of *Seawolf* (SS197) I envisaged not a deadly weapon to be used against our enemy, but a sinister, dark shadow lying in wait to deliver a lethal strike—a U-boat. My fantasy with early American history turned abruptly to the reality of the present time and the business at hand.[3]

Lieutenant Neville and I had much to talk about. Despite his erect and military bearing, his manner was informal and relaxed. His pleasantness was somewhat disarming. While waiting to be served our New England clam chowder and lobster salad, I placed the listing of ships' characteristics on the table, thinking that Neville would pick it up or at least glance at it. But instead, he asked me about my family and my previous duty station. He was curious as to why I was singled out and who briefed me on the assignment. He asked me specifically if I had volunteered. Yes, was my reply. I felt obliged to give him complete yet succinct answers. As best I could, I summarized my brief visit to Washington. He was surprised that so much was accomplished from the time I left *North Carolina* to the present. He was particularly pleased that I had been given the necessary directives, informal as they were, to manage the logistics for the ship, including the hundred-thousand-dollar revolving fund with Riggs Bank. Apparently he was not surprised when I said I felt self-confident, was eager to get on with the job of fitting out the ship, and wanted to get down to the waterfront and take a look at what would become USS *Asterion*.

As if responding to my cue, Neville reached for the paper that gave the characteristics of the ship. It contained a considerable amount of data. He read it in silence. The break in our conversation gave me an opportunity to reflect on our discussion. I had answered his questions politely and with ease; he made me feel comfortable. I realized that his curiosity was both personal and professional. Not only did he have to satisfy himself that I was qualified and competent psychologically and professionally for the assignment, he would also be expected to render a judgment if and when asked by "Captain" Legwen—and that was a certainty! Neville handed the paper to me. "What do you think, Ken?"

The heading on the sheet of paper read "Enclosure (A)." Enclosure to what, we did not know. As part of my response, I read out loud: "USS *Asterion* (AK100)—USS *Atik* (AK101): Tonnage Gross 3209, Length 318' 6", Beam 46'. Cruising Radius 9600 at 9.5 knots." I volunteered my impression: "She isn't very big and she isn't very fast, but she can go a long way." As I glanced ahead, I was pleased to see that she would be well armed: "Four–4"/50 cal. main battery; four–.50 cal. machine guns; six–single depth charge throwers; five–Lewis .30 cal. machine guns; five–sawed-off shotguns; twelve–Colt .45 pistols; fifty–hand grenades." I noted aloud that she would have sonar, QCL echo-ranging and listening, but no radar. Interesting, too, it said, "Vessels have cargoes of pulp wood on board." I was surprised there were no searchlights. Neville expressed his concern regarding the speed of the ship. He doubted that maximum speed was much better than the 9.5 knots. This would be a serious disadvantage when engaging a U-boat, whether she be surfaced or submerged.

The two ships were at Berth 6, less than a thousand feet away. It would be a refreshing walk in the crisp air. We wore our bridge coats and gray gloves to keep our outer body warm, and we had the hot New England clam chowder to sustain the inner self. It was sunny, but below freezing. We walked along Dry Dock 2, a 550-foot dry cofferdam-type dock with the caisson in place to keep out the Piscataqua River water. Soon the two ships came into view. They were still painted in peacetime colors, black hull, white superstructure, and the letter B for Bull Line, A. H. Bull Steamship Company, prominent at the upper end of the tall, slender smokestack. As we walked another hundred feet, the name *Evelyn* became conspicuous on the bow of the closer ship. *Carolyn* was tied up further down the berth. We stopped walking and stood for a few moments in silence. I said to myself, She's no *North Carolina*. Neville broke the silence with three words: "Oh, my God!"

There she was resting at the dock in unimposing modesty: dignified, yes; splendid and formidable, certainly not! The seemingly tired old lady lay there asleep, cold iron. Neville said, "She looks expendable." A period of silence followed. Then I replied: "Maybe we will learn to love and respect her." Neville was a good storyteller, as I learned over time. He continued the theme of our conversation by recalling something he had to memorize at the naval academy, attributed to Alfred Thayer Mahan, U.S. naval officer, strategist, and prolific writer: "The backbone and real power of any navy are the vessels which, by due proportion of defensive and offensive powers, are capable of giving and taking hard knocks." Neville added, "I sure hope the backbone and power of our navy are not too dependent on this vessel." I listened carefully to Neville's words. The application of Mahan's logic to our first impression of *Evelyn* stimulated some sobering thoughts. We both felt some apprehension, some anxiety related to our immediate future. Indeed, the ship looked expendable; she was expendable!

Neville and I walked along the dock toward the bow, which had been rigged to gain access to the ship. We stepped aboard onto the well deck just after the deckhouse. All doorways from the weather deck were open, and the inside temperature seemed colder than the outdoor reading. She was "cold iron" and without shore power. We had not thought to bring a flashlight; it made no sense to wander around in the dark. We made our way to the bridge using outside ladders and peered into the chartroom. Like *Evelyn*, we were getting cold. We needed more than New England clam chowder to warm our bodies and our spirits. Our curiosity regarding the ship was only partially satisfied. Both Lieutenant Neville and I had many questions that only shipyard personnel could answer. We would start with Commander Quinby. So it was back to Building 86 and Quinby's office.

It was very cold walking into the freezing wind. As we fought the headwind, I asked Mr. Neville about himself and his naval service. He provided a verbal résumé. He was born at the naval hospital in Portsmouth, Virginia. His father was a navy construction corps officer, a naval architect. He graduated from the naval academy, joined *Saratoga* (CV3) in the Gunnery Department, next as gunnery officer in the destroyer *Twiggs* (DD127), then to China and the coastal gunboat USS *Asheville*. In 1940 he was detailed to the battleship *Arkansas* (BB33) on convoy operations to Iceland and Newfoundland. He left *Arkansas* in New York to join *Asterion*. I asked if he had had experience in antisubmarine warfare. He said he had none other than working with the U.S. destroyers in the convoys and closely monitoring the Canadian and British DDs and corvettes in company with *Arkansas*.

Walking into the freezing wind drained the energy from both of us. On our arrival at Commander Quinby's office, he offered us a most welcome cup of hot coffee. Neville interpreted the offer of coffee to mean Commander Quinby was agreeable to our spending more than a few minutes with him. Neville told the commander we had been to the ship and observed that no work was in progress. Quinby seemed to welcome the opportunity to talk to the executive officer before the other officers arrived. He emphasized that this was a low-profile job in the shipyard in support of a secret project. Since all ships' personnel were ordered to the shipyard, the commandant, Admiral Wainwright, would have administrative control until the ships were commissioned. But he expected the prospective commanding officers to take charge and detail the officers and men to prepare the ships for their mission. Quinby indicated that when the COs arrived there would be an interface meeting with the construction and conversion planning officer, Capt. Andrew Irwin McKee; the yard supply officer, Capt. M. H. Philbrick; and the ships' officers. A target date of 5 March was set for commissioning. He provided a copy of NAV 331-A, the enlisted personnel allowance for *Asterion*. Neville asked when the enlisted men would arrive. Quinby said the majority were being assembled at the receiving stations in Boston and New York, but certain key petty officers could be brought to the shipyard early. Neville and I thanked Commander Quinby for his briefing.

It was approaching four o'clock in the afternoon. Quinby expected the ships' officers to arrive on the afternoon train, and they had to be processed. He would be busy. He said he would send them to the BOQ where we could meet with them if we so desired. We made our way to our temporary living quarters. The sun was close to the horizon in the southwest; it would soon be dark. It couldn't get much colder. Neville asked if I would join him at seven o'clock and suggested we go to the Officers Club for lobster. I was pleased to accept.

A few minutes before seven o'clock, I knocked on Lieutenant Neville's door. He was dressed and ready for Maine's biggest and best "edible marine decapods." He said Schwaner had arrived and would join us for dinner. The lieutenant was waiting in the BOQ lobby, and Neville made the introduction, a simple, "Dutch Schwaner, this is Ken Beyer." Dutch extended a big hand with a very firm grip. I learned later that he had played varsity baseball, his first love, all four years at the naval academy. Inside the club was warm, and the sparsely populated bar was inviting. Although mild mannered, physically Dutch was a strong, muscular man. We were about the same height, five feet, eleven inches, but he seemed heavier; he certainly had more muscle weight than I did. Lt. Dutch Schwaner was a New Yorker from Saratoga Springs. He graduated from the naval academy in 1936, attested to by his sizable academy ring, much like Neville's. He was married. He had had successive assignments in the battleship *Texas* (BB35), the cruiser *Omaha* (CL4), the stores ship *Yukon* (AF9), and the destroyer *Noa* (DD343). Ordnance was his specialty. We had a pleasant dinner—but without Maine lobster, which was not served on Monday nights. However, we learned from the waiter that the old Rockingham Hotel in Portsmouth offered the best lobster dinners in town. We would be there the next night if at all possible.

At 6:30, Tuesday, 10 February 1942, my alarm clock awakened me from a deep sleep. I was refreshed and wondered what challenges this day would reveal. The executive officer's meeting should be a good starting point for developing an overall plan of action for bringing the crew together, fitting out the ship, and getting ready for commissioning. At commissioning, the officers and crew move aboard, and the ship becomes "a living thing." At 8:30 Lieutenant Neville entered the conference room and asked us to be seated. It was apparent that he had met, either last night or this morning, the two officers absent from dinner on Monday. As a formality, Neville went around the table naming each officer: Lieutenant Schwaner, our gunnery officer and first lieutenant; Ensign Guy Ray, engineer; Ensign Ken Beyer, supply officer; and Ensign John Lukowich, communications officer. Neville's commentary was to the point: Lt. Cdr. Glenn Legwen would be the commanding officer, expected tomorrow or the next day with Lt. Cdr. Harry Hicks, prospective commanding officer of *Atik*, our sister ship. The two merchant ships *Evelyn* and *Carolyn* would become, respectively, USS *Asterion* (AK100) and USS *Atik* (AK101) when commissioned. They would operate as U-boat decoy ships under their merchant names. The duty was secret and hazardous, and he presumed all had volunteered. Then he added, "If at any time you wish to transfer to other duty, speak directly to me or to the captain."

While it was a bit premature, I could not help but wonder about the captain, his knowledge of Q-ship tactics, his perception of U-boat warfare, his appreciation for the several years of experiences that had honed the veteran U-boat commander into a skilled and daring tactician. This was what he—and we along with him—would face. Would he be prepared? Would we? Yes, there was much to think about and to do.

Neville continued his remarks with specifics that established his objectives and leadership style: Get acquainted with each other; plan your work; coordinate your efforts; and eliminate loss motion. He said the ship's commissioning date was 5 March, less than three weeks away. He then addressed our responsibilities: Be satisfied that the shipyard's alteration plan is acceptable; be careful not to interfere with their work; be certain their work is done correctly; and assume nothing when it comes to the fighting ability, the seaworthiness, or habitability of the ship. He encouraged us to talk freely with *Atik*'s officers. He concluded by announcing that after Legwen and Hicks arrived, Commander Quinby would have a meeting to provide information and establish shipyard ground rules.

Meeting and evaluating new shipmates is an interesting endeavor. This was no exception. It's like the first meeting with the coaching staff and teammates for any team sport. Focus is on the key participants. In a small ship, such as *Asterion*, every officer is a key player. And in the Q-ship versus U-boat contest there were no rules. Cunning, deception, trickery, finesse, and craftiness were all in the "unofficial" rule book of the game. In such a contest, the game can be won or lost by the performance of any one key player.

Ens. Guy Brown Ray, the engineer, and I both knew we had much to do before commissioning. We had to determine and procure spare parts, repair parts, and consumable items for the old machinery and electrical systems in the ship. He would specify his needs; I would requisition the items from the Naval Supply System, buy them on the open market, or arrange to have them made in the shipyard. We understood each other and established a relationship of apparent mutual respect, personally and professionally.

Guy-Brown, as we would call him, was a "mustang," an enlisted man, who by virtue of his outstanding professional abilities and deportment, advanced through the ranks to a commissioned officer. He enlisted in the navy in 1919 at age seventeen. He was promoted to warrant machinist in 1929 and commissioned ensign in November 1941. Guy-Brown had served in the battleships *Wyoming* (BB32), *New Mexico* (BB40), and *Maryland* (BB46), in destroyers, and in the aircraft carrier *Lexington* (CV2). For two years he was the repair officer in the destroyer tender *Melville* (AD2). In 1934 and 1935 he was ship superintendent of new construction at the Portsmouth Naval Shipyard. This assignment proved to be a great asset; his familiarity with the yard facilitated communications with yard personnel and served to expedite jobs through the production process. Indeed, Guy-Brown was well qualified for the engineering position. When he finally looked over the main propulsion plant in *Evelyn*, he commented: "My job is not to keep the old steam engine going, it's to get it going, but then I have played with bigger toys than this one!" Guy Brown Ray stood tall as an engineer even though he was less than five feet, seven inches in height. His center of gravity protruded noticeably over his slackened trouser belt. He was married and the father of four children.

John R. "Luke" Lukowich, a graduate of the Naval Reserve Midshipman School in New York, was commissioned ensign, U.S. Naval Reserve, in November 1941. He had a brief tour at Headquarters, Commandant, Third Naval District, New York. There, he had been assigned to the communications office that also supported the commander, Eastern Sea Frontier. He was tall and slender with a quiet, reserved, unassuming personality. What Luke lacked in practical shipboard experience was more than offset by his positive attitude and his eagerness to undertake the tasks at hand.

As we were about to leave the conference room, Lieutenant Duffy and the officers assigned to *Atik* arrived. There were introductions and handshakes and as many brief conversations as there were pairs of officers. Lt. (jg) Ed Joyce, my counterpart, and I agreed to meet later and make a courtesy call on the shipyard supply officer, Capt. M. H. Philbrick. Neville and his entourage left the area. Lt. Leonard Vincent Duffy, USN, took a seat at the head of the conference room table. He began with an authoritative: "Take a chair and be seated." His topics covered in general the same items addressed by Neville. And like *Asterion's* exec, he emphasized the secrecy of the mission, its precarious nature, and the need to place personal matters in order for a long deployment.[4]

Lieutenant Duffy was direct and firm, but not arrogant. His academy reputation followed him into active service: "He could be disagreeable, . . . whether for the sake of argument or just to be ornery. But . . . he has a sparkling sense of humor, and is always ready with a pun." While effective and dependable, his sometimes brusque mannerisms were in sharp contrast with Neville's suavity. Duffy, at age thirty-five, was five years older than and five years senior in rank to Neville. His five years of seasoning as an executive officer and commanding officer of small ships, USS *Heron* (AVP2), a converted mine sweeper, and USS *Napa* (AT32), a 1,030-ton ocean-going tug, probably shaped his attitude and leadership style. The responsibility of command took some sparkle out of his sense of humor and instilled a more serious element into his normally carefree character. The fraternization he enjoyed with his regiment-mates remained at the academy. After graduation his piano playing remained in Smoke Hall, and his jazz band was a thing of the past. He would maintain a respected position among men.[5]

Neville, on the other hand, had experienced more of the formality of the traditional "ship-of-the-line" navy and felt comfortable in dealing with his junior officers in a direct and personal way. As professionals schooled in naval etiquette and tradition, his juniors were expected to conduct themselves within acceptable bounds. Both officers knew that camaraderie was not a requirement of military leadership and, in the opinion of most authorities, should be avoided. Lieutenant Duffy adhered strictly to this principle, whereas Neville was more flexible. Duffy, as executive officer, would function as the executive assistant to the commanding officer. He would take direction from his leader. If Hicks was a strong, active, in-charge, hands-on leader, Duffy's demeanor would complement the command role. However, Lieutenant Duffy, a well-educated, well-trained, experienced, and self-reliant naval officer, could adjust easily to the needs of the command. He would take his cues from Hicks.

Lt. Daniel Bernard Deckelman, USN, was born in Cincinnati, Ohio, in 1913. He graduated from the U.S. Naval Academy and was commissioned ensign on 3 June 1937. At the academy, "Danny" was tagged in the yearbook as "a likable fellow, . . . a member of that party known as the backbone of the Regiment." Upon graduation, Deckelman was detailed to the heavy cruiser *Vincennes* (CA44). His official naval file states that he served in the gunnery department until detached in February 1942 to report to *Atik* as her gunnery officer. At that time *Vincennes* was in New York. She had returned from convoy duty to South African waters. At the New York Navy Yard she was being prepared for deployment and transfer to the Pacific Fleet. Dan Deckelman's style was aggressive but controlled. Even at the naval academy he was "never one to sit idly by and let things run their course." In *Vincennes* as a junior officer he felt restrained, underutilized, and unchallenged. In 1940, according to his official file, he requested transfer to the Supply Corps where he might have more management responsibilities as a "young" officer. *Vincennes*'s commanding officer, Capt. J. R. Beardall, forwarded Ensign Deckelman's request with a less than glowing endorsement: "Ensign Deckelman has shown aptitude for Supply Corps work and in the opinion of the Commanding Officer he is qualified now for line duties and for promotion to Lt. (junior grade)." Rear Adm. C. W. Nimitz, the chief of the Bureau of Navigation

(Personnel), forwarded the request to the selection board for postgraduate instructions. When his request was denied, Deckelman asked for transfer to new construction, preferably one of the new battleships. Instead, Dan was ordered first to *Asterion* and then, for reasons unknown other than error, to *Atik*.

Lieutenant Deckelman would preside over *Atik*'s armament and husband these weapons as his very own. Although almost five years had passed since his naval academy days, he still retained his smart and snappy military bearing. *Vincennes* would demand that of her officers. While apprehensive regarding the mission of *Atik*, he was eager to throw off the yoke of an assistant gunnery officer in the heavy cruiser and be the "gun boss" in another combatant—disreputable as *Atik* might be. Now, after rapid promotion to senior lieutenant and head of the Gunnery Department, Dan Deckelman would flourish in his new assignment. More frequently now than in *Vincennes*, he would sit back in his chair, light up a not-too-expensive cigar, and indulge himself in a brief period of rapture. He felt he had achieved a position of relative prominence that was not available to him in *Vincennes*. He was a ready and able team member.

Lt. Harold James Beckett, E-M, USNR, was a licensed engineer in the Merchant Marine and served in the Army Transport Service during World War I. He was born in New York City in 1898. He went to sea at age eighteen and soon experienced the devastation of U-boat attacks when he survived the torpedoing of the transport *Antilles* and later the transport *Finland*. He continued serving in the Merchant Marine after the war and was commissioned a lieutenant (jg), USNR, in 1928. Beckett was called to active duty in 1940 and assigned to the fitting-out detail of the converted yacht *Intrepid* (YP71) at the Sullivan Drydock and Repair Company in New York City. She was renamed USS *Sylph* (PY12) and was commissioned on 1 October 1940. Beckett served on board as engineering officer and was promoted to lieutenant, USNR, to rank from 21 September 1940. *Sylph*'s commanding officer was Lieutenant Commander Hicks. Accordingly, these two officers needed no introduction. Lieutenant Beckett, at age forty-three, was a professional sea-going engineer. Amiable, knowledgeable, and cooperative, he interfaced well with the shipyard personnel and ship's officers and men. Having already survived two torpedo attacks, had Lt. Hal Beckett been a superstitious person rather than a man of valor, he might have declined the assignment to *Atik*.

Lt. (jg) Edgar T. Joyce, SC-M, USNR, was born in the Bronx in 1910. He attended Fordham University before going to sea with the United Fruit Steamship Company. Joyce was commissioned in the naval reserve in July 1941 and reported for active duty as assistant to the supply officer, Navy Yard, Brooklyn, New York, the following month. From that billet he was ordered to *Atik*. Although as a newlywed he had a natural reluctance to leave his bride, he also felt the deeply embedded yearning for ships and the sea. Here in Portsmouth, he would concentrate as best he could on the many and varied details of his new responsibilities. He was malleable and would easily adjust to duty in a navy ship. But then, would *Atik* resemble a navy ship? Hardly!

The most junior partner in the Atik Shipping Company enterprise was Ens. Edwin Madison Leonard, D-VG, USNR. He completed the roster of *Atik*'s officers. Edwin Leonard was born in Reidville, South Carolina, on 21 January 1919. An ambitious and studious young man, he earned a bachelor's degree at the University of South Carolina and a law degree from the University of Virginia. In March 1941 he accepted an appointment as midshipman, USNR, and commenced officer's training at the U.S. Naval Reserve Midshipman School, New York (USS *Prairie State*). He was commissioned ensign, USNR, in June 1941, and ordered to USS *Washington* (BB56) for duty in communications. From the new battleship *Washington*, Ensign Leonard was transferred to Portsmouth for duty in *Atik*. Edwin Leonard was an intelligent and willing team player. He adjusted well from the formality of the daily routine aboard *Washington* with an embarked admiral to the unceremonious environment of the hurried conversion of SS *Carolyn* to USS *Atik*. His busy life permitted no time for serious romance and marriage. He hoped that would come later.

The arrival of Lieutenant Commanders Legwen and Hicks on the scene on 12 February 1942 shifted the ships' conversion and commissioning process into high gear. Both prospective COs met with their officers. Commander Quinby gave his briefing. The detail plans and sketches for the modification of the two ships to accommodate the armament and the additional personnel were reviewed. Copies were provided. Quinby stated that the shipyard was confident that all alteration work for the two ships would be completed in time for commissioning on 5 March 1942. Quinby reported that shore electrical power and steam had been provided to each ship so spaces could be heated and lighted. A walk-through of each ship by yard and ship personnel was scheduled for the afternoon. Legwen and Hicks were asked to present within the next five days work-requests for items not already in the shipyard plan, as well as names and ratings of key enlisted personnel to be transferred to the ship-yard early to assist in precommissioning activities. There appeared to be few administrative problems; none that could not be resolved. Comman-der Quinby had planned well.

Both Legwen and Hicks had the same two major issues in mind: the seaworthiness and fighting ability of ship and crew, and the tactics to be employed when engaging a U-boat. The first item Legwen and Hicks discussed with their respective ship's officers, asking for their evaluations. But the second issue remained the overwhelming concern of each CO. It was apparent that little substantive guidance would come from Eastern Sea Frontier, the operational commander. Legwen and Hicks knew that tactics would depend on the circumstances, the CO's ability to maneu-ver his ship into a superior relative position, and finally, the ability of his ship and crew to take punishment while responding with deadly force. Each captain would spend many hours contemplating and developing his own strategy and tactics. Based on a few guarded comments by each, it appeared that Legwen was the more aggressive, while Hicks was the more contemplative.

Hicks and Legwen also differed in administrative and leadership prac-tices. Hicks directed, whereas Legwen delegated. Both methods appeared to be equally effective. Neither one adhered to Machiavellian principles of conduct. They were pleasant and professional in their interactions with others. Hicks visited the ship twice a day and expected to see his officers on board overseeing the conversion work. Legwen preferred to inspect the shipyard work less frequently. However, he had a daily meeting with his officers for progress reports, brief discussions of general topics, and resolution of problems. As time passed and the tempo of activity increased, the benefits of mutual discussions between *Atik* and *Asterion* officers diminished and the independence of each ship evolved.

The conversion of the two cargo ships was not a major challenge to the shipyard marine engineers and craftsmen. The discipline and workmanship of the Portsmouth Navy Yard workers were commendable. Most knew the conversion work on the two surface ships was unusual. But they asked few questions and got no answers. Adherence to schedules and specifications and the need for quality work were ingrained in the attitude and workmanship of the craftsmen in this submarine building yard. The pride of the New England shipbuilder was readily apparent. This pride had been tarnished temporarily on 23 May 1939 when USS *Squalus* (SS192) sank in sixty fathoms of water during test dives off Portsmouth and the Isle of Shoals. The cause of the sinking was the failure of the main induction valve, which resulted in the flooding of the after engine room. She was raised successfully, repaired, and recommissioned as USS *Sailfish*. The tragedy that caused the deaths of twenty-six men was a lasting lesson in quality control.[6]

Carolyn and *Evelyn* had been bulk raw sugar carriers. Each had five cargo holds; two forward of the bridge, one aft of the bridge house and forward of the smoke stack, and two aft of the midships deck house. All holds had a tween deck, or a second deck, level below the main. According to the shipyard's plans, the second deck level of hold number 2, second from the bow and immediately forward of the bridge house, would be enclosed with sheet metal around the hatch opening and converted to a crew berthing compartment on the starboard side and a storeroom and workshop on the port side. The number 3 hatch at the same level would also be enclosed and the surrounding spaces outfitted as a crew mess deck and lounge. In both cases the hatch openings would remain clear so pulpwood logs could be loaded into the lower holds. These spaces plus existing compartments provided ample room for the enlarged crew.

The installation of the ships' armament required considerable structural augmentation. Supports for the four concealed 4-inch, 50-caliber cannons made deck understructure reinforcement imperative. One of these guns was located on each side of hatch number 3 on the upper deck level. The existing steel deck plates at these locations were replaced with a leveled platform supported from the deck below by substantial beams of channel iron welded in place so as to absorb the force of the cannon when fired. A canvas drapelike screen, painted gray, was designed to conceal these weapons from horizontal view. The other two 4-inch, 50-caliber guns were mounted on the after corners, port and starboard, atop the deckhouse aft of the smokestack and aft of the lifeboat davits. As with the two forward guns, these required supports that would assure a stable platform under conditions of repeated rapid fire. A plywood "house" concealed these weapons. Panels could be removed on orders to bring the guns into action. This "penthouse" structure altered to some extent the profile of the ship.

The six mark-7 arbor and depth charge projectors for the mark-6 mod-0 depth charges were located and arranged on the after end of each ship. The installation assured a technically effective pattern when the charges were fired simultaneously and detonated at the preset depth. Two projectors were located on the deck below the after 4-inch guns, two on the after well deck abreast number 5 hatch, and two on the poop deck, in each case one port and one starboard. Mounts for the four .50-caliber machine guns were located on the well decks abreast of number 2 hatch forward and abreast of number 4 hatch aft. These mounts were collapsible and could be raised easily and quickly when needed. The mounts, when in the down position, would be out of view of any U-boat. Indeed, even with their armament in place, *Carolyn* and *Evelyn* would be ships "of relatively insignificant appearance." Hopefully, they would appear to be a worthwhile artillery target to the experienced U-boat commander.

With the shipyard work progressing satisfactorily, attention turned to outfitting the ship and orienting the crew. Both Legwen and Hicks provided Commander Quinby a list of the petty officers for the precommissioning detail. Within forty-eight hours, these leading petty officers and specialists were assembled at the naval shipyard. Hicks chose to convene an early meeting of all hands to introduce his officers and to brief the petty officers on the ship's mission and their assignments. Legwen preferred to have his officers, individually, address their personnel. This difference in personnel management was typical of the leadership styles of the two commanding officers. Both were effective.

Lieutenant Commander Hicks addressed his officers and men (see appendix 1 for ship's roster of enlisted men). He confirmed that all present had volunteered for hazardous sea duty. He emphasized that this was not a suicide assignment: "The ship is expendable, but you are not." However, he explained, success and survival depended on how well each person carried out his assigned duties. He then introduced each officer and detailed each petty officer to his respective department (see appendix 2). Hicks emphasized the need for a mobile and capable damage control party. Damage control was an essential survival element, since the pulpwood logs were highly flammable and flood control was necessary to maintain a level platform for the 4-inch guns. He tasked Chiefs McCall, Sparrow, Johnson, and Paredes, and petty officers Smith and Ouellette, under Beckett's direction, to organize, lead, equip, and train to meet all damage control objectives. Lieutenant Commander Hicks dismissed the group with the admonishment that there was much work to be done and only a short period of time in which to do it. He cautioned the group to speak only to family members and then say only that his duty was in a navy cargo ship, USS *Atik*.

Lieutenant Neville mustered *Asterion*'s precommissioning detail and called the roll (see appendixes 3 and 4). Neville, like Hicks, wanted to assure himself that each member of the crew was, indeed, a volunteer and had been given the opportunity to decline the assignment. This he confirmed with each petty officer before proceeding further with his meeting. In much the same manner as Hicks, he explained the mission of the ship, the configuration, the concealed armament, the interface with ship-yard personnel, the urgency and covert nature of the mission, the AK100 misnomer, and he somberly advised each person to put his personal affairs in order. He then announced the names of the officers and their duties, and provided a schedule for each of the petty officers to meet in the conference room with his head of department.

"Swiftness in war comes from slow preparations." This quotation is attributable to Gen. Sir Ian Standish Hamilton, the British commander who in 1915 undertook the land campaign against the Turks on the Gallipoli Peninsula. If this maxim had been applied to the preparations of *Atik* and *Asterion* for war, it might well have foretold the future of this undertaking. The two-week period beginning Monday, 16 February 1942, was a time of intense activity and seemed evanescent, to end before it began. By Sunday, 1 March, the ships were nearing the time for final inspection by the two commanding officers before acceptance and commissioning. Shipyard personnel were turning over the propulsion plants while the ships were made fast alongside the dock. This eight-hour dock trial was to ensure the proper working order of the engines and boilers and to confirm the absence of steam leaks, hot bearings, and other troublesome abnormalities. The discrepancies were corrected. On Tuesday, 3 March, the ships put to sea for underway trials, *Asterion* in the morning and *Atik* in the afternoon. Acceptance inspection of each ship by her commanding officer and moving the crew aboard were scheduled for Wednesday. If all went well, on Thursday, 5 March 1942, the commandant of the yard would place the ships in commission as U.S. Navy vessels.

The commissioning of a naval ship is normally a ceremonious event. The band plays John Philip Sousa marches. Decorative flags and pennants fly from the yardarms and from the fore peak to the fore truck to the after truck to the after peak. Political and civilian dignitaries are present. Senior military officers with swords, gloves, and medals are in colorful array. Shipyard workers and families are in abundance. The ship's officers and crew are in conspicuous ranks. And, of course, newspaper reporters and cameras are capturing the speeches, the accolades, and the festive atmosphere for publication and posterity. Navy ship commissioning, usually, is an auspicious and punctilious occasion. But little, if anything, could be termed "usual" about AK100, AK101, or their commissioning ceremony.

On the clear, cold, bright but waning afternoon of 5 March 1942, at precisely 1615, the officers and crew of *Asterion* stood at parade rest at their designated places on or near hatch number 5. The crew wore dress blues, flathats, and peacoats. The officers presented themselves in dress blues, gray gloves, and bridge coats. At 1620 the navy band from the First Naval District, Boston, arrived by bus, marched on board, and formed ranks. At 1625 Rear Adm. John D. Wainwright, USN, commandant, Naval Shipyard, Portsmouth, New Hampshire, and his party of officers arrived. He took his place at the portable lectern, ready to begin the ceremony at precisely 1630. At 1628 the Boston and Maine's steam locomotive arrived alongside with ten carloads of pulpwood logs. Even the band's best effort at "Anchor's Aweigh" could not compete with the presence of the B and M. The admiral's aide seemed to be the only one concerned.

Notwithstanding the din of discordant sounds and the fragrance of coal smoke, freshly cut pine logs, and air-drying lobster traps, the gallant admiral proceeded with his script. After a few short, inaudible sentences, the significant words could be heard, "I place this ship in commission." Legwen, now the captain, saluted the admiral; the admiral saluted the captain. Neville gave the order to hoist the ensign (American flag), the jack, and the commissioning pennant. Chief Darling ran up the pennant to the main truck; Journey hoisted the ensign on the flag staff aft; and Stansbury raised the forty-eight white stars on the blue field jack to the top of the jack staff. The band played the national anthem, and the B and M went about its business of placing gondola cars alongside the dock and expelling coal smoke with the bellow of a Texas bull loose on a New Hampshire dairy farm. SS *Evelyn* was now USS *Asterion*.

The admiral departed USS *Asterion* flanked by the smartly aligned sideboys and to the shrill of the boatswain's pipe. He proceeded to *Atik* and repeated his performance. Both ships sported their new coat of navy-gray paint, but the white alpha-numeric ship type and number designation normally painted on the sides of the bow, "AK100" for *Asterion* and "AK101" for *Atik*, were conspicuously absent. Oversight? No, intentional. It was also no coincidence that the commissioning ceremony took place in the late afternoon, just before dark and after the daytime shift of shipyard workers had departed. The better the concealment, the greater the security.

Admiral Wainwright returned to his office to have the appropriate entry made in the shipyard's official log. It read as follows: "5 March 1942. USS *Asterion* (AK-100) placed in commission at 1630. Lt. Cdr. Glenn W. Legwen, USN, commanding. USS *Atik* (AK-101) placed in commission at 1645. Lt. Cdr. Harry L. Hicks, USN, commanding." The commandant, Navy Yard, Portsmouth, advised the Office of the Chief of

Naval Operations, Washington, D.C., Rear Adm. W. S. Farber, USN, of the events by confidential speedletter 061310 dated 6 March 1942.[7] The vice chief of naval operations, Vice Admiral Horne, informed the commander, Eastern Sea Frontier, Rear Admiral Andrews, of the commissioning of the two ships by secret letter, which read in part: "Although [the] vessels have been regularly commissioned by the Commandant, Navy Yard, Portsmouth, N.H., by direction of the Chief of Naval Operations, and so recorded in the Log of that Yard, the commissionings are not a matter of record in the Navy Department. . . . Except for personnel records in the Bureau of Navigation there has been no record of acquisition, conversion, and operation of the subject AKs. Pertinent information is contained in a secret file in custody of the Vice Chief of Naval Operations."[8]

Few if any U.S. Navy ships, throughout the two-hundred-year existence of the naval service, have been intentionally denied official recognition as were these two Q-ships. Mystery ships, indeed!

5

Getting Under Way

IT'S GONE WITH THE WIND NOW AND HOPING
FOR A WINDFALL.

Chief of Naval Operations War Diary,
23 March 1942

ACTIVITY SCHEDULES and daily routines for USS *Asterion* and USS *Atik* were quite similar. The two principal objectives were safety and battle practice. The prerequisite was settling the crew in the ship. This would be done on Friday, Saturday, and Sunday, the sixth, seventh, and eighth of March. The watch, quarter, and station bill was developed and posted so each person would know his duty assignment and time period and his battle station. Watch sections were established. Damage control (DC) and fire-fighting parties were organized and drilled. The location of DC lockers with oxygen breathing apparatus and P500 portable pumps, the positioning of fire extinguishers, fire plugs, hoses, and applicators all had to be drilled into the minds of designated personnel. These were but a few of the many tasks to be accomplished in a limited period of time. Battle practice would come soon.

Holiday routine was not observed on Saturday and Sunday. Crew liberty was restricted to personnel with family no further away than Boston. Those few who qualified were cautioned to limit discussions to strictly unclassified matters. The shipyard continued to load pulpwood. Checking and testing equipment, reviewing and updating technical manuals and navigation charts seemed to be a never ending chore. It was a learning process for the crew. It all had to be done. There was no alternative.

On Wednesday, 11 March, Hicks and Legwen were in New York to receive instructions from Eastern Sea Frontier's Operations Office. They made a brief call on Rear Adm. Adolphus Andrews. He greeted the officers with unexpected friendliness. He congratulated them on their new command. He admonished them that much of the success of the project would depend on their own initiative, skill, and daring since the U.S. Navy had no worthwhile experience in this type of naval warfare. He wished them good luck and successful "hunting." Capt. Thomas R. Kurtz, Andrews's chief of staff, and Commander Farley took Legwen and Hicks in tow.

In operations, Farley handed the two COs their Preliminary Operations Order. This op-order was intended to provide Hicks, Legwen, and their officers a training period during which they were to devise a means to catch the German "U-fish": a strategic lure, a tactical bait, and a deadly hook. No chapter in any U.S. naval warfare textbook taught cleverness and adroitness in the ruse of Q-ship operations. Legwen, Neville, and Schwaner, and Hicks, Duffy, and Deckelman, along with their junior officers, were supposed to write the chapter then teach the course to the crew. Training through incessant drilling would provide the crew with the skill and agility necessary to successfully pass the course. They would learn their lessons well; Hicks and Legwen would see to that.

The op-order provided for: (1) a brief period of at-sea training to begin on or about 24 March 1942; (2) direction to report when ready for sea to commander, Submarine Division 101 (COMSUBDIV 101), the local area operations commander; (3) proceeding independently on widely separated courses for shakedown in areas where enemy activity had not been reported; (4) navigating so that one ship should be approximately 480 miles southward of the other after five days at sea; (5) departing the navy yard, Portsmouth, in such a manner that they would appear to all observers as armed vessels regularly commissioned in the navy; (6) concealment at the first opportunity when clear of land and other vessels or guns and depth charge throwers, with commission pennants hauled down and other steps taken to have USS *Atik* and USS *Asterion* present the appearance of merchantmen; (7) reporting to commander, Eastern Sea Frontier by dispatch, on completion of shakedown; at that time, and not before, the second operation plan would be made effective by message.[1]

Hicks and Legwen reviewed the order. One obvious question was, Where had enemy activity not been reported? Commander Farley acknowledged that this was difficult to determine but the western Gulf of Maine appeared suitable for training exercises. He cautioned that the area along the Atlantic Coast from Barnegat Inlet, north of Atlantic City, to Cape Hatteras, North Carolina, had witnessed the majority of attacks during the past sixty days. He added that three attacks had occurred during the past three days: one that morning, a ship off Assateague light, Virginia, near Winter Quarter lightship; another the morning before, the U.S. tanker *Gulftide*, off Barnegat Inlet, New Jersey; and one on the ninth, 110 miles east of Cape May, New Jersey. Finally, he said the British admiralty advised that, based on their intelligence reports, they anticipated an increase in U-boat activity along the U.S. coast to begin at any time. Armed with these data, the two Q-ship captains returned to their commands.

Concealing the conversion of *Evelyn* and *Carolyn* from merchant ships to Q-ships became a concern of navy yard security. The wife of one of *Atik*'s officers reported that "work on these Q-ships was common knowledge in several Portsmouth boarding houses." Navy yard security knew it would be "impossible to conceal the peculiarities of the structures of these vessels from the scores of shipyard civilian workers assigned to the conversion job."[2] They could respond only on a case by case basis and attempt to keep rumors from getting out of hand. Cdr. Tom Ryan's selection of the somewhat remote New England shipyard for the secret conversion project was a calculated one. Portsmouth was a small yard in a relatively small community. And more important, it maintained a workforce of loyal and responsible New Englanders. These patriotic Maine and New Hampshire families treated this sensitive "job" with discretion. The "talk" of the project was short-lived both inside the yard and out. It apparently never left the local area.

U-boat headquarters (BdU) in Lorient, France, did not expect the United States to employ decoy ships as an anti-U-boat weapon. However, a few of the more "cautious" U-boat commanders were suspicious. On 7 March 1942, U-578, Korvettenkapitän Ernst-August Rehwinkel, operating off the Delaware Capes, reported to BdU a vessel that he suspected to be a submarine decoy. He avoided engagement. It was KK Rehwinkel who, on the night of 28 February, had torpedoed and sunk USS *Jacob Jones* (DD130) off Cape May.[3] Then on the night of 11 March, Kapitänleutnant Adolf Piening in U-155 located in the Cape Hatteras area advised BdU he fired a spread of two torpedoes at a freighter. The torpedoes missed and he was attacked immediately by an aircraft that dropped three bombs, all near misses. He observed the aircraft and the steamship working together by means of blue signal lights. He suspected the freighter to be a submarine decoy ship. Apparently, there were other reports, for U-boat headquarters responded with a rebuke in a radio communication to all U-boat commanders. It was included in BdU's War Log under the date 11 March 1942 as follows:

> The great number of reports recently of submarine decoy ships must be treated with great reserve. These reports have been made in most cases by commanders with little operational experience who suspect any vessel behaving in an unusual manner of being a submarine decoy ship. Ensuing defensive measures and misfires are not in most cases attributable to the special observance and expedients of submarine decoy ships but to their own clumsy tactics and lack of firing dexterity. It is scarcely to be expected that the enemy who is so short of shipping should employ vessels that must be valuable to him as submarine decoy ships, especially as the chances of success for these craft in this war have shown themselves to be very small. Submarine commanders are requested to take note of this.[4]

Ironically, only fifteen days after this stern admonition the United States would deploy two such decoy ships.

On Thursday morning, 12 March 1942, Hicks and Legwen held separate meetings with their officers. The subject was the status of machinery and equipment checks and crew orientation and training. The conclusion arrived at was the same for both ships. Independent at-sea training

Getting Under Way

and exercising the ship's equipment and machinery was highly desirable if not essential to ensure the basic operational and combat readiness of the ship and crew. Deckelman and Schwaner, the gunnery officers, agreed they could not properly exercise the gun crews in lowering the camouflage while in the harbor. Further, they wanted to fire each 4-inch cannon and at least one depth charge before leaving the resources of the shipyard. Likewise, Beckett and Guy Brown Ray, the engineers, collaborated and concluded they wanted hands-on, at-sea operation of the old main steam plants while they could still get help from the yard if needed. Duffy and Neville concurred and recommended a two-day at-sea exercise before executing the op-order. Hicks and Legwen obtained permission from COMSUBDIV 101 to exercise *Asterion* on 13–14 March and *Atik* on 16–17 March. The area about forty-five miles due east of Portsmouth and the Isles of Shoals and beyond the hundred-fathom curve east of Jeffreys Ledge was designated for the operation. The officers of both ships involved themselves in, understood, and responded to the importance and seriousness of their responsibilities. Hicks and Legwen expected nothing less.[5]

The only excitement during USS *Asterion*'s two-day excursion was anticipated. Legwen wanted to fire a depth charge off the stern at a pistol depth setting of thirty feet. He was eager to know what the effect would be on the ship and the external sonar gear by this shallow, close-range explosion. Indeed, now not later was the time to find out. Since the K-gun charge could be fired from the bridge, he had all hands on alert and moved forward of the main mast. It was only a precaution; certainly, he did not expect to blow the hind end off old *Evelyn!* The charge was fired. The large, 300-pound canlike shape still attached to its arbor sailed through the air like an overstuffed ballistic pelican and splashed through the surface of the Gulf of Maine. Tension mounted but not nearly as high as the massive geyser that followed the visible shock wave effect on the water and the physical impact that could be felt on the ship. Sonarman Second Class Ralph Moseley of Birmingham, Alabama, thought it a good idea to listen to the detonation with his earphones on. He did, and that was all he could hear for five days! Guy-Brown and the damage control team inspected the propeller shaft and the rudder–steering engine and reported no machinery casualties, leaking seals, gaskets, or open seams; the main engine was still on its foundation. *Asterion* sped on leaving only a cloud of rust behind. She returned to the shipyard at dusk on Saturday, 14 March.

Hicks was pleased with Legwen's brief report. He was prepared to take *Atik* out of the Portsmouth harbor at daylight, the sixteenth. His main concern was the stability of the two 4-inch gun mounts on the after corners of the midships deck house. While *Asterion* had suffered no casualties, he wanted to assure himself that the welds in the network of angle iron supports under the gun foundations would not fail. When *Atik* arrived at the operating area, Hicks had Lieutenant Deckelman man the two after 4-inch cannons. Gunner's Mate First Class Don Taylor, the gun captain, had Gunner's Mate Third Class Willis Clinkinbeard train the gun out ninety degrees and zero elevation. Hicks went below to observe the support structure. Both Hicks and Deckelman wore sound-powered telephones, instruments that generate their own power by sound moving in the field of a magnet. On command, Taylor fired. Insulation on the vertical partitions fell and a few light fixtures broke, but the welds held. Hicks and Deckelman followed the same procedure with the port gun with the same results. Hicks and the gunners were very pleased. On Tuesday evening Hicks brought *Atik* in to the yard and made her fast at the dock astern of *Asterion*.

Atik's and *Asterion's* predeployment exercises satisfied both Hicks and Legwen. But there was much crew training to be done before facing their battle-seasoned German adversaries beyond the Gulf of Maine. Such training is best done at sea with drills and drills and more drills. The new ship captains were beginning to feel the lure of the sea.

In late March the days were getting longer and the time before leaving the shipyard was getting shorter, much shorter. Legwen and Hicks were eager to put to sea, and they agreed that Monday, 23 March 1942 would be departure day. But there was still much dockside work to be done. The stores that had been requisitioned from the shipyard and the items purchased from the open marketplace that had not already been delivered would arrive. Throughout the three-day period, Wednesday the eighteenth to Friday the twentieth, shipyard trucks and vendor deliveries would arrive at the ships: Portsmouth Fruit and Produce Company; Holland Butter Company; S. S. Pierce Company; Swift and Company; Radiomarine Corporation of America; the Babcock and Wilcox Company; and Sears, Roebuck and Company, to name a few. When the Sears, Roebuck truck arrived alongside *Asterion*, Chief Kaiser was surprised that 150 men's suits at $25.00 each had been ordered for delivery to K. M. Beyer, care of the Portsmouth Naval Shipyard. Shortly afterward, Marine Clothing Company of Boston delivered $3,114.50 worth of dungarees, shirts, oilskin coats, sou'westers, sheepskin-lined coats, and other items of special clothing. Chief Kaiser knew this was a strange navy; he signed the receipts without hesitation. No doubt the same masquerade was being acted out alongside *Atik*.[6]

Hundreds of items and tons of material would be checked and disposed of by direct turnover to the ordering department or placed in the storerooms for future issue. The two chief storekeepers, Joe Kaiser and Pete Gayde, and their assistants would take charge and ensure that the vendors' invoices were correct, that accurate receipts were gotten, that proper distribution of material was made, and that no items would go astray. Because of the limited refrigerated storage space for fresh food, the temperature in both compartments of the "reefer-box" was lowered to minus ten degrees Fahrenheit. Accordingly, what was not canned or "dry" foodstuff was frozen and required special handling. The cooks, Chiefs Ed Ragan and Frank Cahalan and six-foot-four "Tiny" Law and cocky "Woodie" Woodside, took charge of that detail.

One day was set aside for receiving and stowing the remaining load of ammunition and depth charges. Lieutenants Deckelman and Schwaner took personal charge of their ammo-handling party. Chief Boatswain's Mates Darling and Arledge supervised the deck gang stowing the extra mooring lines and stocking the paint locker. The carpenter's mates, Barton, Plaushak, Paredes, and Ouellette, took charge of the plywood and four-by-four and six-by-six timbers to be used for damage control. Chiefs Andy "Doc" Fignar and "Rich" Roth, assisted by Bill Chapman and Forrest Bailey, were responsible for the drugs, medicines, and other medical supplies.

Clerical chores were equally important. Chief Yeomen Danny

Kosmider and Charlie Clarke kept busy with personnel matters and last-minute reports and correspondence. Each ship's muster roll had to be kept current and mailed to the Navy Department, Washington, before departure. Storekeepers William Murphy and Chester Maple were the disbursing clerks and maintained their respective ship's payroll and pay allotment records. All these activities were geared to the fixed departure date: 23 March.

Hicks and Legwen granted enlisted personnel whose families lived within one hundred miles of the Portsmouth shipyard a special twenty-four-hour liberty. Hicks, with strong prompting from Duffy, permitted officers' wives to visit the area. Legwen discouraged it. All personnel were again admonished to maintain the utmost secrecy regarding the mission of the ships. Home leave meant different things to different people: a home-cooked meal to savor; a familiar bed and the privacy of the old room; a night out with the boys, or the girls; a period of play with the kids; privacy with the wife; or hours of joy for mom and dad. Few let the fact that they had volunteered for imminent hazardous duty prey on their minds. Armand R. "Frenchy" Ouellette, carpenter's mate second class aboard the *Atik*, was one of the few.

Frenchy Ouellette was born in 1909 in New Bedford, Massachusetts, of Canadian parents. His speech and mannerisms reflected the French-Canadian culture of his bilingual, Catholic household. He joined the navy at age eighteen, and in true navy style "saw the world." Frenchy's visit home on 21 March 1942 is told by his niece, Dolores M. Ouellette of Westminster, Massachusetts. She was twelve years old at the time. He was twenty years her senior.

One day, I was seated at the kitchen table doing homework. My uncle came to the kitchen door and knocked. With great surprise my mother opened the door and said, "What are you doing here? You were home just a short time ago!"

I looked up to see a sad face and his hands reaching out to my mother, who was his favorite sister. My dad joined them and they immediately moved to the dining room and sat at the table. We four children were told to stay in the kitchen.

What he told my parents was that he had volunteered for a suicide mission and that this would be the last time they would ever see him. He then went on to say that it all began when the ship's captain had asked them to report on the deck. When all hands had reported they asked for volunteers to serve on a special patrol.

My uncle had been in the navy since 1927 and was considered one of the "old men." As an example to the younger men, he stepped forward. The usual response was to have others step forward to provide a choice for the officers. Men close to retirement were rarely selected in recognition of their service. But no one stepped forward but my uncle. The Captain approached him and asked him again if he wished to volunteer. Knowing he had no family and suddenly realizing that he didn't want to go back on his commitment, he had no other choice but to say yes again.

They immediately sent him home on leave before reporting to Portsmouth. He told my mom and dad that he was sending his trunk with all his things in the next few weeks. He also told [my mother] that he was turning his life insurance over to [her] for our education.

Needless to say, they tried to reassure him that he would survive, but he was beyond convincing. The next day or two, I don't recall how long, was a whirlwind visit and parties of friends and relatives. My uncle seemed to be in a constant mellow state of drunkenness, semi-laughter, and semi-tears. His leaving was filled with embraces and kisses from everyone. My mother gave him a rosary and told him to pray. He never once told us where he would be sent. After he left, we said the rosary on our knees every night. . . .[7]

Irene Swann Beckett, Ethel Schoenberg Deckelman, and Cora May Joyce all visited their husbands in Portsmouth. They were suspicious of the mission of this navy cargo ship. Cora May and Ed Joyce had been married less than a year. He would bid farewell to his bride a contented man. She would return to New York to her work and to the uneasiness of mind normally experienced by military wives whose husbands go off to war. Most adjust; some do not.[8]

Irene Swan Beckett was the veteran, the housemother. Older and more mature than the other wives, she had married Harold in 1935; they had no children. She knew the sadness of departures and the joys of returns. Harold had survived World War I and intended to see the end of World War II. Irene was not as optimistic but supported her husband in his ventures. She, too, had a hint of the hazardous assignment for which Harold had volunteered. But she knew Hicks and had the utmost confidence in the sound judgment and capabilities of him and her husband.

Ethel Deckelman was an intelligent and independent person. Daniel and their year-old son, Damon, were the focus of her love but not necessarily her life. She knew Daniel loved her deeply, but she did not understand his love of the navy. However, she dared not force him to choose one love over the other. Aware of the hazardous nature of Daniel's assignment, she scorned the navy for its plan and wanted him to transfer to other duty. Ultimately, she succumbed to the inevitable.

By midnight, Sunday, 22 March 1942, all was in order in both ships for departing the shipyard on the next day. Weekend liberty for all hands expired. All were aboard. Last mail would leave the ships at 1000. At 1300, 23 March 1942, USS *Atik* cast off all lines and, with the help of a navy yard tugboat, turned around and pointed her bow down the Piscataqua River channel. The strong flood tide pushed her abreast of *Asterion* before she completed her maneuver and gained headway. Legwen, Neville, Schwaner, and I were on *Asterion*'s bridge waiting for *Atik* to clear the turning basin. Hicks on *Atik*'s bridge and Deckelman with the anchor detail on the forecastle could be seen plainly some one hundred yards away.

When the tug let go *Atik*'s line, Hicks moved to the port wing of the bridge and ordered half speed ahead. He then turned toward *Asterion*, facing where we four officers were observing his departure, came to attention, raised his right hand to his cap's visor, and held a most military salute. Legwen, Neville, Schwaner, and I automatically snapped to attention and saluted in return. Deckelman followed suit, as did many of *Asterion*'s sailors who were on deck at the time. We wished *Atik* and her men hail and farewell. The salutes represented a silent demonstration of praise and respect; a sincere wish for good hunting, good shooting, and good luck; and a prayer for their safety and well-being. No doubt Hicks and Deckelman conveyed the same sentiment in their gesture: an appropriate expression between comrades-in-arms. The adventure was about to begin.

Atik moved ahead against the current, eased left around Henderson

Point on Seavey Island, and kept to midchannel for the mile run to the flashing green buoy where she began her right turn around Fort Point. The captain had the "conn," and the navigator, Lieutenant Duffy, was plotting the bearings as called out by Chief Dalton. From Fort Point, Duffy located Gunboat Shoal buoy bearing 174 degrees. Hicks called out to the helmsman, Quartermaster First Class Roy Burgess, to steady up on course 174 degrees. When *Atik* cleared Kitts Rocks and the flashing red whistle buoy to port, Hicks brought the ship around to course 90 degrees and passed north of the Isles of Shoals. *Atik* was soon clear of land. *Asterion* followed an hour later.

By 1500 on 23 March 1942, both ships were clear of the channel and heading for open water. Those on deck who could look forward upon the open water—and pause and meditate—would recognize the symptoms of that age-old lure of the sea. As Irvin Anthony wrote in his book *Down to the Sea in Ships:* "The spell of the sea fever will reach him and thrust him out over the grey wastes of reckless waters."[9] The lure of the sea, that strong, compelling attraction, that state of enchantment, is felt by every true seaman, whether he be the ancient mariner running before the wind in full sail, the modern day merchantman guiding his vessel on the trade routes through fair weather and foul, or the present-day navy man in time of war leaving the sanctuary of the safe harbor to face the restless waters and other warriors eager for combat. In the mid-nineteenth century, Henry Wadsworth Longfellow wrote of the seaman:

> He scorns to sleep 'neath the smoking
> rafters
> He plows with his ship the raging deep,
> Though the storm king roars and the winds
> howl after,
> To him it is only a thing of laughter,
> The sea king loves it better than sleep.

Many have gone to sea when their country called in time of need. Why? For various reasons or for no reason other than patriotism. They, too, have respected the raging deep. They have heard the roaring storm, felt the howling winds, sought out and faced the persistent foe. But not all have laughed. And not all return.

In the Office of the Chief of Naval Operations at the Navy Department, Washington, a few monitors maintained a dutiful vigil. Upon being notified that the two "mystery" ships had departed Portsmouth, one of the officers wrote in the official Chief of Naval Operations War Diary, "It's gone with the wind now and hoping for a windfall."[10]

6

Advancing toward Destiny

THE BEST PROTECTION AGAINST THE ENEMY'S FIRE IS
A WELL-DIRECTED FIRE FROM OUR OWN GUNS.

Adm. David Glasgow Farragut,
U.S. Navy, 14 March 1863

ON 2 MARCH 1942, activities that would eventually bring two deadly adversaries face to face were taking place simultaneously at different locations. Lt. Cdr. Harry Hicks, U.S. Navy, was in the Naval Shipyard, Portsmouth, New Hampshire, on board the ship that he would command when the 3,100-ton converted merchantman SS *Carolyn* was commissioned as USS *Atik*. Some thirty-one hundred miles to the east, Kapitän-leutnant Reinhard Hardegen of the Undersee arm of the German navy, on the bridge of his command, U-123, a type IXB, 1,050-ton submarine, departed U-boat bunker Keroman 3 on the Port Louis Bay in Lorient, Occupied France. Hardegen was en route to the western Atlantic to join his cohorts in American coastal waters.[1]

USS *Atik* and USS *Asterion* were commissioned on 5 March 1942. The two ships sailed from the Naval Shipyard, Portsmouth, New Hampshire, on the afternoon of 23 March. Hicks took *Atik* due east for approximately thirty-five nautical miles to 70 degrees west longitude, and at 1800 local time changed course to 147 degrees, a southeasterly direction to clear Cape Cod, Massachusetts. At 2300 *Atik* reversed course and slowed to four knots. Hicks would wait until morning to commence a period of day-and-night exercises to drill the crew for topside discipline, gunnery practice, and depth charge exercises. He knew that his own cunning and the shooting skill of his gun crews would mean the difference between victory and defeat, life and death. Hicks, Duffy, and Deckelman collaborated on the schedule for drills and exercises. Carpenter's Mates Barton, Ouellette, and Paredes spent the night building a ten-foot-by-ten-foot raft with an eighteen-foot-tall canvas pyramid that would be launched and used for target practice.[2]

Reveille on 24 March was sounded at 0630. Civilian clothing was issued and all naval uniform items were packed in seabags and stored under lock and key. A hearty breakfast was served, and there were drills until late supper. No more than twenty crewmen were allowed on the weather decks at any one time. Deckelman, the "gun boss," drilled his 4-inch gun crews. Hicks waited until dusk before granting permission to fire on the homemade target. Then, at fifteen hundred yards, each 4-inch fired two rounds during the remaining daylight. Hicks then closed on the white canvas target to five hundred yards to exercise the .50-caliber machine-gun crews. The light red tracers would provide a display of morbid celebration. The target remained unscathed except for the .50-caliber hits at the closer range. There was little more to be accomplished this first day. The next day would be better: Hicks would demand "well-directed fire from our own guns."

Hicks added damage control, fire, and abandon ship drills to the plan of the day. The abandon ship drill was limited to two boats and a total of twenty-five men, primarily off-watch seamen and firemen. There would be no officers in the boats. There were to be no communications with U-boat personnel, and only the coxswains would carry sidearms, the use of which was limited to maintaining discipline in the boat. Lieutenant Duffy had suggested at a meeting in Portsmouth with Legwen, Hicks, and Neville that the boat crews be armed with shotguns, submachine guns, and hand grenades and make an attempt to approach the surfaced submarine and attack the U-boat's gun crews and bridge. He was overruled and the tactic was not discussed again.

While Lieutenant Duffy was conducting the various drills, Deckelman continued working with his gun crews and the gunner's mates assigned to the depth charge detail. Hicks concluded the gunnery exercises with a single round fired from each 4-inch cannon at a range of a thousand yards. Although no depth charges were expended, Lieutenant Deckelman repeatedly schooled Gunner's Mates Don Ray and John Rice and their teams on depth charge handling procedures, especially on the charges' safety features. A copy of the procedure was given to each handler and was committed to memory:

> During shipment and stowage, the inlet valve is closed by a plain safety cover screwed onto the valve body. This plain cover is removed by hand on command before the projector is fired. Removing the cover permits water to enter the pistol.
>
> The Mk. 6 pistol has nine possible settings of the index pointers, indicated by the figures 30, 50, 75, 100, 150, 200, 250, and 300 and the word SAFE stamped on the pistol flanges. The figures indicate the depth in feet beneath the surface at which the pistol will fire when the pointer is adjacent to any given setting. When a pistol is set at SAFE, it cannot fire.
>
> A safe setting lock prevents the shock of gunfire, bomb hits, or underwater explosions from moving the index pointer off the SAFE setting. This lock consists of a short piece of copper wire rove through holes in lug of the index pointer and wrench stop. The ends of the wire are twisted together. The index pointer is thereby secured in the SAFE position and cannot be moved until the wire is broken. The wire will be broken by the application of force to the depth setting wrench handle at the time the index pointer is moved, upon command, to the specified numerical setting. Whenever the index pointer is reset to SAFE a new piece of wire MUST be inserted.[3]

Hicks was satisfied that his crew was well instructed and conditioned to their new tasks. Continuing the concentrated training would become less productive. Hicks felt he had achieved an important psychological goal: the arduous training exercises diverted the crew's concern about the exigencies of their mission. How his officers and men would act under fire could be learned only under fire. By late afternoon Lieutenant Commander Hicks decided it was time to seek out the enemy. He was prompted by intercepted distress messages from SS *Empire Steel*, SS *Dixie Arrow*, and SS *Narragansett*, all to his south. At 1700, Hicks changed course from 147 degrees to 180, due south. This course took *Carolyn* through the Great South Channel between Nantucket Shoals and Georges Bank. Hicks advised Eastern Sea Frontier by radio that he was ready in all respects to implement op-plan number 2. ESF acknowledged.

Lieutenant Commander Legwen took *Asterion* due east from Portsmouth. His plan was to proceed on a course of 90 degrees until he reached the 65th meridian, then turn south, clear Georges Bank, and enter the open Atlantic. Between 0800 and 2000 on 24 March, in the general area southwest of Cape Sable, Nova Scotia, he exercised his crew at various drills and gunnery practices. Like Hicks, Legwen was ready and eager to enter into the Battle of the Atlantic. At 2000 Eastern War Time, on 24 March, some twenty nautical miles south of Cape Sable, Legwen advised commander, Eastern Sea Frontier that *Asterion* had completed ship exercises. ESF directed the commanding officer to carry out op-plan number 2.[4]

The period of independent ship exercises for each ship followed generally the same pattern. The ships were identical in characteristics and indistinguishable in crew training objectives. Legwen and Hicks had discussed together the strategy and tactics of U-boat warfare. Each could offer only his limited experience and the fragments of useful information provided by ESF. In essence, Q-ship tactics reverted to a very basic contest of outwitting the opponent. The variables of any confrontation with a competitive and experienced U-boat commander were inexhaustible. The solution was to be ready for any contingency and to use the element of surprise to full advantage. With this tactic in mind, Legwen and Hicks conditioned their officers and key petty officers to expect physical hardship and mental stress, and to show leadership and courage in the true sense of the words. The crew members would follow the strong leader, would stay at their stations until properly relieved, and would use their weapons in the proper manner so long as they were able. Hicks and Legwen, after only thirty-six hours of intensive drilling, were satisfied that their teams were ready to enter the competition.

Both captains had been briefed on the op-plan developed on 11 March by Cdr. Tom Ryan and Lt. Cdr. Louis Farley. All had agreed to the target date of 25 or 26 March for the completion of individual ship exercises and to the routing to be taken by each ship to the operating area. The plan, summarized below, was intended as general guidance for the two captains.

1. Operate independently in the waters roughly two hundred miles off the U.S. Atlantic Coast.
2. Ship identity must remain secret until action is joined.
3. Action should be joined only when an enemy submarine is at sufficiently close quarters to ensure its destruction by superior gunfire, followed by depth charge attacks if it succeeds in submerging before destruction.
4. Enemy submarines have been attacking during darkness; they are rarely seen until after the target vessel has been struck by a torpedo.
5. If challenged by a friendly ship or aircraft, use as identification SS *Carolyn* and SS *Evelyn*, owned by the A. H. Bull Steamship Company.
6. If challenged by an enemy ship, reply in accordance with international procedure, using the calls and identifications: *Atik*: SS *Vill Franca*, Portuguese Registry, Call: CSBT. *Asterion*: SS *Generalife*, Spanish Registry, Call: EAOQ.
7. For port calls, notify commander, Eastern Sea Frontier, who will inform the U.S. Maritime Commission. A commission representative will provide logistics support. Costs will be paid by "company" check to the U.S. Maritime Commission.[5]

During the meeting in New York on 11 March, several topics discussed with Legwen and Hicks were prudently excluded from the written op-plan. One, do not expect immediate assistance from U.S. Navy units. Two, avoid capture by all means. Although Hicks had inquired about the status of military crews in civilian disguise under international law or the provisions of the Articles of War of the Geneva Convention, a direct answer was not forthcoming. The concern of the two COs was the treatment of the crew as spies or enemy combatants without uniforms versus their status as prisoners of war if captured. Unlawful combatants, Legwen contended, could be punishable by military tribunals rather than civilian courts of law and thereby dealt with more harshly. The unofficial response from the Navy Department was "avoid capture." Legwen and Hicks shared this implied order only with their officers.

USS *Atik* and USS *Asterion* now shed all outward signs of a warship and donned the cloak of innocent merchantmen, "a ship of relatively insignificant appearance." *Evelyn* was the first of the two mystery ships to experience, as Legwen would express it in his diary, a "somewhat dubious" U-boat contact.[6] At 2105 Eastern War Time, 24 March 1942, while still on course 90 degrees, Seaman First Class Gil Ciucevich, operating the sonar, reported receiving two "pings" in quick succession. Legwen brought the ship to General Quarters so all battle stations would be manned. At that time *Evelyn's* sonar was not capable of providing true bearing of the target; therefore, the precise direction of the source of the "pings" could not be determined. Legwen wrote in his diary:

> All doubt as to whether we had encountered a submarine was settled by the receipt of two "pings" in quick succession. At infrequent intervals we received more "pings." Each time two "pings" were made in quick succession. Contact was maintained for about a half hour, but the submarine was never seen. At 2245 we proceeded southward. We later received a submarine summary showing the presence of a submarine in approximately the same position in which the contact was made, which was latitude 41-40 N, longitude 65-14 W.[7]

Unknown to Legwen, German submarines at that time were not equipped with "active" sonar and, therefore, were not capable of "pinging." What Ciucevich heard and reported were probably Canadian navy ships doing routine search operations. Nevertheless U-552 (Kapitänleutnant Erich Topp) was in the area and torpedoed the Dutch tanker *Ocana* at latitude 42-36 N and longitude 65-30 W about two hours after *Evelyn's* incident. While contact with a U-boat was not made, *Evelyn's* crew responded in a mature and professional manner. Legwen and Neville were pleased. *Carolyn* and *Evelyn* proceeded south on parallel courses some 250 miles apart. Now they would seek out the enemy and introduce a new dimension to the U.S. Atlantic coastal campaign.[8]

On 2 March, U-123, with Kapitänleutnant Hardegen in command, departed bunker Keroman 3 on its eighth war patrol, its second to America's Atlantic coast. During the brief period of postpatrol refurbishment, some changes in personnel were made. Oberleutnant Heinz Schulz, the engineer, or LI, was given a Leutnant (Ing.) Mertens as an LI student. Oberleutnant zur See Rudy Hoffman was transferred to other duty. Von Schroeter fleeted up to number one watch officer (IWO) and surface attack officer. The new number two watch officer (IIWO) would be Leutnant zur See (Ensign) Wolf-Harold Schüler. Also new to the U-123 wardroom was Fähnrich zur See (Midshipman) Rudolf Holzer, a supernumerary for training as a deck watch officer. Many of the veteran crew members were reassigned to U-123, which pleased Hardegen. Technical knowledge, sound, logical thinking, foresight, attention to details, and a bold character: These are traits of successful U-boat commanders. Hardegen possessed them all. He advised BdU that to conserve fuel and be able to stay on station longer, he would travel a modified great circle route across the Atlantic, thus evading the anticipated bad weather around the Newfoundland Bank. Hardegen was conscious also of the limited number of torpedoes he had been allotted. He admonished von Schroeter that with only seventeen "eels," he must choose his targets carefully. By noon on 3 March, U-123 had "steamed" 141 nautical miles toward her destination, Cape Hatteras, still 3,750 miles to the west.[9]

U-123 progressed on her westward course, on the surface at night and submerged during much of the day. Hardegen exercised the crew with alarms and deep dive drills. He practiced leveling and trimming at various depths by using the bow and stern planes. These were critical maneuvers. Hardegen was eager to check out his planesmen. Their dexterity was crucial to quick and accurate maneuvering under emergency conditions. These exercises included the "unlikely" procedure for scuttling and abandoning the boat. Hardegen observed that the crew was now "settled-in" in the boat. The U-boat would continue its cautious transit westward at an economical speed averaging five to eight knots. On Friday, 20 March, U-123 was 2,543 miles from her French base. Almost three weeks had passed since leaving Lorient. Hardegen adjusted course to a new great circle pattern that would take U-123 directly to Cape Hatteras.[10]

Sunday was not a day of rest. At 0935 local time, after completing a check of the sea water ballast transfer system and the dive and trim system, U-123 surfaced. The overcast sky and good visibility made it reasonably safe to run on the surface and recharge batteries. Twelve minutes later the bridge watch officer, Leutnant Schüler, reported a target. U-123 pursued and at 1257 local time launched a G7a compressed air torpedo from six hundred meters and struck the ship in the engine room. In sixteen minutes the U.S. tanker SS *Muskogee*, 7,034 gross registered tons, gently sank beneath the waves. The crew's noon meal was its last.

On 23 March U-boat headquarters advised KK Schuch (U-105), KL Lassen (U-160), and Hardegen: "Free maneuver in total coast areas from Marine Quadrant CA50 to Quadrant DM52." The northernmost point of marine quadrant CA50 was at or near Manasquan, New Jersey, north of Barnegat light. Quadrant DM52 extended south and west to include Key West, Florida, the approach to Havana, Cuba, and all the Straits of Florida. This message gave Korvettenkapitän Heinrich Schuch in U-105, Kapitänleutnant Georg Lassen in U-160, and Hardegen authorization to hunt along the Atlantic coast wherever allied shipping was the most concentrated. With the abundance of targets in the assigned area and the limited number of torpedoes in each boat, the length of the patrol would surely be shortened while the tonnage-sunk tally would reach new levels. It was good news, indeed, for these U-boat commanders.

On 23 March, as Hicks in *Atik/Carolyn* and Legwen in *Asterion/Evelyn* departed Portsmouth and entered the Gulf of Maine, Schuch and Hardegen were busy some 500 to 550 miles to the south. Korvettenkapitän Heinrich Schuch in U-105 at 1500 local time was on the surface chasing a steamer on course 130 degrees at ten knots. Wind was from the west at twenty-five knots and the seas were high at twelve to twenty feet. The following sea raised the stern of the 251-foot U-boat and caused the propellers to break the surface of the water. With the reduction of resistance on the propellers, the engines raced and the increased revolutions drew more fuel from the diesel tanks. Further, the LI and the enginemen were constantly adjusting the throttles to minimize the stress on the diesels. After three hours forty-five minutes, an anxious Schuch noted the steamer had turned on her lights. Schuch continued his pursuit only to see the brightly illuminated Argentine flag painted on the side. She was the *Uruguay*, a neutral ship. In disgust, KK Heinrich Schuch broke off his attack. Schuch had every reason to be disgusted. He had had problems with the weather, with his batteries, and with chasing neutrals. So serious was his overall situation that on 24 March he radioed U-boat headquarters that he required fuel replenishment (at sea) because of his high fuel consumption and excessively high battery temperature. BdU responded that fuel replenishment was not possible.[11]

Kapitänleutnant Hardegen and U-123 also had a busy evening on 23 March. He had brought the boat to the surface at 1700 local time, dusk. At 1723, at latitude 36-20 N and longitude 64-10 W, steering base course 260 degrees on the gyro compass, the port lookout sighted mast tops. She was another tanker. Hardegen must have been jubilant. At 2002 local time, he called down the voice tube to man battle stations: "Auf Gefechtsstationen!" He planned to close the range rapidly, make a clean shot from a bow tube, turn away, and if necessary, launch a second torpedo from a rear tube. He ordered tubes 2, 3, and 5 to prepare for firing.

At 2057 local time U-123, with the moon blocked by a strong thunderstorm behind her, was at a range of five hundred meters. Von Schroeter fired tube 3. The sonarman reported the torpedo was running. Hardegen turned the boat hard to starboard to escape any blast effect. He waited for impact and detonation—nothing happened. Astounded, he commented: "To miss at this short distance is impossible!" The bow torpedo room reported a "tube runner" in tube 3. Now Hardegen realized the torpedo was "running," but it did not leave the tube. It was stuck with the air-driven propeller spinning. Hardegen's brain was humming, too, with rapid-fire thoughts: "How can the sonarman, the 'talker,' make such a mistake? Why didn't I get the report from the torpedo room sooner? Had I gotten the report of a tube runner sooner, I could have fired tube 2 at an eighty- or ninety-degree angle. It was ready. This mistake has undercut my attack plan. Surely by now the tanker watch has seen me." Now Hardegen had to save the attack. He called for hard right rudder in order to fire tube 5, the one of the two stern tubes that he had made ready. Von Schroeter was frantically attempting to program new guidance data when the after torpedo room reported that tube 5 had fired.

"Halt, sichern!" (Halt, secure!) commanded Hardegen. Rather than let the confusion escalate, the U-boat commander brought a halt to the attack. The tanker's watch by now had seen the U-boat, maneuvered in a short zigzag pattern, and attempted to hide in the darkness. U-123 followed at a respectable distance so as not to provoke an artillery response. In quick order, the U-boat commander determined that the "tube runner" in 3 was a mechanical failure; the breakdown in communications and the premature launch of the torpedo in tube 5 were human errors, for which he took immediate corrective action—he relieved the "mixer" and the "talker." He would summarize the details in his KTB when he completed the attack. This would be followed by quick and appropriate disciplinary action. Hardegen without doubt was both angry and chagrined: disappointed with his crew for their mistakes, distressed by the potentially dangerous situation in which the human errors had placed the boat and the crew, and embarrassed to have to write the details of the mishaps in his log for Dönitz and the staff to read. There would be time later, under less stressful conditions, to write his report. Right now his attention was focused on the serious game at hand.

U-123 was on the surface running at full speed to regain a forward position relative to her prey. Rafalski reported that the tanker had radioed a U-boat distress warning. She was the British motor tanker *Empire Steel*, 8,150 gross tons, built in 1941. She reported her position as some ten miles south of Kaeding's DR (dead reckoning) location. Hardegen was still concerned about the guns on the tanker. It was atypical of the Brits not to put up a good fight. The cautious commander decided to fire a spread of two eels from a longer distance than normal.

It was 2201 local time. Hardegen had had *Empire Steel* in sight some four and a half hours. But he was not weary. This was the game he loved to play. U-123 had pursued the tanker for about sixteen miles to the northeast. Hardegen saw his opportunity and seized it. Tubes 1 and 2 had been prepared for firing. The range was nine hundred meters, angle seventy-five degrees, and target speed twelve knots. Von Schroeter and Schüler had completed their data entry tasks and the guidance systems in the two torpedoes had been programmed. The attack officer fired the spread. The eels left the tubes and sped toward the tanker. The commander observed the dark column that engulfed the target. She was still floating on an even keel and was burning badly forward. Hardegen was not satisfied. He was concerned that after the foreship had burned out she might be able to proceed with intact engines. Hardegen ordered his crew to man their gun stations. Six rounds of cannon fire penetrated the ship's engine room. She began to settle by the stern. More projectiles set afire the aft bunkers. The entire ship was now ablaze. At 0152 local time the tanker capsized to port while her bow rose steeply some twenty meters out of the water. The hull was torn apart from keel to railing. At 0256 U-123 departed the scene on course toward Cape Hatteras.

U-123 continued her westward course on the surface. Her speed was five knots. At 0927, when Hardegen was considering submerging, a bridge lookout sighted an airplane under the cloud cover and at a range of ten thousand meters. U-123 crash dived to avoid detection. The commander felt confident that at that range and with the numerous whitecaps on the disturbed ocean surface, the aircraft's crew had not spotted the diving submarine. At 1100 on 24 March 1942, Kaeding logged the daily weather report: "Wind west 7–8 [fresh gale, 30–35 knots]; 8/10 cloud cover; sea 6–7 [high seas, 20–30 feet]; visibility 8 nautical miles." U-123 was some 485 miles due east of Norfolk, Virginia. With the rough sea condition and the possibility of aircraft remaining in the area, Hardegen thought it prudent to remain submerged. He would save fuel and get better speed beneath the pounding waves. Hardegen turned his attention to Midshipman Holzer.

Fähnrich zur See Rudolf Holzer was twenty-two years old and had completed his basic courses at U-boat school. U-123 was his first assignment, his first war patrol. Hardegen had assigned him to various officers for orientation, and from time to time he would stand the bridge watch with von Schroeter. Other than to observe and stay out of the way during attacks, he had no specific duties. Hardegen found him in the small wardroom, the officers' mess, and engaged him in a friendly dialogue on such topics as the weather, habitability, and some technical aspects of the U-boat. He observed that the midshipman was a fine young German who, in time, would make a good U-boat officer. Von Schroeter and Schulz both spoke well of him, agreeing that he was an intelligent and inquisitive officer, eager to learn and to contribute. Hardegen was pleased.

At 1800, U-123 surfaced. Weather and sea conditions had improved, but the sky was still overcast. Hardegen suspected the seaplane encountered earlier was based in Bermuda, which was approximately 250 miles to the south. He was aware that U-123 was approaching potentially dangerous waters. Hardegen contemplated his sortie along the U.S. coast. Then he remembered that over the past several days his radioman, Rafalski, had been giving him copies of attack reports by the other U-boats already on station on the U.S. Atlantic coast. When he sorted out the messages and assimilated the data, he felt mixed emotions. To his surprise and disquietude, he noted that his rival, Korvettenkapitän Johann Mohr in U-124, already had attacked ten ships: one on 14 March, two on the seventeenth, two on the eighteenth, two on the nineteenth, two on the twenty-first, and one the day before, 23 March. At one level, no doubt, Hardegen was pleased at the apparent success of his comrade; at another, he was a bit annoyed by the strength of the competition. He now had a fixed goal to exceed. Rivalry within the U-boat service was serious and spirited.[12]

Hicks in *Carolyn* and Legwen in *Evelyn* on 24 March continued their journey southward. Hardegen, in U-123, advanced through the quadrants on his trek westward. And Schuch, in U-105, seemed content to chase his rudder if not his torpedoes. They were all approaching that illusionary point on the chart called Destiny.

7

The Mystery of the Mystery Ship

SHORTLY BEFORE THE ATTACK, TARGET CHANGED
COURSE TO STARBOARD. . . . IN THE BOAT WE HEARD
THE TORPEDO HIT THE TARGET; NO DETONATION.

Korvettenkapitän Heinrich Schuch,
Commanding U-105, 26 March 1942

BY 1000 LOCAL TIME, 25 March, U-123 was 3,303 miles from Lorient
and 325 miles east of Cape Hatteras. With no further attack reports from
KK Mohr in U-124, KL Hardegen turned his attention to KK Schuch,
the poor fellow with difficulties. He was approximately a hundred miles
southeast of U-123, roughly midway on a line drawn between Atlantic
City, New Jersey, and Bermuda. Hardegen considered Schuch an
intruder and thought it prudent to be aware of his presence.[1]

KK Heinrich Schuch continued to have problems. Twice during the
past forty-eight hours he had had to adjust his estimated position by some
twelve to eighteen miles. In each case he was farther to the north than he
had plotted by dead reckoning. Then he pursued a neutral ship for six
hours, using fuel from his already low supply. Early in the morning on
the twenty-fifth Schuch started an attack run on a large tanker. He fired
a spread of three torpedoes from his bow tubes from fifteen hundred
meters. The spread missed. He turned and launched a spread of two from
his stern tubes at a range of a thousand meters. This spread also missed.

He reloaded tube 1, turned, closed to six hundred meters, and fired. After thirty-four seconds, the torpedo struck aft near the engine room. KK Schuch could see the tanker was not sinking, so he decided to fire a Fangschuss, a coup-de-grace shot. At 0018 he fired tube 4 from a range of eight hundred meters and observed a hit in the foreship. The tanker radioed its position. She was the British tanker *Narragansett*, 10,389 gross registered tons, fully loaded. Schuch observed the tanker afire and sinking stern first. Admiral Dönitz and his staff surely would question the Korvettenkapitän's use of seven torpedoes on the tanker. Further, KK Schuch would be interrogated about his eight-hour pursuit of the target considering his low fuel state.

Schuch's misfortunes continued. At 0629 U-105 passed into the general area where he had first sighted *Narragansett*. His hydrophones detected propeller noises bearing 176 degrees. He turned toward the bearing, and with periscope up he observed a medium-size steamer zigzagging on base course 315 degrees at twelve knots. At 0923 U-105 surfaced to give pursuit. For eight hours the unfortunate KK Schuch pursued a ship that he could not catch. Then his lookout reported masts bearing 348 degrees. The capricious Kapitän again reacted. He recorded his response and intention in his KTB: "Giving up pursuit of first steamer and intend to attack second freighter for which I am in a better forward firing position. In addition, my advanced maneuvering is favored by wind and sea from astern. Target zigzagging around base course 135 degrees; speed ten knots." For several hours KK Schuch chased his new target. At 1400 local time 26 March, based on estimated position, U-105 and U-123 were less than two sailing hours apart. Apparently, neither U-boat commander knew the exact location of the other. At this time Lieutenant Commander Hicks in *Carolyn* was on a southerly course in the vicinity of latitude 36-15 N, longitude 70-00 W, also an estimated position. Lieutenant Commander Legwen in *Evelyn* was some 250 miles to the east-northeast. *Evelyn*'s radioman had intercepted *Narragansett*'s distress call so Legwen knew there was at least one U-boat in the general area.

On 26 March 1942 an unheralded yet notable episode in U.S. naval history occurred. When the obscure and tenuous fragments of recorded data were revealed and analyzed, the irony of the drama began to unfold. Exactly what happened and precisely where it happened are not known, and little has been written about the incident. A chronology of probabilities associated with actual events provides some clues. This narrative is based on what I think could have happened. It is an effort to piece together the known facts and the probable events into a plausible account.

Thursday, 26 March, was an extraordinary day indeed: a fateful day for the men aboard the mystery ship *Carolyn* and for the commander and crew of the German submarine U-123. For the officers and men of *Carolyn*, their valor can be known only to themselves and God. For the commander of U-123, this day would never be forgotten: He would suffer his first personnel casualty, and he would have his protective shield breached. For the Korvettenkapitän in U-105, his role in this action was probably more significant than he could know. As for *Evelyn*, she would remain in the wings of the stage on which the drama would unfold and await her cue. It would come at another time and another place, in the final act.

At 1703 on this Thursday afternoon, a lookout on the bridge of U-123 reported smoke clouds on the starboard beam. Hardegen was summoned to the bridge. He and von Schroeter counted six or seven separate clouds on the horizon and concluded that it was probably a convoy. U-123 changed course toward the potential targets. It soon became obvious to the German officers that it was a single steamer on course 215 degrees. The wind was shifting between west-northwest and north at a velocity of about ten knots. It carried the clouds of heavy smoke toward the U-boat. The range was approximately eight miles. Initially, the U-boat commander was suspicious, thinking the freighter was artificially producing this dense smoke. But he studied the ship's profile and, except for a high superstructure behind the funnel, concluded she was a normal freighter of medium size, about 3,000 tons. No other structures were unusual and she gave no hint of armament. Hardegen adjusted his speed and course to lie behind the freighter. He intended a surface attack with a torpedo from the ship's port quarter soon after darkness, in about three hours. However, at 1800, as darkness approached, the target started zigzagging and appeared to no longer belch out heavy smoke. Hardegen adjusted speed and course and maintained his relative position. He considered attacking this target with artillery but ruled that out because of the anticipated worsening of sea conditions and the darkness. He adhered to his original plan. Meanwhile, Korvettenkapitän Heinrich Schuch in U-105 was also in the area pursuing an unidentified freighter that was zigzagging and on an estimated course of 135 degrees. KK Schuch was ahead of his target, with the wind and moderate seas to his back. He would wait for the range to close to within two thousand meters before attacking.

At about 1800 Seaman Second Class Robert E. Bell, the port bridge lookout in *Carolyn*, reported a sighting on the port quarter. Lt. Leonard Duffy was the underway watch officer and responded immediately to Bell's report. Duffy studied the object with his binoculars, and in his mind there was no doubt about its being a submarine on the surface in pursuit of *Carolyn*. He sent the messenger on the double to summon the captain to the bridge. Captain Hicks and Duffy agreed the object was a U-boat and that the range was about six thousand yards, or approximately three miles. Hicks inspected the surfaced U-boat and concluded the German was indeed in pursuit but would wait for darkness and close the range to within a thousand yards before attacking. He hoped she would stay on the surface and make her move before it got too dark. In response to Hicks's orders, Duffy passed the word by messenger and telephone to man battle stations.[2]

In a matter of minutes, all hands were at their battle stations. Talkers with sound-powered telephones were located at key positions throughout the ship: the engine room with Lieutenant Beckett; damage control party on the mess deck with Chief Metalsmith Herb McCall; a roving talker with Lieutenant Deckelman near the 4-inch batteries; aft with Gunners Mate First Class George Smith in charge of depth charges and the after machine guns; and Chief Yeoman Daniel Kosmider on the bridge with Captain Hicks. Hicks took the bridge phone temporarily, summarized the situation, and cautioned that this was a waiting game, relax for now, but be ready to respond to commands.

To provoke an attack before darkness, it is theorized that Hicks commenced an abbreviated zigzag pattern and gradually slowed from nine to six knots. The U-boat followed suit. Hicks waited in the enclosed bridge house. He, like Legwen, would prefer an artillery duel in daylight so the decoy would have the advantage with her superior gunfire. But the U-boat commander did not take the bait when *Carolyn* reduced speed to six knots. The ever-patient commander held his position for two long hours. Then, at 2005, Hardegen increased speed to close on his target. It was dark; the moon was hidden behind partially broken but thick clouds. He directed his attack officer, von Schroeter, to approach on the surface to within seven hundred meters and fire tube 2. At a six-hundred-meter range, the G7e electric torpedo was launched. Hardegen expected a quick and easy kill and had invited Midshipman Holzer topside to observe the sinking. The three officers and two lookouts were on the bridge. The time of launch was 2037.[3]

Lieutenant Deckelman, in the deckhouse shielding the two after 4-inch guns, looked through his binoculars. They were fixed on the U-boat's dark gray-black tower and then on the white water being pushed and cut by the prow. He was the first to detect the phosphorescent wake of the torpedo not more than nine feet below the surface of the Atlantic. He called his report on the sound-powered phone to the bridge. Hicks called "torpedo" to Duffy who was standing on the port wing with the lookout. Duffy saw the wake coming straight for the spot at the waterline beneath where he was standing. A moment of immobility, then instinctively, he turned to run away from the railing at the deck's edge. Three paces, he returned, grabbed Bell, the lookout, who was transfixed by the sight of the silvery-green luminiferous wake rushing toward him. Before the two men could clear the wing of the bridge, the torpedo struck below them just forward of the superstructure. Hicks saw in front of him the rush of water upward, the canvas cover and hatch battens of number 2 hatch blown into the air, and a momentary flash followed by splintered pulpwood logs. The port side windows of the bridge were shattered by the violent detonation. Hicks ignored the deafening sound and the physical shock of the blast that knocked him to the deck. Then the sea water from the geyser cascaded down. He could not see Duffy and the lookout through the deluge. They were not there. The wing of the bridge where they had been was no longer there. Hicks was not concerned with the smoke pouring from the blasted open hatch nor did he realize he was bleeding and his body was numb. He turned to Chief Dan Kosmider and asked for a telephone report on damage assessments.

In rapid order Hicks received the reports: All was not well, but USS *Atik* could still fight. Deckelman reported the deck under the forward, port 4-inch gun mount was thrust upward and the gun was not usable except in dire emergency. He also reported the U-boat had turned to starboard and was passing slowly astern at a range of three to four hundred yards. Beckett stated that the engine room had received a bad jolt. He wanted to stop the engine. He was checking the boilers for dislodged fire brick and for loose boiler tubes. No major steam leaks had been noted. Chief McCall reported a bad rupture on the port side of the transverse bulkhead between number 2 and number 3 holds. Because of the pulpwood logs, he would not be able to brace it. The pulpwood in hold 2 was on fire, but he would have it under control. Gunner's Mate George Smith reported no casualties aft.

Hicks spoke directly to his communications officer. He took the sound-powered phone from Dan Kosmider and called to Ensign Leonard to send the standard SSS (submarine sighting) and SOS messages, giving the best estimated position, and to state that the ship was burning forward, but not bad. The message was transmitted on the 500 kilocycle band at a stated time of 0055 GMT (Greenwich Mean Time). Hicks was either not aware that he was growing weaker from loss of blood or he chose to ignore it. As he walked to the starboard wing of the bridge, he ordered the helmsman, Quartermaster First Class Roy Burgess, to come right, easy. With the phone still on his chest, he told Deckelman he was dispatching the panic party and turning right; he instructed him to drop the camouflage and to commence firing when the guns bore on the submarine. The captain spoke a few words of encouragement, telling Deckelman to make every shot count.[4]

Chief Signalman Robert Temte hoisted the American flag and the commission pennant. Deckelman passed the word to his gun captains, Ray Roberts and George Kaiser on the two starboard 4-inch cannons, and to George Smith who was directing the two .50-caliber machine guns. Gunners Mate Third Class Charles De Witt, on the after, starboard .50-caliber gun was the first to open fire. He raked the conning tower and the deck guns with his .50-caliber common and tracer projectiles. As the U-boat and *Atik* reached a near parallel course, the 4-inch guns commenced firing.

After the first few salvos, the darkness, the flashes, and the smoke from the muzzles all but blinded the gun pointers and trainers. At a range of three to four hundred yards, Hicks had the starboard depth charge pistols set for thirty-foot depth detonation, the safety covers removed, cleared personnel from the K-guns, and fired. The three, three-hundred-pound charges of TNT sailed into the air toward the U-boat. The submarine turned hard right and, still on the surface, ran away on a perpendicular course from *Atik*. Deckelman ordered "cease fire," then called Hicks to say the U-boat could no longer be seen. Hicks replied in a weakened but determined voice to continue firing: shoot where you last saw her; shoot where you think she is. Hicks reasoned that the U-boat commander, if not badly hit, would be back for an easy and final shot at the slowly sinking ship. He told Ensign Leonard to send another message from *Carolyn* requesting assistance even though he knew none, other than *Asterion*, might be available. Edwin Leonard acknowledged, saw that his captain was in a state of collapse, and sent for a corpsman.[5]

Chief Pharmacist Mate Richard Roth took the unconscious Hicks in his arms. The captain's pulse was so weak Roth was not certain he felt it, but he was still breathing. His trousers were soaked in blood. The crimson fluid had filled his shoes. Pharmacist Mate First Class Forrest Bailey was holding the flashlight as Roth searched for the bleeding wound. He found it in the abdomen. Only the tight inflatable life belt around his waist had kept Harry Hicks alive—till now. His breathing stopped; his heart stopped; there was no more blood to pump. The captain had given his last order. Roth looked for Lieutenant Duffy. He was told the exec was lost overboard. Roth then took the phone from around Hick's neck and handed it to Chief Kosmider. The chief called to Lieutenant Deckelman to announce that both the captain and the executive officer were dead.

Lieutenant Deckelman had fired eight or nine more rounds into the darkness, "where he thought the U-boat was." Then he ordered cease fire. The depth charges had detonated but apparently not close enough for a "kill." Deckelman had called to the bridge, but got no answer. Now he knew why. He made his way forward to the bridge to take command. Roth and Bailey took Hick's body below to his cabin, which was in shambles from the torpedo hit. They placed him on the mattress on the deck near where his bunk had been. Both the forward and the outboard bulkheads of the captain's corner cabin had been blown away, along with the port bridge wing on the deck above. There was no cabin. As the two corpsmen left their captain's body, they closed the door behind them. Now they had the wounded to attend to. The dead would be buried later.

Lt. Daniel B. Deckelman had been thrust into a new and demanding role. When he reached the bridge, he sent a messenger to find Lt. (jg) Ed Joyce, who was below deck standing by at damage control center and instructing crew members as to their duties if ordered to abandon ship. Deckelman then noticed the ship was losing headway. He took the phone from Kosmider and called to the engine room for Lieutenant Beckett. Deckelman announced that Hicks and Duffy were both dead and that he was now in command. Beckett said he had major problems in the engine room. One boiler was damaged and the main engine had to be stopped to cool off a hot bearing. Equally serious, the forward bulkhead separating the boiler room and the engine room from number 3 hold was ruptured. Unless stopped, sea water would flood the whole compartment. Frenchy Ouellette and his damage control party were trying to shore up the bulkhead and stop the major leaks. Beckett said he wanted to stop the main engine for fifteen to twenty minutes.

Deckelman agreed. Moving ahead slowly might buy some time, but it might also aggravate the problem of flooding. The ship's sound gear was knocked out, so the location of the submerged U-boat could not be determined. *Atik* was getting an increasingly heavy port list, and she was sinking forward up to the main deck. There was much to ponder. Lt. Ed Joyce arrived on the bridge and seemed unsurprised by the damage. Deckelman briefed him on the current state of affairs. The U-boat might return if it was not severely damaged, or the German might think the battle won and leave the scene. Although Deckelman had no way of knowing for sure, he anticipated another attack, probably with a torpedo. Deckelman asked Joyce to check casualties and evaluate damage as best he could. He also asked to have the panic party in the boats stay near the ship, to be picked up in about an hour. Joyce went on his way. Deckel-man, in his own mind, called "time out." He had to think—about actions and reactions, initiatives and defenses.

The decoy was a new and unexpected experience for Kapitänleutnant Hardegen and the crew of U-123. The keen-witted U-boat commander was snared by the deadly trap, *eine U-Bootsfalle*. His crafty calculations and patience, and a lot of luck, had saved him and his crew from certain destruction. He had planned his attack to take advantage of the dark-ness, and he had had the patience to wait several hours to play his game. Darkness was his ally. Although he had been stalking *Atik* for three and a half hours, he waited until after nightfall to make his move. Hardegen described the details of the attack and counterattack in his KTB:

> The moon was well hidden behind the clouds. At 0237 CET [2037 local time], I fire a torpedo from tube 2 at a range of 650 meters. Hit at forward edge of bridge. I suspect she is going to sink soon because of her own speed of ten knots. It starts burning and listing to port and sinking by the bow. She radios name *(Carolyn)* and position. The wind is com-ing from the north and it is overcast. Sea state is 2–3 [slight to moder-ate], abated a little.
>
> After I fire my torpedo, I turn to starboard around its stern. A lifeboat is lowered into the water; the second is in its davits. The situation seems normal so far, and there is nothing suspicious. I now have the feeling it picks up steerage way, because the range suddenly decreases. I am turn-ing off to starboard, but he is following. His angle is 90 degrees. I am turning hard to starboard, and then all of a sudden flaps and tarpaulins are falling down and he fires with at least one cannon and two machine guns. Fortunately, the deck gun is first short and then long and to the sides. I can clearly see the splashes. The 2-centimeter bullets from the machine guns are hitting the bridge hard and whistling uncomfortably close around our hats.
>
> I evade right away with all ahead full. Our engines develop some smoke, which gives us cover. I see large pieces flying through the air. Shortly after, fierce detonations shake the whole boat. I suspect a torpedo hit. Closing all bulkheads. Then I see high water columns and I realize he has thrown depth charges at us.
>
> I have been had! Fooled like a bloody beginner! I have been snared

by a heavily armed U-boat trap. When we receive the first machine-gun burst, Midshipman Holzer is wounded. It is difficult to get him through the tower hatch. Because of the wounded midshipman, the many hits on the bridge casing, and the closeness of the depth charge explosions, I cannot crash dive immediately. I have to wait to see if the submarine is still leakproof. In time, we are almost out of firing range and the U-boat trap stops shooting. A low pressure test indicates that the boat is airtight.

Holzer was the only one injured. We had amazing, unheard of luck. The next day I counted eight 2cm hits on the bridge alone.

After we were out of artillery range I went below deck. I saw that the condition of Midshipman Holzer was hopeless. Apparently a 2cm projectile had exploded in his right upper thigh and torn open the flesh from the hip joint to the knee. Much of the muscle was torn away. I could not determine clearly how badly the bone had been shattered. The leg was connected only by small pieces of skin. We applied a tourniquet as best we could and wrapped a towel around the large wound. Our first-aid supplies were not sufficient. I realized that for such an injury, even a doctor on board the submarine, under normal conditions, could not help.

Since we were many miles from the nearest neutral port, I decided to make it as easy as possible for him by injecting an ample dosage of morphine. Holzer himself behaved very courageously. He was still conscious after an hour. He did not complain at all. He told me of his severe pain only when I questioned him. He lost consciousness around midnight.

The U-boat commander kept U-123 at periscope depth and pulled away to a safe distance from the crippled *Carolyn*. He ordered von Schroeter to keep the target in sight. He did not know whether the decoy would run or stay to fight. Then he thought further: If she has sonar, she will be after me, but I don't think she has the speed to catch me. I will not give her another chance. Hardegen again turned to his number one watch officer, von Schroeter, to prepare tube 1 for a submerged shot, and to keep the target under surveillance until he returned to the tower. He had matters to see to below.

Below deck the crew was in tumult. A boisterous segment of the crew, even some senior petty officers, were arguing that the decoy tactic was a dastardly act. They proposed that the U-boat-trap should be sunk without mercy and that all those who manned it should be shot. A smaller number of the crew contended that modern naval warfare had few rules and that fairness was not one of them. The captain's presence quieted the debate. He left the assembly a matter to ponder: "Is being harmed by a U-boat-trap any less fair than sinking an unarmed merchant ship?"

At 2044, some seven minutes after KL Hardegen fired a torpedo and hit *Carolyn*, KK Schuch in U-105 began his attack on his target, a 3,000- to 4,000-ton freighter. At 2056 he launched a torpedo from a range of fifteen hundred meters and two minutes later another from a thousand meters. The Korvettenkapitän recorded in his KTB this account:

> Shortly before the attack, target changed course to starboard. Consequently, the angle of firing is quite large. In the boat, we hear the torpedo hit the target; no detonation. Fuse failure? On the bridge, it is observed the steamer is listing to the port side. I decide to fire a second torpedo in spite of angle being too large. At an estimated range of 1,000 meters, I fire tube 2 at 0258 CET [2058 local time]. Second shot has no effect on target. Probable miss forward. At 0306 CET [2106 local time], after turning off, I start a new attack run. A shadow is sighted at 174 degrees true. Made out as tanker. I decide to attack the tanker as a more valuable target. Tanker's course 40 degrees, speed 9.5 knots.[6]

KK Schuch made his exit from the scene. He recorded no further report of this attack and gave no further description of the target. Could it have been *Carolyn/Atik* that he attacked some 270 miles east of Nags Head, North Carolina, and 320 miles south of Nantucket Island, Massachusetts? Circumstantial evidence supports this thesis. He was in the area near where KL Hardegen reported his attack. Exact locations were not known; positions were estimated on the basis of dead reckoning, which is not a precise measurement. Schuch's tracking chart, a part of his KTB, clearly shows many corrections and indicates a pattern of changes that tends to position him further north than he had estimated. On the basis of this argument, U-105 could have been in the vicinity of *Atik* at the time of Hardegen's initial attack. If U-105 were in the immediate area of the attack, would not Hardegen have known it? Not necessarily. KL Hardegen was busy reacting to the potentially deadly Q-ship. His approach and first attack on *Atik* was on the surface, and during this phase his sonar was not manned; therefore, he would not have heard U-105. Did KK Schuch

Q-SHIPS VERSUS U-BOATS

know U-123 was in the area? Probably not. He too was preoccupied chasing targets and firing eels. Furthermore, he was some distance away from the target and probably on the opposite side from U-123. Didn't he hear U-123 hit *Carolyn/Atik* some nineteen minutes before he started his attack on the same target? Apparently not. Hardegen stated it was a muffled explosion. This is understandable if the sound was partially absorbed by the pulpwood logs in *Carolyn*'s forward holds. And from a distance of more than two thousand meters, in the darkness of night, Schuch would not have seen the geyser that erupted. But why Schuch did not hear *Carolyn*'s depth charges detonate is a mystery.

Nineteen minutes after Hardegen's first hit, Schuch fired his first torpedo at the target. He heard it hit, but there was no detonation. He observed "the steamer is listing to the port side." Also, he noted, "Shortly before attack, target changed course to starboard." Hardegen also reported that *Carolyn*, after his torpedo hit at 2037 turned to starboard and took on a port list. Coincidence? The existence of two different freighters of 3,000 tons in the same general location, turning to starboard, and carrying a port list, all in the same approximate time frame is highly improbable.[7]

Aboard *Carolyn/Atik* an atmosphere of relative calm prevailed. It was now twenty-three minutes since the attack began. Lieutenant Deckelman had little time to adjust to the awesome responsibilities thrust upon him. He had to establish his priorities. Priority one was caring for the injured. Priority two was maintaining a strong defense posture. Priority three was keeping *Atik* afloat if at all possible. And priority four was to save the engineering plant for electricity, freshwater, and heat. All were equally important.

Lt. Ed Joyce returned to the bridge to give Deckelman his evaluation of conditions below. He began with his rough count of the dead, wounded, and missing. Then he described the damage: Destruction was considerable on the port side and the after end of hold number 2. Hold 3 was also flooding. The torpedo hit below the mess deck. Most of the casualties were the men assembled on that deck on the port side. The port, forward machine gun was gone, and the two men manning that gun were missing. The forward, starboard machine gun was knocked off its collapsible mount but was in working order. The forward, port 4-inch gun was out

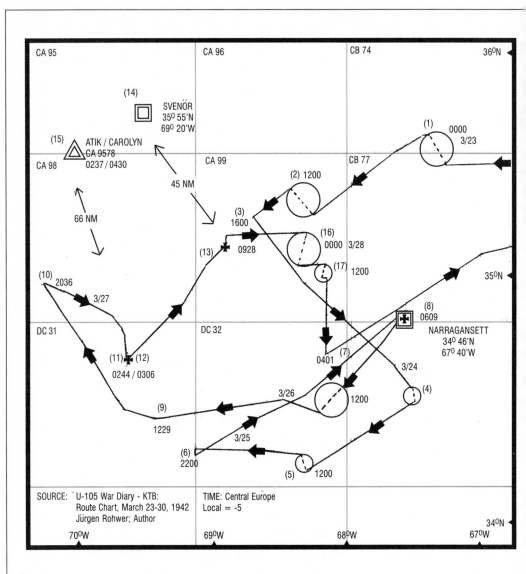

CA 95

CA 96

CB 74

36°N

(14)

SVENÖR
35° 55'N
69° 20'W

(15)

ATIK / CAROLYN
CA 9578
0237 / 0430

CA 98

CA 99

CB 77

(1)

0000
3/23

45 NM

(2) 1200

66 NM

(3)
1600

(16)

0000 3/28

(13)

0928

(17) 1200

35°N

(10)

2036

3/27

(8)
0609

NARRAGANSETT
34° 46'N
67° 40'W

DC 31

DC 32

(11)

(12)

0244 / 0306

(7)

0401

3/24

(9)

3/26

1200

(4)

1229

3/25

(6)
2200

(5)

1200

SOURCE: U-105 War Diary - KTB:
Route Chart, March 23-30, 1942
Jürgen Rohwer; Author

TIME: Central Europe
Local = -5

70°W

69°W

68°W

67°W

34°N

U-105/U-123/SS *Carolyn*/SS *Narragansett*/SS *Svenör*

1. 23 March   0000   Position correction: 8nm

2. 23 March   1200   Position correction: 8nm

3. 23 March   1600   Sighted ship, commenced pursuit

4. 24 March   0230   Broke off attack, neutral ship; transmitted message to BdU requesting fuel replenishment

                0300   Position correction: 6nm

5. 24 March   1200   Position correction: 6nm

6. 24 March   2200   Sighted smoke 260°; tanker course 60°

7. 25 March   0401   Fired spread 3 torpedoes, 1500m; missed

                0408   Fired spread 2 torpedoes, 1000m; missed

8. 25 March   0609   Fired single torpedo, 800m; hit. Tanker radioed position: 34°46' N, 67°40' W

                0618   Fired single torpedo, 510m; hit. SS *Narragansett* sunk; position: CB7779

                1200   Position correction: 8nm

9. 26 March   1229   Sighted steamer on course 315°; pursued

10. 26 March   2036   Gave up pursuit. Sighted masts; target course 135°, 10 kn

11. 27 March   0256   Fired torpedo, 1500m. "Heard torpedo hit target, no explosion. Fuse malfunction. Listing of steamer to port side observed."

                0258   Fired torpedo, 1000m; missed. "Target changed course to starboard."

12. 27 March   0306   Started new attack run, then broke off to pursue new target (tanker), course 40°

13. 27 March   0928   Fired torpedo, 400m; hit tanker, no effect. Fired 2d and 3d torpedoes; hits. Target sunk; position: CA9945

14. 27 March   Target radioed: SS *Svenör*, position 35°55' N, 69°20' W

15. 27 March   0237   *Atik/Carolyn* position: CA9578 (U-123 KTB)

16. 28 March   0000   Position correction: 8nm

17. 28 March   1200   Position correction: 4nm

of commission. The foundation was ruptured and heaved upward. The small port lifeboat was gone, blasted away. The forward bulkhead separating the boiler room and engine room from cargo hold number 3 was leaking. The damage control party was attempting to shore it up. The major leaks seemed to be under control. Joyce recommended the boats and the panic party be brought back on board. Deckelman agreed.

Deckelman turned to the bridge talker, Chief Kosmider, and asked for Ensign Leonard to come to the bridge. Deckelman noted that the chief was bleeding about the face and asked if he was all right. Kosmider said he was; the shattered glass from the windows had struck him when the torpedo hit. Ensign Leonard was in the adjoining compartment, the radio room, and responded quickly to the summons. Deckelman asked Leonard to draft an SSS SOS message: Surface torpedo attack, major damage and settling forward, but not sinking, require medical help. This short message, Deckelman reasoned, might entice the U-boat skipper to approach on the surface again. He might think he could sink the ship with gunfire. Deckelman thought the German would be foolish if he took the bait, but he proffered it, just in case. Deckelman again turned to Dan Kosmider and asked for Lieutenant Beckett to come to the bridge.

Hal Beckett arrived on the bridge in about three minutes and reported that the boilers were still in operation, but he was concerned that if the ship kept settling by the bow, the propellers would be pushing air, high and dry. Beckett confirmed that it was a major effort to keep the bulkhead forward of the boiler room from giving way. Frenchy Ouellette and his damage control gang were working hard to keep the water from flooding the boilers. If that bulkhead went, it would be lights out! Deckelman suggested that only a minimum of men remain in the engine room. Beckett acknowledged; he would be there if needed.

Deckelman's attention then turned to his guns. He had Chief Kosmider call Gunners Mate Don Taylor to the bridge. Gunners Mate First Class Don Taylor was the type of petty officer every gun boss wanted. He knew his weapons. He could operate every position. He would tolerate no dry grease fittings; he would tolerate no smudges or dust. The breech block and the barrel and the pinions of his guns had to be spotless and have just the right amount of lubricant or protective grease. His ammunition handlers were trained to care for each piece of fixed ordnance as if it were a baby. He cared for his depth charges equally as well. Deckelman told Taylor he was now the gun boss. He shared his thoughts that the U-boat skipper must know by now that *Atik* was a trap. The camouflage should be down and the guns manned. The ship obviously had taken on a considerable port list and was down by the head. The port 4-inch gun could be elevated to 45 degrees to bear on a target, but could the starboard guns be lowered enough to bear on a surfaced target at close range? They might bear only when the ship rolled to starboard. Deckelman told Taylor to exercise his trainers and pointers. Depth charges were Deckelman's next concern. He didn't think they would be needed again; therefore, he wanted to make sure that on each charge the index pointer was on Safe and a safety cover was screwed onto the valve body. He didn't want the charges to detonate if the ship sank. Deckelman made sure Taylor understood his instructions.

Chief Metalsmith Herb McCall had been forward near the exposed cargo hold when U-123's torpedo struck. He had climbed down the hold's ladder with a flashlight in one hand and an oxygen breathing apparatus over his face. Many of the pulpwood logs had been blown out of the port side of the hold, and others were being washed out as the hull was blown open up through the main deck. The blasted hole on the side was at least thirty feet wide. Some impacted logs on the starboard side were still smoldering but would soon be extinguished by the rising water. McCall swept his flashlight around so he could report his findings and evaluation to the bridge. Then he saw it. At first, he couldn't believe his eyes. He looked closer, focusing on the object some twenty-five feet away. "It's a torpedo," he thought. Then he said it aloud. He knew no one could hear him, but he had to say the words out loud to overcome his disbelief. Partially embedded in the pulpwood logs on the starboard side was a long, cylindrical object with propellers. "Jesus," he said to himself, "it can't be! Is it armed? It has to be a dud! Thank God." His DC party waited for him above on the main deck. He said nothing about what he had found. He directed his men to return to the mess deck area and assist with preparing the dead for burial. There, Edwin Dana had already collected dog tags and listed the dead and missing. McCall went to the bridge to report his findings. Lieutenant Deckelman listened carefully and calmly to McCall's report. He agreed it must be a dud, what else? He concluded that the U-boat must have fired two fish several seconds apart, and the second one, with an apparent faulty trigger, had come to rest among the pulp wood logs. A dud fish presented no imminent danger.

At 2053 two East Coast marine radio stations copied *Carolyn*'s first message. Both stations, Manasquan, New Jersey, and Fire Island, New York, passed the transmission to the New York District Coast Guard and COM3, the joint communications office of the commandant, Third Naval District, New York, and the commander, Eastern Sea Frontier, at 2057. Both radio stations took bearings on *Atik/Carolyn*'s signal, but the distance was too far for accuracy although they did place the transmission about three hundred miles east of Norfolk, Virginia. *Carolyn*'s second message, which also stated "0055 GMT" (2055) as the transmission time, was recorded by the two coastal stations at 2132 and by the marine radio station at Surfside, Massachusetts, at 2133. Again bearings were taken and again the discrepancies were too great to plot a precise position. The second message was delivered to Eastern Sea Frontier communications at 2134. The thirty-seven-minute time difference between *Carolyn*'s stated 0055 GMT for the second message and the radio stations' time of receipt may have been caused by the confusion on board the ship following the torpedo hit. In any event, the distress messages from *Carolyn* fell on deaf ears in Eastern Sea Frontier. ESF's War Diary states "the dispatch from SS *Carolyn* resulted in no immediate action." Just another merchantman.[8]

At 2125 *Asterion/Evelyn* intercepted Hicks's SSS SOS message. Legwen changed course. He advised his officers that *Atik* had made contact with a U-boat and he was proceeding to the position given. U-123 remained submerged after its frantic retreat from the decoy's counterattack. Hardegen kept his boat at a respectable distance from his adversary; close enough to keep *Carolyn* under surveillance but distant enough to provide reaction time to any more of the "trap's" tricks. At 2200 von Schroeter, who had been making frequent observations through the periscope, advised Herr Kaleu (a respectful and abbreviated form of Kapitänleutnant) that the U-boat trap had not sunk: "She seems to have

PRIORITY   COMMUNICATIONS THIRD NAVAL DISTRICT   **PRIORITY**

```
PD V CG NR9                                    27MAR42FS
PT V CG NRS-A
            Z QUAY Q ZONA Z NMY Q QUAY ZMJ 500 0132/34 SSSS SOS
            FROM:  COMNYDIST CG
            INFO:  COMTHREE
36.00 N 70.00 W APPX SS CAROLYN TORPEDO ATTACK BURNING FORWARD REQUIRD
SSISTANCE 0055 GMT
NFK 147 AT 0132 (MANASQUAN)
NJY 143 AT 0132 (FIREISLAND)
C WA FORWARD REQUIRE


TOD 0137 HA CG
R PT BU
```

CONFIRMATION

PRIORITY   COMMUNICATIONS THIRD NAVAL DISTRICT   **PRIORITY**

```
PD V CG NR3                                    27MAR42FS
PT V CG NR3-A
            Z QUAY Q ZONA Z NMYQ QUAY ZMJ 500 0053/56 SSS SOS
            FROM:  COMNYDIST CG
            INFO:  COMTHREE
LAT 3600 N LONG 7000 W CAROLYN 0055 BURNING FORWARD NOT BAD


BEARINGS FROM MANASQUAN 150 AT 0053
            FIREISLAND 146 AT 0053


TOD 0057 HA CG
R PT BU
```

CONFIRMATION

a buoyant cargo. She lay stopped, and the crew has gone back aboard." Hardegen responded, "I have decided this time to make a submerged attack." Hardegen took control of the boat once again. He prepared tube 1 for launch. He then maneuvered U-123 to a zero-degree bearing-on-target and a zero-degree angle-of-fire, as if he were aiming the U-boat at the starboard broadside of the apparently lifeless *Carolyn*. At 2030, 26 March 1942, from a distance of five hundred meters, Hardegen launched his G7e, serial number 21921, for a point-blank shot at *Carolyn*'s engine room. It took only twenty-four seconds for the eel to reach its mark.[9]

Aboard *Carolyn* there was no warning. With 90 percent cloud cover, there was no moonlight to illuminate the periscope. As U-123 moved ahead cautiously at three knots, the wake of the extended scope was inconspicuous. The electric G7e hit in the engine room, on the starboard side, at a speed of thirty knots. The detonation of eleven hundred pounds of high explosives was an instant death blow for all in the enclosed area: Lieutenant Beckett and his engineering gang; Frenchy Ouellette and his damage control team. The explosion carried away the upper decks on the starboard side above the point of impact, killing or wounding many of Gun Capt. Ray Roberts's crew and putting another 4-inch out of commission. Deckelman was startled, but not surprised. He had expected the second torpedo, but not this soon. He had hoped for another fight, but he knew no smart U-boat commander would accept the challenge unless he was without torpedoes. Hardegen was smart and he had more fish.

Dan Deckelman needed no further damage reports. On the bridge he felt the blast. He saw the yellow-red flash over his right shoulder. He heard the debris fall on the charthouse and pilothouse roof above his head. He thought the water cascading from above would never end. It took a few minutes for his eyes to once more adjust to the darkness, and he was amazed at how well he could see. He quickly scanned the ocean's surface on the starboard side, hoping the submarine would appear. Then he became aware of *Carolyn* settling deeper by the bow. He wondered if she was going to founder or if the pulpwood logs would, as intended, give her enough buoyancy to stay afloat, even partially submerged. He thought about his guns—would they remain usable even if the water was up to the main deck? He did not want to think beyond that point, but the situation demanded his full attention.

Lieutenant Deckelman was not ready to give up the ship. He had two choices: fight or quit. He had never been taught to quit. As long as he had a platform and a gun and a few able men, he would fight. Edwin Leonard came out of the darkness and reported that all radio communications were down, even the battery backup. Ed Joyce announced his presence and stated that one 4-inch gun on each side was manned and ready, and both after machine guns were intact, but the forward crew living spaces and the mess deck were flooding. Deckelman acknowledged and told Joyce to check the availability of rafts and to split the "idle" crew members and put as many as half the boat's capacity in each of the two remaining boats and have them stay near the ship to pick up those in the water if the ship sank. Joyce went below.

On the darkened and damaged bridge, an eerie stillness prevailed. No one uttered a word. Leonard, Kosmider, Burgess, and Deckelman stood there in silence. The gleam of a flashlight illuminated the bridge from the charthouse. It was Chief Quartermaster John Dalton. He had been at the chart table maintaining the ship's rough logbook, double-checking the positions plotted by dead reckoning, and until power was lost, listening in the radio room on 500 KCS for a message from the several marine radio stations that might give a bearing on the last radio transmission. Dalton joined the group. Ensign Leonard broke the silence with a rhetorical question: how much more punishment could the ship take? He knew Deckelman had no answer, and none was offered. Everyone knew the old girl had already taken more abuse than he thought possible. The main deck was awash up into the forward superstructure, and the propeller was out of the water. Deckelman probably intended to stay with the ship as long as she stayed afloat, reasoning that the survivors would be safer there than in rafts and small boats in rough seas. He would risk another torpedo hit. His concerns were the guns and gun crews. His concerns were resolved at 2350, Thursday, 26 March 1942. The destruction was instant and total, and exactly what happened is still a mystery.

Kapitänleutnant Hardegen was an anxious spectator to the decoy's final moments. He kept U-123 submerged after he fired his coup-de-grace at 2230, then moved away from *Carolyn* some two thousand meters. His second eel was not, as intended, a "stroke of mercy," for *Carolyn* remained afloat for another eighty apprehensive minutes. He observed through the periscope the crew going into the lifeboats again. He saw the forecastle sink deeper and the water engulf the main deck up to the base of the midships superstructure. She appeared to list more to port. The stern showed the propeller out of the water and free in the air. At 2327 U-123 was brought to the surface, still a safe distance from *Carolyn*, its slender gray-black tower hidden in the darkness of the moonless night. Hardegen recorded the following: "The steamer is still exactly as I saw it before with the periscope observation."

At 2350 Hardegen witnessed the destruction of SS *Carolyn*/USS *Atik*. He later recorded his observations in his KTB: "27 March 1942. 0550 CET. Now come the heavy detonations, either the boilers or the depth charges and ammunition. I don't see her anymore. I can see no wreckage." Hardegen recalled three distinct explosions occurring an hour and twenty minutes after he fired his second torpedo. Twenty minutes before these unexplained blasts, he observed *Carolyn* still afloat in the same attitude, forecastle sunk with water covering the main deck to the superstructure and the propeller out of the water, as he saw her shortly after his second torpedo hit. Apparently she was not sinking further, or when surveyed from a distance, the rate of sinking was imperceptible. He suspected the detonations were caused either by the boilers or the depth charges and ammunition. It could not have been the boilers, for they were demolished already by the second torpedo over an hour earlier. Nor could it have been a magazine. *Atik* had no magazines. Her gun ammunition was stowed in ready-lockers by each 4-inch gun. They would not destruct as a single or triple heavy detonation, nor would the depth charges self-destruct.

Depth charges are designed for stowage in a fail-safe mode. They are detonated by a hydrostatic pistol. *Atik*'s depth charges were either secure in their stowage racks or mounted securely on the K-gun launchers. The ship was still afloat at the instant of the three rapid explosions, according to Hardegen; therefore, with the stern above water and all depth charges high and dry, the hydrostatic pistols could not fire. A plausible explanation

Q-SHIPS VERSUS U-BOATS

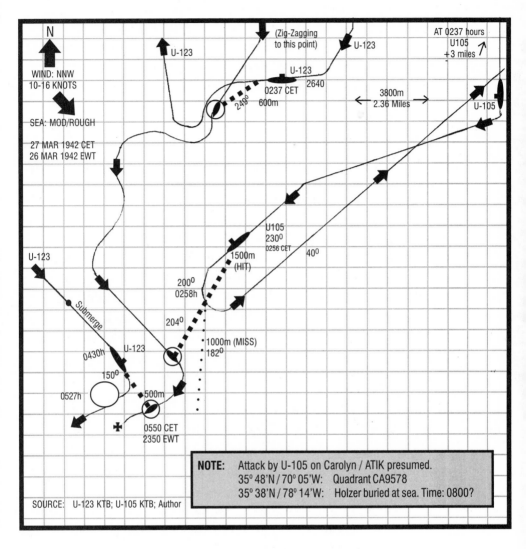

26–27 March 1942: U-123/U-105 attack on SS *Carolyn*/USS *Atik*

is the possibility of a wayward torpedo lodged in cargo hold number 2. It is conceivable that a nearly spent torpedo could have entered *Carolyn*'s hull through the large hole made by U-123's first torpedo and come to rest embedded in the exposed hold among the disarrayed logs without a proper contact with the firing mechanism. U-105 could have been the source of that torpedo. KK Schuch in U-105 recorded firing two torpedoes, one at 2056 and the other at 2058. The first one struck the port side with no detonation and the other one missed. This was nineteen minutes after Hardegen's first hit. It is reasonable to assume that as the ship continued to settle by the bow or was rocked by wave action, the torpedo or logs moved and triggered the firing mechanism.

A normal sequence of events would follow: The exploding torpedo would break the back of *Atik* at or near hatch number 3, just forward of the smoke stack. The after end of the ship, which had been suspended in the air, would come crashing down into the sea. The exploding torpedo, falling debris, and the sudden shift in gravity would dislodge and damage and somehow detonate two of the remaining twenty-one depth charges. The resulting explosions would tear asunder the ship and kill or fatally injure the personnel on board and in the nearby boats. The destruction of *Atik/Carolyn* would be complete. There were no survivors. Hardegen made no report of lifeboats or life rafts. The U-123 commander's deed was done, perhaps with some contribution by KK Schuch in U-105. The brave navy men of USS *Atik* and their gallant old ship passed into history. Their valor and sacrifice were absorbed by the secrecy of their mission and by the more auspicious and celebrated naval engagements that would follow: Midway, Coral Sea, the Philippine Sea, and eventually the victory over the U-boats.

On U-123, Reinhard Hardegen turned his attention to Midshipman Rudolf Holzer, who lay at peace after dying quietly during the second attack on *Carolyn*. Hardegen recorded, "We have lost a good comrade. Around 0800 hours CET [0200 local time], after a brief but solemn ceremony, we gave his body to the sea. He is laid to rest in the seaman's grave at 35-38 North and 70-14 West."

Hardegen, understandably, was disturbed by the Q-ship incident.

Except for his KTB entry and a brief radio report to BdU of his engagement with a U.S. U-boat trap and the loss of an officer, he took no further steps to provide Admiral Dönitz with the details of the engagement. Inwardly, Hardegen was grieved by the loss of his midshipman and by his ineptness in not recognizing *Carolyn* as a trap. He was troubled with self-condemnation; he realized full well that it was only extreme good luck that had saved him, his boat, and his men from the fate he finally inflicted on his opponent. Outwardly, he was anticipating his arrival at Cape Hatteras and its bountiful targets. He set course 270 degrees, due west, a straight line to his "happy hunting grounds."

Lt. Cdr. Glenn Legwen, in *Evelyn/Asterion*, recorded that at 2125 on 26 March he was informed of the attack on *Atik*. Chief Radioman Richard Turja handed the captain *Carolyn*'s first 0055 GMT message. Legwen asked Neville, who also had a copy, to meet with him in the charthouse. Legwen advised Guy Brown Ray, the watch officer on the bridge, that *Atik* had been attacked and was burning. He directed a course change to 269 degrees and informed the engine room to go to full power. Neville, who remained in the chartroom, had measured the distance to *Atik*'s position. He advised Legwen that it was about 275 miles to *Atik*'s reported position. At 9.5 knots, it was approximately twenty-nine hours away. An estimated arrival time in the area would be the early morning of the twenty-eighth.[10]

Turja entered the chartroom with *Atik*'s second message and gave it to Lieutenant Neville. Neville read it aloud to Legwen who responded that *Atik* must have been surprised by a couple of well-placed torpedoes and then shell fire; otherwise, she should have been able to fight back. He reasoned that unless she met with a real catastrophe, she should still be afloat. He concluded that it would serve no purpose to radio Hicks. There could be other ships closer, and hopefully Eastern Sea Frontier would vector a navy ship or aircraft to the scene. Both officers pondered *Atik*'s fate and hoped for the best. Both were anxious for further information. None was forthcoming.

These first several days at sea in the "war zone" provided a firsthand opportunity to observe Legwen and Neville under pressure. While the "pressure" was not as intense as an actual submarine attack, to the uninitiated and inexperienced decoy officers, any unusual observation or extraneous event brought all hands to battle stations. These false alarms occurred on the twenty-fourth, the twenty-fifth, and the twenty-sixth: Flares, "pings," propeller noises from "friendly" ships, especially fishing vessels, and the sighting of any lights on small boats all precipitated a call to General Quarters.

The captain and the executive officer formed a harmonious pair. Lieutenant Commander Legwen was aggressive, quick to react, and dauntless. Lieutenant Neville, while showing no fear, was more calculating, evaluating, and restrained. The restraint may well have been intentional to offset the boldness of Legwen, with whom he enjoyed great rapport and understanding. I held both men in high regard. My position in relation to the other officers was somewhat unusual. I was a supply corps officer, a staff officer not in the line of command. My primary responsibilities were logistics and finance. I was the treasurer of the bogus Asterion Shipping Company and was the only person authorized to draw on the company's account at the Riggs National Bank in Washington, D.C. As a staff officer, I was not called upon to stand the underway officer-of-the-deck watch.

Ensign Lukowich was the communications officer and stood watch in the radio room. He served as backup bridge watch officer whenever needed. Lt. Larry Neville was the navigator as well as the executive officer. As navigator, he would "shoot stars" each morning and evening, weather permitting, and would spend about twenty minutes in the charthouse determining the ship's position based on his sextant sights and calculations. I suggested to Neville that since I had no watch to stand, I would be pleased to be his junior watch officer on each of his two daily watches. We all believed it was during this period of twilight that we were the most vulnerable to a U-boat attack. Neville accepted my offer and so advised Legwen. Both knew from previous discussions and observations that I knew the ship, the rules of the road, the armament, and shiphandling — though there was little need for that in the middle of the Atlantic. Apparently, too, I had displayed to their satisfaction a sense of responsibility. My night vision was particularly good, and because of my keen interest in ships as a youngster, I was familiar with characteristics of many vessels, both foreign and domestic. In a very short period of time, the bridge became my watch station as well as my battle station.

Asterion/Evelyn moved westward along the 36th parallel. Legwen came to the bridge quite often for discussions with Neville. I seldom participated in these conversations, but I was never excluded. Legwen assumed we would find *Atik*. He was interested in the condition of the ship, the damage sustained, the effect of the pulpwood on buoyancy, and the detailed attack sequence of the U-boat. Neville played the role of the pragmatist. He recognized the position given by *Atik* was approximate and that small boats would be blown about by the surface winds if the ship had sunk. Although Neville knew the operations officer at Eastern Sea Frontier had stated that assistance was not available, he felt that a search aircraft might be dispatched, and it would be better suited than surface craft to locate survivors. He asked Ensign Lukowich to monitor the various frequencies for any radio traffic relating to *Carolyn*'s distress message. While Legwen was confident he would find survivors, Neville was not optimistic.

At about 0330, 27 March, Ensign Lukowich awakened Neville and gave him a copy of an SSS SOS message from the Norwegian tanker *Svenör*. The ship reported its position as some 35 miles east of *Atik*'s stated location and due west on *Asterion*'s course.[11] Neville took the copy, dressed, and went to the charthouse. His quick calculation placed *Svenör* some 160 miles due west. He noted the close proximity of the position to *Atik*'s and concluded that the same U-boat must be attacking targets in that area. He would wait until after morning star sights to notify Legwen.

By 0715 Neville had fixed the ship's position and was ready for discussion with Legwen. He sent the bridge messenger with a copy of *Svenör*'s distress signal to the captain. Neville's mind was racing ahead, considering possible near-term events. There could be survivors from both *Atik* and the Swedish tanker. Would we have enough food, clothing, and medical supplies for these men? He shared his thoughts with me on the bridge. We had ample food, but my concern was the medical requirements. We had a corpsman staff, but no medical officer. I suggested we alert "Doc" Fignar, the chief hospital corpsman. Neville dispatched the messenger to have Doc come to the bridge. Chief Andy Fignar reported to the bridge rather promptly. Doc was a serious-minded person, independent, and regulation. He was the closest thing to a doctor and chaplain that we had on board. The exec summarized the situation and advised Doc to be prepared to treat survivors and to report any anxiety among the crew. Neville's sense of duty and his consideration of Doc Fignar's responsibility and capability were noteworthy. He sensed the physical strain and mental stress we all felt but chose to conceal as best we could. He knew Fignar would have a stabilizing influence on the men below deck. Neville appreciated Doc's father figure among the crew, especially the younger sailors. My fondness and respect for Mr. Neville grew as time went on. His mental agility and calmness relieved much of the concern I had for when we would engage our first U-boat. I felt confident he could manage any situation under fire as long as he was physically able to do so.

Neville and I were relieved by Guy-Brown a few minutes before 0800. We went directly to the wardroom for breakfast and a few minutes of relaxation. We were both tired, having had little sound sleep during the past ninety-six hours. Legwen came into the wardroom. He had *Svenör's* message in hand. He said he had already had breakfast and was going up to the charthouse and bridge for a while. Neville offered to join him, but Legwen declined. "Larry," he said, "you had better get some rest. We may have a busy night tonight." It was obvious that the attack and apparent loss of *Atik* weighed heavily on the captain's mind. He wanted revenge. But against which U-boat? Any U-boat! Legwen had no way of knowing that at 1600 that day he would be less than fifty miles from U-105. After sinking *Svenör*, KK Schuch sailed east-northeast on a direct line to his home base in Occupied France.

KL Hardegen, after the burial of Midshipman Holzer, moved in the opposite direction. Still markedly disturbed by his encounter with the U-boat trap *Carolyn* he would seek comfort by adding more tonnage to his tally. After this patrol he expressed his remorse in a pamphlet entitled "Auf Gefechtsstationen!": "We couldn't immerse ourselves in sad thoughts. For the first time the war had claimed a victim from us. That only forced our hand. Our sights were set on looking for the enemy and crushing him, loyal to our motto: Attack! Advance! Sink!" Hardegen was anxious to reach the Atlantic Coast of the United States. There his revenge would be abundant and sweet. He would be there in seventy-two hours.[12]

At 1400 on 27 March, Legwen and Neville were called to the bridge. Lieutenant Schwaner and the starboard lookout had sighted a partially submerged lifeboat. Legwen stopped the ship alongside for a close inspection. The boat apparently had been in the water for several months. The stern was stove in and there were no identifying marks. The boat was left as it had been found. At 2000 *Asterion* slowed to five knots and made a wide circle at *Svenör*'s reported position. There was enough moonlight to provide visibility; however, the hour-long search was fruitless. Legwen gave orders to proceed westward to *Atik*'s position, another three to four hours away.

Commencing at 2200 the wind from the west freshened. In an hour's time it had increased to a moderate gale force, a velocity of thirty knots. Large waves had formed and *Asterion* slowed to about two knots. Legwen became concerned about the additional delay in arriving at *Atik*'s position and the effect of the worsening weather on possible survivors. Daylight, Saturday, 28 March 1942, *Asterion* was still not at her sister ship's reported location. The wind had increased to force 9, a strong gale with high seas. Legwen took his ship westward for three more hours. He then turned south for two hours, then east with the wind and seas astern for three hours, then north for one hour, then westward again. By dusk there was still no sign of *Atik* or her crew. All during the search extra lookouts were posted on the flying bridge, one deck above the navigation bridge. The daylong scrutiny of the rough seas was a strain on both the crew and the ship. That night the steering gear jammed and was freed only by rigging a block and tackle system to relieve some of the strain on the rudder. The failure of the rudder was an added concern for the already anxious captain.[13]

At daylight on Sunday, 29 March, Legwen continued his search. This time he followed a downwind, zigzag pattern. But once again the steering gear malfunctioned. The ship's rudder thereafter had to be operated from the after steering compartment in the poopdeck housing. Apparently the old *Evelyn* was not accustomed to the rigors of flank speed in a pounding sea. She reacted further to her "unaccustomed abusive treatment" by springing several bad leaks in the bottom of a boiler's steam drum. More feed water was being used than could be made. With some reluctant but convincing arguments from Guy-Brown, Legwen broke off the search and pointed *Asterion's* bow toward Norfolk, Virginia. Guy-Brown and his "black gang," as the engineering crew was called, would make the necessary repairs while at anchor in the calm water of Hampton Roads. We arrived off Cape Henry on 31 March, picked up Capt. Hugh Foster of the Virginia Pilot Association, and proceeded to our anchorage off Old Point Comfort. Legwen left the ship soon after anchoring to make his way to the naval district commandant's office and to report to Eastern Sea Frontier Operations. Neville commented that since the captain was in civilian dress, he would have to use his most persuasive talent to avoid security and make it to the commandant's office without being arrested. We all had the utmost confidence in our commanding officer.[14]

Asterion had many superior petty officers on board. Certainly two of the most outstanding were Chief Quartermaster Lionel Cook and Quartermaster Second Class Roger Metz. Chief Cook was probably the oldest man in the ship's company, between fifty-five and sixty years old. He was a big man, with a strong, well-built physique. His hands were large and, like his face, were leathery from years of exposure to the sun and the sea. He was not a gregarious person. He seemed always to be in the charthouse or on the bridge checking the wind and the sea. He often took star sights and noon-sun-lines with Lieutenant Neville, and, like Kaeding in U-123, he took pride in his dead reckoning accuracy. He was old school navy and found it difficult to accept the imposed informality of nonregulation dress in this bastard-Q-ship duty. He would often be heard saying, "On my ship sailors are sailors, not slobs!" His shipmates said he stayed in the charthouse because it was centerline and midships, the farthest point away from a torpedo blast. That might be true. If so, it showed good judgment. Cook always positioned himself so that the person speaking to him was on his right side. Metz was of the opinion that Chief Cook had little or no hearing in his left ear and suspected he could not hear too well with the other. Metz reasoned that that was why he spoke so loudly most of the time—"and always yelled at the sailors." Metz, in his mid-twenties, respected and catered to Chief Cook and was rewarded in turn with shared knowledge, instructions, and friendship. Both men were professional navy petty officers of the highest order.

After anchoring, Chief Cook and Roger Metz took bearings to mark the exact location of the ship. With the log entry made and checked, Chief Cook released his tension by relating to Metz the battle of *Monitor* and *Merrimack* in 1862 near the very spot where *Evelyn* was anchored. Metz listened politely and then wondered aloud if the chief had been there at the time. Chief Cook turned his deaf ear toward the young quartermaster.

While still at anchor on the morning of 4 April, Legwen went ashore to again contact Eastern Sea Frontier Operations. All repairs to the boilers had been completed, and the ship was again ready for sea. Atlantic Fleet Headquarters provided Legwen with a secured telephone line to New York. Commander Farley at Eastern Sea Frontier advised Legwen of the recent U-boat attacks close in along the coast of Virginia and the Carolinas. Legwen copied the list as Farley spoke:

26 March	Tanker *Dixie Arrow* 34-55 N/75-02 W
27 March	Freighter *Equipoise* 36-36 N/74-45 W
29 March	Freighter *City of New York* 35-16 N/74-25 W
31 March	Tug *Menominee* and three barges 37-34 N/75-25 W
01 April	Tanker *Tiger* 36-50 N/74-18 W
01 April	Freighter *Rio Blanco* 35-18 N/74-18 W
02 April	Tanker *Liebre* 34-11 N/76-08 W
03 April	Freighter *David H. Atwater* 37-57 N/75-10 W

It was apparent the attacks were close in to the coastline, generally within sixty miles. Legwen suggested to Farley that *Asterion* remain in coastal waters rather than the two hundred miles offshore called for in the op-order. Farley agreed. Further, with the loss of *Atik*, Farley gave Legwen freedom of operation from New York to the Straits of Florida. Legwen advised Farley that *Asterion* was ready for sea and that he would leave Hampton Roads at 1300 and proceed southward toward Cape Hatteras where most of the attacks had occurred.

Before the conversation concluded, Farley said he had no information on the loss of *Atik* and there was still hope for survivors. He also stated that Admiral Andrews was interested in Legwen's views as to what happened to *Atik*. Legwen welcomed the opportunity to voice his opinion. He believed *Atik* had been surprised and disabled by one or more torpedo hits. Then in the darkness the submarine surfaced at close range and shelled the bridge, the radio room, and the superstructure with its deck guns. Hicks no doubt returned fire as best he could with his 4-inch cannons and the .50-caliber machine guns. He could have inflicted casualties among the German deck gun crews. The U-boat commander, in turn, must have been surprised and angered, and in retaliation fired another torpedo at the slowly sinking *Atik*. As a final act of vengeance, the U-boat commander might have destroyed the life boats and rafts. Legwen stated that he was surprised he did not find wreckage or survivors, even though the weather was very bad. His personal opinion was that the Germans were merciless and bent on total destruction of the decoy. He was convinced that Hicks's radio had been hit and put out of service early in the engagement. He had expected him to radio some details of the attack. Legwen was concerned that because of the similar characteristics of *Atik* and *Asterion*, he would be identified as a decoy and either avoided or made a sought-after target for a submerged attack. With that in mind, Legwen said that unless otherwise directed, he intended to initiate an attack on any U-boat that he judged vulnerable, rather than wait for the submarine to strike first. Farley thanked Legwen for his opinion. He said *Asterion* should proceed as scheduled and that if Admiral Andrews disagreed with the intended tactics he would provide other instructions. Legwen returned to his command.[15]

There are many perplexing matters in the loss of the mystery ship USS *Atik*. But none is more puzzling than the question why Hicks did not grasp the initiative and attack the U-boat before nightfall. U-123 was within close range; *Atik*'s 4-inch battery gunners had a clear view of the target; and the ship's maneuverability was not yet impaired. It is possible if not probable that Hardegen commenced his assault only seconds before Hicks's intended attack.

The saga of the loss of USS *Atik*, also known as SS *Carolyn*, was almost complete. The next of kin of the 139 officers and crewmen were notified by the Navy Department of their status as "missing following action in the performance of their duty and in the service of their Country." Not until May 1944 did the Navy Department make the official notification of the presumption of death of USS *Atik*'s officers and men due to enemy action in the North Atlantic.

"Have you any news of my boy Jack?"
    Not this tide.
"When d'you think that he'll come back?"
    Not with this wind blowing and this tide . . .
"Oh, dear, what comfort can I find?"
    None this tide,
    Nor any tide,
        Except that he did not shame his kind —
    Not even with that wind blowing, and that tide.

                                Rudyard Kipling, "My Boy Jack," 1916

8

The Search for the Unknown

HE PASSES THROUGH LIFE MOST SECURELY WHO
HAS LEAST REASON TO REPROACH HIMSELF WITH
COMPLAISANCE TOWARD HIS ENEMIES.

*Thucydides, History of the
Peloponnesian Wars*

GLENN LEGWEN PONDERED the fate of *Atik* and Harry Hicks. He tried
to reconstruct the sequence of events that had led to the attack and
apparent loss of *Atik* and all hands, but he had so little information it was
an exercise in futility. However, he resolved that *Asterion*, his command,
would not suffer the same fate and that somewhere, sometime, and somehow he would even the score. He did not know how, but he would pre-
vail. His verbal report to Farley only fueled his determination. He could
imagine the humiliation of an entrapped U-boat commander. He could
not imagine Hicks not sinking him. Notwithstanding Neville's views to
the contrary, Legwen could not dismiss from his mind the thought of an
enraged U-boat commander and his dastardly retaliation. Glenn Legwen
would show no complaisance toward an entrapped enemy.

When Legwen returned to the ship, Neville met him at the accommodation ladder. They went immediately to the chartroom to plot the positions of the attacks provided by Farley. Neville, when he read about the
attack on the tugboat and three barges, wondered facetiously if that U-boat

114

commander, when he saw the long string of lights on the tow, thought he was attacking the *Queen Mary*.[1] Both officers were seeking a pattern that would reveal the number of U-boats located off the coast and their designated operating area. There appeared to be four groupings of the recent attacks. The first involved the tugboat and the barges and the freighter *David H. Atwater*. They were located on the ten-fathom curve, one north and the other south of Chincoteague Inlet, Virginia. The attacks were three days apart. A second pair of attacks, SS *Equipoise* and SS *Tiger*, were sixty-four and eighty-three nautical miles, respectively, east of Cape Henry light tower. These attacks were also three days apart. The third group, SS *City of New York* and SS *Rio Blanco*, were only six miles apart and some forty-three and forty-nine miles, respectively, east of Diamond Shoals. Group four, SS *Dixie Arrow* and SS *Liebre*, were both to the southeast of Cape Hatteras: *Dixie Arrow* nineteen miles to the southeast of Diamond Shoals and *Liebre* seventy-one miles to the southeast of the Shoals and only fifteen miles off Cape Lookout Shoals buoy. Considering the overall pattern, Neville and Legwen concluded there could be at least four U-boats operating in the general area and that, based on the time intervals between attacks and the locations, it was impossible to predict with accuracy the precise location of future attacks.

Legwen thought it was logical to expect the U-boats to concentrate where shipping was the densest. That would be the area off the coast between Cape Henry (Virginia) and Cape Fear (North Carolina), off Frying Pan Shoals and out to the Gulf Stream. That's where he would "expose" *Evelyn* to the German marauders. Unbeknownst to the officers of *Evelyn*, on that day, 4 April 1942, there were no fewer than seven enemy submarines operating along the coast: U-71, KK Walter Flachsenberg; U-123, KL Reinhard Hardegen; U-160, KL Georg Lassen; U-203, KL Rolf Mützelburg; U-552, KL Erich Topp; U-571, KL Helmut Möhlmann; U-754, KL Johannes Oestermann. More than one of these commanders could have *Evelyn* under surveillance after she left Hampton Roads.

At 1300 on 4 April, Virginia pilot Capt. W. S. Hudgins arrived on board to guide *Evelyn* of the Asterion Shipping Company to Cape Henry. *Evelyn* weighed anchor and proceeded around Willoughby Bank into Thimble Shoal Channel to Cape Henry. There, at 1620, Hudgins debarked and the expendable Q-ship continued eastward on course 97 degrees to clear the entrance to Chesapeake Bay. At 1715, after the evening meal, Legwen brought the crew to battle stations. It was a precautionary measure. Shortly afterward a destroyer passed astern heading down the coast. In the near darkness it was impossible to read the small numbers painted on its bow. I commented to Neville, who was standing beside me on the bridge, that while I felt comforted by the sight of that destroyer, it was the last thing we wanted to be associated with. Neville responded that that was a paradoxical statement if he ever heard one.

At 2000 Legwen turned south toward False Cape buoy, some twenty miles away. At exactly 2247 a huge ball of fire lit up the night. The explosion was off our starboard bow, only a few miles away, and on a compass bearing of 190 degrees true. The fire ball was followed by a high column of flame that spread rapidly through the mid- and after sections of a tanker. Legwen directed John Lukowich to transmit the standard SSS message. *Evelyn*'s position was approximately five miles south of bell buoy number 6, east of Caffey Inlet. The water depth was a mere ninety-three feet. The exploding tanker was eight miles northeast of the beach at Kitty Hawk, North Carolina. From 2250 to 2255 numerous star shells were sighted, presumably fired by the destroyer seen earlier. (Star shells are projectiles that are fired into the air, detonate, and release an illuminating flare suspended by a parachute.) These pyrotechnics illuminated the area to the east of the burning ship.[2]

For several minutes *Evelyn* was like a stagehand caught in the middle of a well-lighted stage. The sharp reports of cannon fire could be clearly heard. Those of us on the bridge used the opportunity of the near-daylight condition to search the area for a surfaced U-boat. We could see clearly the burning tanker, which was still heading in a northerly direction. We looked for gun flashes, thinking the submarine if still on the surface could be shelling the target. At 2300 the sound room reported a distant high speed propeller noise bearing 186 degrees true and moving slowly to the east. Legwen assumed this was the U-boat on a course that would take it across *Evelyn*'s bow from starboard to port. He ordered the curtains concealing the 4-inch guns removed and alerted Lieutenant Schwaner to be prepared to fire to starboard on a surfaced U-boat. By now *Evelyn* was in partial darkness; the burning tanker was a large and bright beacon.[3]

I had stationed myself on the starboard wing of the bridge to gain an unobstructed view of the ocean surface. The bearing of the propeller noise was to the left of the burning ship. I intentionally avoided sweeping my binoculars through the bright light of the flaming oil, which had now spread to the water surrounding the burning tanker. We could still hear cannon fire. Neville called to all on the bridge to report immediately any flashes from gunfire or wakes from torpedoes. We all assumed the U-boat had seen us and was moving into a forward position for an optimum attack angle. In the darkness it was impossible to know whether she was on the surface or submerged. As I stood on the bridge searching for the long, low shape of the U-boat, there was no doubt in my mind that we would be attacked. I knew she was there. It was just a matter of time before a flash would be reported and the sound of an incoming projectile would be heard. Or the tell-tale phosphorescent trail of a torpedo would be seen.

I sensed no feeling of fright as I concentrated my attention on the dark waters, yet I experienced a physical phenomenon completely new to me. With the ball of my right foot firmly on the deck, my right heel began to move up and down uncontrollably. It was not a violent spasm, but it was definitely noticeable. Even when I concentrated on shifting my full weight on to my twitching heel, I could not stop the motion. This lasted some thirty to thirty-five seconds. Perhaps I had not experienced this degree of subconscious fear before. I was pleased that this incident did not manifest itself in a more onerous or ostentatious display. Throughout this brief episode, my mind remained clear, and I never for a moment considered turning away from my duties and responsibilities. I had sensed the bittersweet taste of trepidation. It never happened again.

Legwen turned *Evelyn* sharply to port, to the southeast, and forward of the changing sonar bearing. He was attempting to put the U-boat broad on *Evelyn*'s beam to give our gunners a better angle on the target. In this maneuver in the shallow water contact was lost. It is possible that the submarine also made an abrupt turn toward or away from *Evelyn*, thus providing a much smaller target for the inexperienced sonarman. Contact was never regained. Both *Evelyn* and the U-boat lost an opportunity to add to their tally. We remained in the vicinity of the attack until 0330 searching toward the open sea and offering our ship as an additional target— for a price. Since we were not fired upon, we assumed the U-boat commander was aware of the destroyer in the area and was eager to seek deeper and safer water. Legwen brought the ship close by the still-burning hulk, which we later learned was the U.S. tanker SS *Byron D. Benson.* We could see small craft in the area, presumably Coast Guard boats, so we turned and proceeded on a southbound course. The sinking of the ship was the work of Kapitänleutnant Erich Topp in U-552, the same boat that had torpedoed the Dutch SS *Ocana* on 24 March in the general vicinity of *Evelyn* and south of Cape Sable, Nova Scotia. Would Topp become Legwen's first adversary? The veteran Kapitänleutnant would be a noteworthy opponent.[4]

KL Erich Topp in command of U-552 made his debut on the U.S. Atlantic coast by sinking the small freighter (2,438 GRT) SS *David H. Atwater* on 3 April 1942, 6 miles off Chincoteague Inlet, Virginia, and 1.4 miles southwest of Winter Quarter lightship. Topp sank the ship with ninety-three rounds of 8.8-centimeter cannon fire. But even before this incident, KL Topp had made his mark in U.S. naval history. Although not known by name to the U.S. Navy at the time, on 31 October 1941, Topp torpedoed and sank the destroyer USS *Reuben James* (DD245) some 600 miles west of Ireland. The destroyer was struck near the bow, probably causing the forward magazine to explode. No officers and only 45 of the ship's complement of 160 were rescued. She was engaged in escort duty of convoy HX156 at the time. KL Topp may not have intended to torpedo a U.S. destroyer, but his "mistake" was condoned by the Nazi high command.[5]

Ironically, three incidents involving U-boats and U.S. destroyers, including U-552 and *Reuben James*, played into President Roosevelt's impatient hands. The president's policy regarding the European War from 1939 until 11 December 1941, when Germany and Italy declared war on the United States, provided for a carefully tailored plan of gradual escalation from strict neutrality to actively supporting the Allies, especially the British, to the extent "permissible" short of war. At home, opposition to the Roosevelt policy was deeply rooted. Congress had passed the Neutrality Act of 1935, with later amendments, which the president signed reluctantly because of its binding restrictions. The general public, with the sacrifices of World War I still in mind, was not eager to again enter into a European conflict. Yet Roosevelt, convinced that Britain could not alone defeat the Axis powers, would persist in "pulling rabbits out of the hat" to circumvent the obstacles placed before him by the isolationists. The U-boat attacks provided a few "rabbits."[6]

On 4 September 1941, USS *Greer* (DD145), en route independently to Iceland and southeast of Greenland, was advised by a British patrol plane of a U-boat in the area. *Greer* made contact and tracked the submarine for three hours while the British aircraft engaged with depth charges. The U-boat, U-652 (KL Georg-Werner Fraatz), attacked *Greer* with a spread of two torpedoes, thinking the destroyer had delivered the depth charges. *Greer* responded with a single depth charge run. All participants left the scene unscathed. Roosevelt called the U-boat attack on *Greer* "legal and moral piracy" and instructed the navy to "shoot on sight." This was followed by a request from the president to Congress for an amendment to the Neutrality Act to permit trade with warring countries, the arming of U.S. merchant ships, and the restoration of the right of these ships to enter into the war zones.[7]

The second incident involved USS *Kearny* (DD432). On 17 October 1941, USS *Kearny*, while escorting convoy SC48 some 350 miles southwest of Iceland, was torpedoed and damaged by U-568 (KL Joachim Preuss). Eleven of *Kearny*'s crew were killed. The destroyer diverted to Reykjavik, Iceland, for repairs. Even though this was the first incident of U.S. bloodshed, little reaction was discernable from the apathetic American public.

> Even this "incident" was taken pretty much as a matter of course by the American people who always have considered the men in their regular armed forces—Navy, Army and, most of all, Marine Corps—as rugged mercenaries who signed up voluntarily, as do policemen and firemen, for hazardous service; it was, of course, tough luck when any of them were killed in line of duty in a Central American revolution, or on an

accidently sunk submarine or on a deliberately sunk gunboat, . . . but it was still all in the day's work. There was little or no self-identification of the normal American soldier or sailor. In the case of the drafted men, however, the attitude was entirely different. They were "our boys" who must be kept out of harm's way at all costs. Since there were no drafted men in the Navy at that time, there was no great popular indignation against Hitler for the attacks on the destroyers; but what is most important is that neither was there any serious popular indignation against Roosevelt for his responsibility in thus exposing our ships. The American people were merely waiting, in a seemingly apathetic state.[8]

And so it was with the sinking of USS *Reuben James* by Erich Topp on the morning of 31 October. Except for the bereaved families of the 115 officers and men lost, the general public seemed to show little interest. However, as the president had requested, Congress passed the amendment to the Neutrality Act, which Roosevelt signed on 17 November with great satisfaction. It was a close vote in both houses. The irony is that Topp, Preuss, and Fraatz, the latter two of little-known reputation, by their actions directly and greatly assisted President Roosevelt in his determination to pressure Congress and to prepare the country for the inevitable involvement in the war in Europe. But Roosevelt was running out of "rabbits." The attack on Pearl Harbor removed the obstacle of isolation, and the U.S. people accepted the wartime leadership of their president. Roosevelt, in his radio speech on Tuesday night, 9 December, declared: "We may acknowledge that our enemies have performed a brilliant feat of deception, perfectly timed and executed with great skill. It was a thoroughly dishonorable deed, but we must face the fact that modern warfare as conducted in the Nazi manner is a dirty business. We don't like it—we didn't want to get in it—but we are in it, and we're going to fight it with everything we've got." America was at war, officially and unequivocally. However, rhetoric brought no overwhelming countermeasures to the increasing U-boat activities along the Atlantic coast. Project LQ, the decoy ship program with *Evelyn* and *Carolyn*, was a desperate and immediate response. In time some additional coastal craft, especially trawlers and aircraft, would be assigned to antisubmarine duties, and the formation of escorted coastal convoys would materialize.[9]

Q-SHIPS VERSUS U-BOATS

After sinking *David H. Atwater* with gunfire, KL Topp moved U-552 down the coast to the Nags Head area. There, almost in view of the Wright Brothers National Monument and only a few miles from *Evelyn's* position, Topp torpedoed and sank the American tanker SS *Byron D. Benson*. Here on the night of 4 April, Legwen was taunting a skilled and venturesome adversary. Legwen was equally bold and daring, and he was eager for an engagement with any of the veteran U-boat commanders. But on this very night back at commander, U-boat headquarters, now in Paris, Admiral Dönitz's office reported the torpedoing of the freighter SS *Evelyn*.[10]

There are many unresolved mysteries concerning U-boat operations in the Atlantic west of the 66th meridian. One such puzzle was the reported torpedoing of *Evelyn*. In U-boat headquarters War Log dated 4 April 1942 appeared this terse entry under the heading of "Reports on the Enemy": "Torpedoed: 'Evelyn,' 3141 BRT, in CA7653." Marine quadrant CA7653 was located immediately off the coast east of Albemarle Sound and the communities of Nags Head and Kitty Hawk, North Carolina. Neither the date and time of the reported attack nor the U-boat making the report was identified by BdU. *Evelyn* left the Hampton Roads anchorage at 1300 on 4 April. At 2200 both KL Topp in U-552 and *Evelyn* were in marine quadrant CA7653.[11]

Forty-seven minutes later Topp torpedoed the tanker SS *Byron D. Benson* in CA7652, the six-mile square contiguous to CA7653. At that time Legwen transmitted on the normal merchant marine radio frequency his SSS message, announcing to the world the submarine attack and the location. The U-552 KTB makes no mention of either sighting or attacking *Evelyn*. According to Admiral Dönitz's war log, no other U-boats were in that immediate area that evening or the next morning. Since *Evelyn* was not torpedoed, why was an attack reported in the daily war log? There are two possible explanations. Headquarters staff misread a report from KL Topp, or the B-Dienst communications system misinterpreted Legwen's SSS message. But Erich Topp did not transmit his situation report for the period beginning 4 April to BdU until 11 April. The error, then, must have been a misreading of *Evelyn's* SSS message.[12]

The B-Dienst, or Funk-Beobachtung-Dienst (radio observation service), was the German central worldwide radio monitoring system. The navy branch copied all naval and merchant shipping radio transmissions. B-Dienst or BdU could have misread *Evelyn*'s SSS message as an SOS. BdU would then compound the error by assuming she was torpedoed and by adding the tonnage, 3141 BRT, from Gröner's handbook wherein such data are available. Gröner's reference book also includes the characteristics of the ship, the horsepower, the type of propulsion plant, the builder, the year built, the owner, the operator, and the names of other ships of the class, including in this case *Carolyn* and *Evelyn*. And this highlights the second curious point. Would it not be reasonable to associate the two ships and to suspect that *Evelyn* also might be a decoy or U-boat trap? There seemed to be ample evidence on which to base that conclusion. Several recent events should have alerted Admiral Dönitz's staff to the sinister mission of *Evelyn*. The BdU war log of 5 April 1942 included the report: "U-123 situation report (badly distorted W/T [wireless transmission] message): After torpedoing her, surprised by U-boat decoy ship in CA9578 with D/C [depth charges] and gunfire. Decoy ship sank after second hit. Midshipman Holzer dead."

That BdU statement followed a 26 March entry, also based on Hardegen's situation report, that read: "SOS from steamer *Carolyn* (3209 BRT) in CA9573. Fore part of ship ablaze, torpedo attack completed." The discrepancy between the quadrant location, CA9578 and CA9573, no doubt, was a typographical error and of no significance. But the failure of the BdU staff to associate the several pieces of intelligence—the depth charge and gunfire attack by *Carolyn*, Hardegen's explicit identification of the U-boat decoy ship, the death of Midshipman Holzer, the more recent report of the torpedoing of *Evelyn*, and the reference to the information in Erich Gröner's merchant fleet handbook—deprived the U-boats operating in American waters of the true identity of *Evelyn*. Had the BdU staff been alert, its intelligence personnel should have recognized that the Americans were employing more than one decoy ship and at the very least have retracted or amended Dönitz's report of 11 March 1942, which stated in part: "The great number of reports recently of submarine decoy ships must be treated with great reserve." No such reference or retraction was ever made.

The phantom ship *Evelyn* proceeded down the coast on 5 April. The attacks by KL Hardegen and KL Topp and their comrades-in-arms became profoundly apparent. At 1205 several bodies floating face down were observed. Legwen took the ship through the shallow waters of Diamond Shoals. Then in rapid order we came upon the partially submerged hulks of three victims of earlier attacks. This scene was noted by all aboard the decoy and all the crew members were keenly aware that we were engaged in a very serious contest. Some became angry and some had their carefree spirits dampened. The majority accepted the inevitable and hoped their fate would not be that of the *Atik*'s crew. Legwen passed the word for all hands not on watch to rest. He suspected there would be much activity during the coming night. Indeed, the U-boats brought the war to our doorstep. At times, the crew of *Evelyn* felt their ship was the last line of defense. They accepted the challenge.

Lieutenant Neville and I attempted to identify the sunken hulks. We had the attack listing and positions provided by Eastern Sea Frontier. As best we could determine, the three ships were the American tanker SS *Australia*, sunk on 16 March; the Greek freighter SS *Kassandra Louloudis*, torpedoed on 17 March; and the American cargo ship SS *Liberator*, sunk on 19 March. Not known to us, of course, were the U-boats involved. BdU had recorded these attacks and had credited Kapitänleutnant Johannes Liebe in U-332 with *Australia* and *Liberator*, and Korvettenkapitän Johann Mohr in U-124 with *Kassandra Louloudis*.[13] Also unknown to us was that KL Hardegen was proceeding southbound a day ahead of *Evelyn* and KL Topp was also headed south only a few miles in advance of the Q-ship. The officers in *Evelyn* had little knowledge of U-boat tactics. After the fact, an analysis of KL Topp's operation, in contrast with that of Hardegen's, revealed the unpredictable pattern of U-boat tactics, which made it difficult if not impossible to devise an effective defense. *Evelyn*, in essence, was a sitting duck, waiting for the first blow and any that might follow if the U-boat chose not to surface and fight. Even an artillery duel in the darkness of the night would be a more even contest.

Kapitänleutnants Reinhard Hardegen and Erich Topp were the most successful, in terms of Allied ships attacked, of the seven U-boat commanders operating off the Atlantic Coast during the period 1–15 April

1942. Hardegen attacked seven ships, although two were salvaged. Topp sank six. But their patrols were not yet finished. They would sink more. KL Topp's KTB differs from Hardegen's, and a comparison of the two reveals the differences in the two men. Hardegen's log entries are detailed and reflect the attention paid to each particular event, usually followed by well thought out decisions. KL Topp, on the other hand, recorded events in a crisp, terse chronology. His log entries were similar to those of KK Heinrich Schuch in U-105. Like Schuch, Topp had problems with his torpedo attacks and recorded his misses without a lengthy discourse on theory, cause, or effect. It is evident he was inclined to launch his torpedoes at a long range and without the technical and precise skill shown by Hardegen. Perhaps this was a habit developed from attacking multiship convoys where the primary target might be missed only to hit another ship. No doubt KL Topp was surprised by the number of escort vessels observed, making him more cautious than daring. He might have had in mind Reinhard Hardegen's report of his first patrol in January along the American coast, which stated that little or no opposition was encountered. It was a fact that in January 1942, Eastern Sea Frontier's armada consisted primarily of small cutters from Coast Guard stations along the beaches and transiting destroyers. But by mid-April, ESF's antisubmarine resources had increased to the following:

- 2 Gunboats (PG)
- 5 Patrol Vessels (PY)
- 4 165-foot Cutters (CGC)
- 8 125-foot Cutters (CGC)
- 3 173-foot Patrol Vessels (PC)
- 1 110-foot Patrol Vessel (PC)
- 19 Trawlers (Canadian and British)
- 5 Eagle Boats
- 72 Naval Aircraft
- 54 Coast Guard Aircraft[14]

Topp's log also reveals the high number of targets-of-opportunity along the Atlantic Coast in early April 1942, and Topp did note the increased number of U.S. Navy escort and antisubmarine vessels as compared to the initial period of Paukenschlag, January–February 1942. Finally, KL Topp's KTB provides some understanding as to why, with so many U-boats (seven or eight) operating at any one time off the coast from New Jersey to Florida, they did not sink more Allied ships. Indeed, the ratio of attacks to available targets from January to April was very low. The ratio of sinkings (total loss) to available targets was even lower since not every attack resulted in a total loss. Topp's reports, as with Schuch and Hardegen, illustrate the problems and challenges experienced by U-boat commanders in effecting a successful attack even when there were an abundance of undefended targets. For example, Topp recorded the following, beginning at the time of his arrival twelve miles off the Virginia coast, east of Chincoteague Inlet, on 31 March 1942 (all times are adjusted to local Eastern time zone). Some events are summarized for brevity:

31.3.1942 [31 March 1942] 0100 CA5748 Winter Quarter lightship position reached.

0950 Went to periscope depth. Sonar reported propeller noises. 4 steamers. Nothing to be seen.

1240 Went to periscope depth. 5,000 GRT steamer. Shooting range too large. Course northerly.

1342 To periscope depth. 6,000 GRT steamer. Course 40 degrees. Set up attack for 2,500-meters range.

1430 CA4999. Fired tube 1. Missed.

1459 New propeller noises. Two tankers on southerly course; one tanker on northerly course. Set up attack on tanker running in ballast since he was closest to me.

1534 Fired tube 2. Range 700 meters. All this maneuvering took place while sea was smooth but with a high swell that was in front of the periscope and obscured the view of the target. Nevertheless, I fired. This was probably the reason for missing.

1550 Aircraft in periscope. Went to deeper depth. Boat was touching ground at 18 meters. Aircraft did not see us.

1700 New propeller noises. At periscope depth (14 meters), tanker, 5,000 GRT, northerly course. Set up attack. Range was too large— about 3,000 meters.

1927 In periscope sighted 10 steamers, listened to but did not sight another 9 steamers.

2120 Surfaced after propeller noises were reported. Pursued on the surface, unsuccessful.

Kapitänleutnant Erich Topp's war diary of his initial operation along the coast of Virginia revealed a somewhat unpredictable U-boat commander. He was anxious to attack and he didn't always show caution and self-restraint. Unlike KL Hardegen who was content to seek targets only under the cover of darkness and to attack at close range, Topp initially seemed to disregard the time of day and would shoot from random ranges, usually in excess of 700 meters. During the two and a half days near Winter Quarter lightship, he sighted or heard no fewer than fifty-eight ships, including five patrol craft. He fired five torpedoes. All missed. The ranges varied from 2,500 meters to a relatively short 700 meters. He could ill afford this expenditure of eels without a hit. He had only fourteen torpedoes. U-552 was a Type VIIC boat, smaller than Hardegen's Type IXB. At 2316 hours on 1 April, U-552 encountered a destroyer that dropped "one small-caliber depth charge." The U-boat sustained little damage.

Noted also in Topp's KTB was his questionable method for estimating the speed of his targets: "Target speed according to revolutions 9 knots." This calculation, it would seem, would be grossly unreliable since so many variables are involved in arriving at an accurate answer: the size, shape, and number of blades that make up the propeller; the size of the ship and its draft; wind force, wind direction, and sea condition are all elements to be considered. Topp appeared to ignore these essential factors. Therefore, it is not surprising that so many of his torpedo attacks were unsuccessful.

At 1811 on 3 April 1942, Topp transmitted his periodic report to BdU. It read as follows:

From Topp: Situation: Three days Cape Cod no traffic. From Cape May to Cape Henry heaviest traffic along the buoys. Traffic stops during the night. Effective air and sea surveillance. For eight days high pressure weather cloudless moon nights. 75 cbm [tons] fuel left. Main transmitter failing. Request wireless repeater. 25 March Qu. CB1363 *Ocana* loaded torpedoed. 4 hours burning out. Destroyed. 3 April CA5744 sank

Atwater with artillery. One G.A. failure, two unexplainable, two explainable misses. 6 plus 2 torpedoes.

Topp reported that he had 75 tons of fuel remaining. The Type VIIC boat had a capacity of 113.5 tons; therefore, 66 percent remained. Of more significance was the number of torpedoes still available. He left St. Nazaire with fourteen. He had expended six with only one hit, *Ocana*. He stated "6 plus 2," meaning he had six below deck in the torpedo rooms and two above deck in reserve, or a total of eight remaining. At some point, he would have to surface and undertake the arduous task of transferring the two reserve eels to the torpedo room below. Unless KL Topp's shooting record improved dramatically, he would have considerable explaining to do upon his return to St. Nazaire and U-boat headquarters.

Topp searched in the vicinity of Kitty Hawk, North Carolina, for the remaining hours of 3 April with no worthwhile contacts. Then in the early hours of 4 April he moved southward some twenty-five miles to Wimble Shoals. There he encountered heavy air cover. He placed U-552 on the bottom. He had had sixteen "unquestionable" periscope and hydrophone contacts but attacked none. At 1750, near dusk on 4 April, KL Topp took his boat off the bottom and motored at periscope depth. He was still in the vicinity of Wimble Shoals, some twenty miles north of Hatteras. His KTB entries for the next six hours reveal his frustration, his persistence, and his eventual reward. First his surface or attack periscope sealed lens became clouded with moisture followed by his air search optics. He heard loud hydrophone noises but could see only the "ghostlike [shapes of] two tankers protected by an escort." Then his gyro compass failed: "Nothing seems to go right today. Nothing can be seen through the periscope, but hydrophone bearings are good." Although it was still daylight, he surfaced to pursue at high speed. After an hour the diesel coupling overheated and he stopped the starboard engine. For a full two hours Topp chased the two tankers. Finally, he reaped his reward. His KTB reads as follows:

2230 Shadow on port bow. Tanker. After all the obstacles I still reach the tanker. The second tanker is not to be seen. Cannot search for her long for the moon is coming up soon. Am running up on starboard side and starting my attack run.

2247 In CA7652. Westerly breeze, flat sea, cloudless. Firing tube 3 on estimated firing data, range 1,000 meters. Hit aft after 1 minute, 8 seconds. Heavy explosion. Flame column many hundreds meters high. Tanker is enveloped in a gigantic ocean of flames. It was a large ship of about 10,000 tons. Now we are being shot at with star shells by the escort, which is in a position with the second tanker further ahead. Nothing is to be seen of the escort vessel, which we have passed by. Turning off at high speed at 90 degrees to gain deeper water. Escort continues to fire star shells.

2330 Reducing speed and slowly turning to the south.

Kapitänleutnant Erich Topp had torpedoed the American tanker *Byron D. Benson*. *Evelyn* was seaward and only a few miles to the north. Those of us on the bridge, including Legwen, witnessed the attack. All felt certain this would be the time and place we would engage one of Hitler's emissaries and test our mettle. Legwen was eager and resolute. While Legwen was determined to engage, the U-boat commander chose deeper water. U-552 apparently crossed *Evelyn*'s southerly course undetected at a distance of less than several thousand meters and then proceeded south on a parallel track.

At daylight on 5 April, KL Topp put his boat on the bottom at eighty meters. This placed him in the area south of Oregon Inlet, either on Platt Shoals or on the northern reaches of Wimble Shoals, and only some three miles off the beach. He would stay on the bottom for the next four hours. It was probably during this period that *Evelyn* passed by her expected adversary on her slow movement southward. According to Topp's KTB entry, at 1000 U-552's hydrophones picked up "piston engine noise." Topp went to periscope depth and sighted a steamer on the hazy horizon, "but she was already beyond a reasonable attack angle." Could this have been *Evelyn* with her noisy old three-cylinder triple expansion piston engine pounding away? Perhaps.

Evelyn's captain might well have remained in the Cape Hatteras area. This had been the location of considerable U-boat activity. But Legwen reasoned that the northern exit of the narrow Straits of Florida was a logical area for U-boats to find the loaded tankers moving oil from the refineries of Texas and Louisiana to the East Coast, Canada, and Great Britain. Furthermore, he did not want to raise the suspicion of a perceptive U-boat commander observing an "inconspicuous" freighter remaining in the area of Hatteras and Cape Lookout. So Legwen took *Evelyn* southward past Kapitänleutnant Erich Topp. U-552 and *Evelyn* would not meet again. Legwen went south to find his U-boat while Topp sought targets in the Cape Hatteras–Cape Lookout area. Topp's adventures in American waters continued for six more days. He added three more tankers and one large freighter to his tally: *British Splendour* and *Lancing* in the Cape Hatteras area, and *Atlas* and *Tamaulipas* off Cape Lookout.[15]

Kapitänleutnant Erich Topp's deeds on this patrol were done. Course 70 degrees started him on his voyage home. His final task was to report his accomplishments. On 11 April 1942, KL Topp released the following radio transmission:

> To: BdU
>
> From: Topp
>
> Situation: Cape Henry, Hatteras Lookout, heavy traffic, large part of it branching off Hatteras to SE and SSE, surveillance by destroyers. Important coastal traffic protected by patrol vessels. Favorable area: Wimble Shoals and Raleigh Bay, 40-meter curve. Have not detected air cover during night hours. Patrol vessels without ASDIC. Wind from WSW 5, barometer rising, temperature plus 27 degrees [centigrade]. Further successes: 5.4 [5 April] Qu. CA7652, escorted tanker, full cargo, 10,000 GRT, sunk burning *[Byron D. Benson]*. 7.4 Qu. CA7969, escorted, full cargo, left sinking *[British Splendour]*. In Qu. CA7991, escorted giant freighter of about 14,000 GRT, torpedoed. [This ship was the SS *Lancing*, Norwegian, 7,866 GRT.] Shortly afterward, internal explosion. Did not observe sinking. One tube runner. 9.4 Qu. DC1165, tanker 8,000 GRT, full load, sunk burning *[Atlas]*. 10.4 Qu. DC1246, escorted tanker, 10,000 GRT, fully loaded, sunk burning *[Tamaulipas]*. With that altogether 43,832 GRT sunk, destroyed, that is, and 14,000 GRT torpedoed. No more torpedoes. Fuel state 60 cbm. Returning to base.[16]

KL Topp stated his tonnage for this six-day period at 43,832 plus 14,000. The actual tonnage for his entire patrol was 45,730, including the seven ships he attacked and sank, one by gunfire, beginning with *Ocana* on 25 March. It was not unusual for the estimated tonnage reported by the U-boat commanders to be somewhat inflated.

Noteworthy, too, is the fact that Topp expended all fourteen torpedoes, including one tube runner, resulting in the sinking of only six ships. This is a ship sunk/torpedo rate of 42.9 percent. To what extent this seemingly low percentage was caused by poor shooting or torpedo failures was not determined. It is known that in February 1941, a year earlier, Topp encountered considerable problems in attacking a convoy northwest of Scotland. He reported firing separately three torpedoes at ranges of 300 to 600 meters, another at 3,000 meters, and a spread of three at 1,500 meters, all failing to detonate. The cause of the failures was not known, but it was suspected that the malfunction was the result of the deterioration of the engine lubricant. By way of comparison, during Hardegen's first patrol in U.S. waters, he expended fifteen torpedoes, including one tube runner, and sank seven ships, one with the additional use of artillery. This ship/torpedo rate is 47 percent, comparable to that of Topp's, and indicative of the "efficiency" of U-boat attacks.

Fuel was the other principal factor limiting the time on station of the U-boats. Erich Topp's boat was a Type VIIC with limited design range when compared to the larger IXB boats. It was the practice to utilize some auxiliary tanks, possibly freshwater tanks, for extra fuel to extend the 113-ton design capacity. Topp reports his fuel state at 60 cubic meters, or approximately 60 metric tons. With about 50 percent of his fuel remaining and all torpedoes spent, he started his return transit to Saint-Nazaire, France, on the Bay of Biscay. He might have remained on station longer to attack with his artillery. Even experienced U-boat commanders could use questionable judgment, and U-boats operating along the American Atlantic coast were not without their problems. Indeed, Topp must be given credit for overcoming the difficulties encountered.[17]

The Third Reich was satisfied with KL Erich Topp's actions and expressed satisfaction with the following wireless messages:

11 April 1942

To Kapitänleutnant Topp: In thankful appreciation of your heroic risks in the battle for the future of our nation, I am awarding you the Oak Leaves to the Knight's Cross of the Iron Cross as the 87th soldier of the German Wehrmacht. [Signed:] Adolf Hitler

From Supreme Commander (Navy) to Topp: On the occasion of the award of the Oak Leaves I am conveying to you my best wishes in thankful appreciation of your outstanding accomplishments which you and your crew have achieved, Topp. [Signed:] Grossadmiral Erich Raeder

12 April 1942

To U-552. For your hard-fought and well-deserved award congratulations to you and your men. [Signed:] Flag Officer U-boats [Admiral Karl Dönitz]

While KL Topp's patrol to the Atlantic coast is not central to the basic story, it is related here for several reasons. One, the close proximity of U-552 to *Evelyn* for a period of some twelve hours without contact is an example of the uncertainties of engagement in antisubmarine warfare, especially with the Q-ship acting in a passive mode. Two, with as many potential targets at close range as Topp encountered, one would expect the successful attack rate to be higher than what U-552 achieved. And three, U-552 remained in the Virginia Capes area, Virginia Beach to Cape Hatteras, where ship traffic was densest. Here, logically, is where Admiral Andrews employed an ever-increasing number of escort vessels and patrol craft, including aviation units. It is apparent from Topp's experience that these added defensive resources were beginning to impact on Dönitz's "happy times." Less than ten days after U-552 left the Capes for the journey home, the U.S. Navy made its first kill of a U-boat. On the night of 14 April, USS *Roper* (DD147), commanded by Lt. Cdr. H. W. Howe, USN, attacked and sank U-85 (Oberleutnant Eberhard Greger). The location was east of Kitty Hawk, North Carolina, and a few miles south of where Erich Topp had torpedoed *Byron D. Benson*, familiar water to both U-552 and *Evelyn*. Beginning in mid-April, U-boat successes along the East Coast began to decline, due primarily to the increased numbers of patrol craft and the introduction of escorted convoys. Indeed, "happy times" in U.S. waters were coming to an end.[18]

Now with Kapitänleutnant Erich Topp and U-552 departing the scene, Lt. Cdr. Glenn Legwen and his mystery ship must venture further into the unknown to seek another adversary. Fate or circumstance kept *Evelyn* and U-552 from a deadly engagement. Glenn Legwen would continue his search for an opponent. He would persist with no complaisance toward this enemy.

9

Confrontation

HE THOUGHT WE WERE FINISHED.

Kapitänleutnant Reinhard Hardegen,
11 April 1942

LOOK FOR THE WHITE CAP.

Lt. Cdr. Glenn W. Legwen, 11 April 1942

LT. CDR. GLENN WALKER LEGWEN spent many wakeful hours in the solitude of his stateroom pondering his attack plans. He felt certain that action would come soon. He could not imagine why he had not been attacked already or been given the opportunity to be the aggressor. He smoked his pipe incessantly as he thought, diagrammed, calculated, and recalculated. The "aroma" of his corn cob furnace permeated the entire wardroom area. A lighted pipe in hand did not quite fit his character. He had a youthful, clean-shaven face, and boundless energy that carried him to the bridge at rather frequent intervals, especially when Larry Neville was on watch.

Legwen used Neville as a sounding board. He would then engage Dutch Schwaner and me to play his role as the tactical officer. He would be the U-boat commander to test our skill. It was a serious game, and Legwen used these sessions to train his officers and to fine-tune his own skill. On one occasion Legwen asked Dutch what he would do if under attack by two U-boats, one dead ahead and the other one astern. Dutch thought a moment and then replied, "I would increase speed to flank toward the forward submarine, zigzag moderately to bring my main battery to bear, ram and machine-gun the first boat, then concentrate fire on the second." Neville and Legwen then discussed the pros and cons of Schwaner's solution. I listened intently, for I knew I would be next to expound a theory. I would be bold.

As expected, Legwen turned to me, "What would you do, Ken, with two U-boats?" "Captain," I said, "I would cheat. Go neutral. Confuse the enemy, if they are not already confused, trying to figure out who shoots first." Legwen laughed, as did Neville and Dutch, then said, "Wait one minute, Ken has the right idea, the right answer. I would cheat, too. I'd hoist the Spanish flag and signal by light to each boat 'Spanish ship *Generalife.*' Hopefully that would interrupt their attack and give us enough time to maneuver into position to fire on both boats. Interesting! What do you think, Larry?" The last must have been a rhetorical question, for Legwen patted me on the shoulder and left the bridge.

On 5 April *Evelyn,* moving southward along the coast, cleared Cape Hatteras and Diamond Shoals lightship. There *Evelyn* passed close by the three hulks sunk earlier by KL Liebe in U-332 and KK Mohr in U-124. KL Erich Topp's trophies, SS *British Splendour* and SS *Lancing,* had been sunk in this very location only a few days after *Evelyn* left the scene. By 1400 on 6 April, on a clear, bright afternoon, *Evelyn* passed Frying Pan lightship. Twelve hours later, on 7 April, Legwen took *Evelyn* past Georgetown light, some forty-five miles north of Charleston, South Carolina. Here another slight course change would take the Q-ship toward the sea buoy nine miles off the mouth of the Savannah River. That marker was reached at 2300, and the course was changed again to take the ship past Brunswick, Georgia, to the St. Johns lightship off Jacksonville Beach, Florida. There, at approximately 1330 on 8 April, *Evelyn* was intercepted and challenged by a seventy-five-foot patrol boat of the U.S. Coast Guard. The events that unfolded began as a comedy but rapidly changed to near tragedy.

Capt. Glenn Legwen, master of the American steamship *Evelyn,* and Lt. Cdr. Glenn Legwen, commanding officer of USS *Asterion,* one and the same person, was challenged by a young Coast Guard officer. Legwen could not reveal his true identity and mission. This subplot was unexpected. The small Coast Guard patrol boat could be seen about a mile ahead and off the port bow. As *Evelyn* approached, the cutter pulled alongside within hailing distance. A young officer called out: "Captain, there is an enemy submarine reported ahead, will you please go behind the breakwater and anchor for the night."

Lt. Dutch Schwaner, the officer of the deck, summoned Legwen to the bridge and slowed the ship to about four knots. With the change in engine revolutions, both Neville and I went to the bridge. Legwen was in the port wing of the bridge in a shouting conversation with the Coast Guard officer. Legwen was saying, "Thank you for the notice, but my orders are to proceed south. I'll be careful." "Sorry, Captain," the Coast Guard officer replied, "my orders are to have all merchant ships enter the St. Johns river and anchor for the night. You are so ordered." "Thanks again," Legwen responded, "but I am proceeding south." With that, Legwen called to Schwaner to increase speed to "full ahead." Schwaner complied.

As *Evelyn* started to pull away from the small cutter, a sailor could be seen manning the .50-caliber machine gun on the bow of the small vessel. Shortly thereafter, the tat-tat-tat-tat of gunfire could be heard and the splashes ahead of *Evelyn* were all too visible. Legwen stopped the ship and called over to the cutter, which was now about fifty feet abreast of the port bridge: "This is a special ship on a special mission for the United States Navy." Still, the Coast Guard officer persisted. The young officer's persistence outlasted Legwen's patience. "Mr. Schwaner, lower the camouflage on the port side and train on the cutter," ordered Legwen. Neville intervened. "JESUS, Captain, you can't do that," yelled Neville, who then ran over to Legwen and said, "Glenn, don't do that." Legwen said nothing. Schwaner complied with the captain's order. The two 4-inch cannons trained out, and to the personnel in the cutter, the two black holes at the end of each cannon barrel must have looked like the entrance to the Holland Tunnel. The cutter cleared away at flank speed in a cloud of black exhaust smoke from his racing engine. Neville ran toward the radio room and switched into the voice frequency. He could hear the excited voice reporting: "An armed enemy surface raider, position off Jacksonville Beach, send air cover immediately. This is urgent, repeat urgent."

Neville reported the message to Legwen. Legwen stopped the ship, trained in the 4-inch, and sent a flashing light signal to the Coast Guard cutter, now some distance away, to come alongside. After approximately ten to fifteen minutes, when army aircraft were circling overhead, the cutter returned. By this time Legwen had the port accommodation ladder lowered. He invited the cutter's commander to send over a boarding officer who had a Secret security clearance. Legwen thought this approach would be both impressive and convincing. It wasn't. Round one of the "Battle of the Breakwater" went to the Coast Guard.

The Coast Guard officer indicated he would come alongside only to pick up one of the ship's officers. A now-subdued Legwen agreed. Neville volunteered to go. Legwen accepted and admonished him to contact Eastern Sea Frontier. He was to speak only to Captain Kurtz, Commander Bunting, or Lieutenant Commander Farley. With Neville on board and aircraft circling overhead, the cutter raced toward the entrance to the St. Johns River. *Evelyn* waited a mile south of the lightship. It appeared that round two might also go to the Coast Guard.

Lieutenant Neville was away for about five hours. He was taken to the air station at Mayport under armed guard. At Mayport, he was treated courteously but firmly until he was in the company of the senior officer available. He was a Coast Guard lieutenant and accepted Neville's navy identification card only after Larry produced his naval academy ring. Neville would comment later that it was worth its weight in gold. Considering the circumstances, its value was understated. A telephone call was made by secured line to New York. The lieutenant asked for any one of the three officers mentioned by Neville. Cdr. Sydney Bunting, the assistant chief of staff to Admiral Andrews, was available to speak to the lieutenant. The matter was explained to the satisfaction of the Coast Guard officer, and Neville was given the phone to speak to the commander. Bunting seemed to be unconcerned with the incident, and he was pleased that no harm had come to anyone and that the security of the mission was not compromised.

Bunting then gave Neville some details about two U.S. tankers that had been attacked off Brunswick, Georgia, that morning, and asked if *Evelyn* had passed in that vicinity and was involved in the incidents. Neville responded that *Evelyn* had passed that area between 0600 and 0800 but had neither received a distress message nor sighted any unusual activities. Bunting indicated that neither tanker had caught fire and, therefore, there was no beacon to be seen. Neville suggested that ESF might consider developing a communications system that would provide encoded messages to *Evelyn*, giving current U-boat attacks with time and positions. With that intelligence, Legwen could better determine where to patrol. He indicated that while the emergency radio frequency was constantly monitored, SSS and SOS transmissions were not always heard and copied. Bunting said he would look into the matter. He wished Neville and *Evelyn* "good hunting" and said to tell Legwen to pick up a U-boat commander's white cap for the admiral. Neville replied that the admiral could have the second one. That ended the telephone conversation. The Coast Guard personnel were asked to respect the secret nature of the ship's mission. Neville thanked them for their courtesies and asked to be returned to his ship. This was done. The Coast Guard lieutenant's parting remark was, "Lieutenant, you don't know how close you came to being bombed."[1]

Lieutenant Neville arrived on board *Evelyn* at 1730, just before dusk. He made his way to the bridge to brief the captain. "I trust," said Legwen, "they treated you as an American naval officer and not as a POW. Am I in trouble? Are we cleared to proceed?" Neville, unruffled by his experience, responded that the ship was cleared to proceed and there were no problems. He then briefed Legwen on the details of his conversation with Bunting, including the request for the white cap for the admiral. Legwen was pleased that Neville had mentioned to Bunting the need for a better system for advising on current U-boat activities. However, Neville's comment that *Evelyn* could have been bombed caught Legwen's attention. For the first time, he expressed his concern that this continued cruising in a passive mode and without some direction seemed to be contrary to even the most liberal interpretation of naval strategy and tactics. Also relying on "chance" is unscientific, and it plays hell on the nerves of those engaged in the experiment. Then, reflecting on the *Atik* incident,

Legwen remarked, "A terrible price has already been paid with the loss of Hicks and his crew. We must do better or. . . ." Neville finished the sentence: "Or die trying?" Legwen was quick to respond and vented more frustration: "No, Larry, that's not what I was going to say. We will do better or we will make Andrews give us what we need so that we have the advantage: a modern and faster ship or even a tanker. And we must have time to train our crew properly with a friendly submarine. It was unfortunate that Harry Hicks got caught so early in his deployment. His crew was not seasoned as well as we are now." Legwen then said, "Let's see where *Oklahoma* and *Esso Baton Rouge* were hit." The two officers went to the chartroom.

The *Evelyn* versus Coast Guard incident off St. Johns lightship was of little concern to Admiral Andrews and the Eastern Sea Frontier staff. The lack of serious concern was evident in the perfunctory entry in ESF's war diary of October 1943:

> The first cruise of USS *Asterion* (alias SS *Evelyn*) began with the shake-down, and continued until April 18, 1942. The incidents of importance in that cruise were many, and they included several sound contacts with U-boats, the sighting of torpedoed merchant vessels and life boats, the rescue of survivors. Furthermore, several contacts with friendly surface craft and aircraft led to awkward situations which required tact and ingenuity on the part of the commanding officer.[2]

"Awkward situation"? No question. "Tact and ingenuity"? Captain Legwen won the Battle of the Breakwater because the Coast Guard bowed to higher authority.

Cdr. Sydney Bunting at Eastern Sea Frontier had provided Neville with some data. His notes read: "SS *Oklahoma*'s position at 0200, 8 Apr., at time of attack: 31:18N/80:59W. Submarine surfaced about 0300, fired twelve rounds at the partially floating hulk, and then disappeared at 0310. SS *Esso Baton Rouge* torpedoed between 0223 and 0243, 8 Apr., at 31:02/80:53. Neither ship caught fire." Neville marked these two positions and times on the chart. The locations were about seventeen nautical miles apart. If the positions were correct, one U-boat could not have torpedoed both tankers at the times noted. Legwen and Neville agreed

Q-SHIPS VERSUS U-BOATS

that if the times and positions were correct, there were two U-boats involved. Although unknown to either the captain or the exec, the source of Bunting's information was the verbal reports of survivors of the two tankers recorded shortly after they were rescued. The accuracy of such data gathered under these circumstances is, at best, questionable. In any case, Legwen and Neville were certain that one or more U-boats were not far away. The two officers were anxious to plot out and see just how close *Evelyn* was at the time of the attacks.

At 0200 on 8 April *Evelyn* was on a course of 199 degrees twenty-two miles north of *Oklahoma*'s reported position. The Q-ship passed within six miles some three and a half hours later, with the torpedoed tanker to starboard, or shore side. At 0800 *Evelyn* passed five miles to the west of where *Esso Baton Rouge* was attacked, if that tanker's position was accurately reported. Neither ship had been sighted. This information infuriated Legwen. He wanted to know why a distress message had not been copied on the radio emergency frequency. He expected the U-boat was still in the area when *Evelyn* passed by.

Legwen was both angered and perplexed. Had he known of the attacks soon after they happened, he could have spent more time in the area before dawn in order to bait the trap. Neville suggested that the tankers might not have been able to send out a distress call and that the U-boat or U-boats could still be in the area, which was why the Coast Guard was directing merchant traffic to the breakwater and St. Johns River. Neville agreed that the German subs were working their way down to the Straits. Legwen calmed down and studied the chart for a few minutes longer. It seemed logical to Legwen that the Germans were interested in northbound tanker traffic. He decided to continue to Canaveral, turn around there as planned, and then work slowly up the coast, hopefully in company with some loaded oilers. Larry Neville responded with an agreeable: "Sounds good to me."

It was standard procedure for the Office of the Chief of Naval Operations to investigate each U-boat attack, interrogate survivors, and summarize the findings. Ensign A. J. Powers, USNR, had the task of writing the summary statements of the two tankers SS *Oklahoma* and SS *Esso Baton Rouge*. These reports apparently served as the official and legal record of the attacks. Regarding *Oklahoma*, his report, dated 21 April 1942, contains several interesting items:

The ship was torpedoed on April 8, 1942, at 0200 EWT in 40 feet of water and remained afloat for approximately 45 minutes.

Location: 8 miles, 25 degrees from second buoy off Brunswick, Ga. Its stern sank and touched bottom.

The bow remained above water.

The tanker did not catch fire.

The main radio transmitter was damaged. An SOS was sent on the emergency transmitter.

Submarine surfaced at about 0300 and fired about twelve rounds.

At 0310 the submarine disappeared toward the east.[3]

The following pertinent points are extracted from Ensign Powers's summary of 21 April 1942 on SS *Esso Baton Rouge*:

The tanker was torpedoed at 0223 on April 8, 1942, thirteen miles, 23 degrees from Brunswick light buoy.

The torpedo struck the starboard side between bunkers and engine room.

Engine room flooded immediately.

The ship sank by the stern, the stern resting on the bottom and the bow draft reduced to 17 feet.

The radio was put out of commission by the explosion.

The crew heard a voice from the submarine say, "Come over here and we will save you."

The submarine surfaced about 20 minutes after the attack and could be seen clearly in the moonlight.

The tanker *Oklahoma* passed the *Esso Baton Rouge* northbound about an hour prior to the attack.[4]

Presumably, the information gathered and analyzed by qualified investigators such as Ensign Powers is more reliable than initial statements made randomly by survivors still in a state of shock. The two attack positions reported by Powers placed the tankers only four to five miles apart. This did not match the locations, seventeen miles apart, as stated by Commander Bunting in his discussion with Neville. But using Powers's positions, it would be possible for one U-boat to attack both ships. The times given by Powers, duly analyzed and verified by knowledgeable survivors, also conform to a possible one-submarine attack pattern. Regarding distress signals, Powers's report states that only *Oklahoma* transmitted an SOS. She used her emergency transmitter. It is probable the transmission was weak and not heard more than twenty or so miles from the ship. *Evelyn*, further away, could not have copied it. Lastly, since the attacks occurred in darkness, it is probable the U-boat remained on the surface but was unobserved except at the times stated. Ensign Power's statements, of course, were not available to Bunting, Legwen, and Neville at the time of Neville's telephone conversation. The apparent misinformation unintentionally provided by Bunting left Legwen with the impression that two U-boats were involved in the two attacks. This false impression, in the overall scheme of things, probably was of little consequence except to emphasize the stress implicit in the Q-ship's passive strategy. However, the U-boat's log related dramatically the maneuvering by her crafty commander.

The attacking U-boat was none other than U-123. Kapitänleutnant Reinhard Hardegen was adding more tonnage to his score sheet and, no doubt, an Oak Leaf to his Knight's Cross. Had Glenn Legwen known that it was U-123 that successfully attacked *Atik*, and that the same boat was now in his immediate area, his blood pressure, from his eagerness to engage and his impatience, could have been measured in terms of meters of mercury rather than millimeters. Of course he didn't know these things. Nonetheless, the two warriors unknowingly were in relatively close proximity to each other.

Once again KL Hardegen provided a detailed record that revealed his skill and adroitness in the technique of U-boat warfare against merchant shipping in the western Atlantic theater. His description of these two almost simultaneous attacks was extracted from his KTB. All times have been converted to Eastern War Time.

7 April 1942

2230 I am close to the end of the northern breakwater at the St. Johns River lightship, on the surface. Supposedly there are anchor sites here, but I see no ships. All lights on as in peacetime. The lightship has a very bright light, which is very disturbing. To the south there appears to be an airfield, for the higher buildings show red warning lights, and on the ground there are many red lights indicating a landing system. The coastline can be seen clearly, and the resort area south of the breakwater is fully illuminated.

2250 A silhouette at the lightship. Appears to be a northbound steamer. I am well positioned ahead of it. I move laterally toward its path. Suddenly I see a huge, wide shadow to starboard. A southbound tanker. I intend now to make it my objective. I move around its stern and see that the first steamer is also a tanker. Since this northbound tanker is loaded, I decide to attack it. I am soon rewarded because another tanker appears behind it also on a northerly course. A pair! It is faster, and when passing the first northbound ship, it briefly turns on its running lights. I have to attack this faster one first and then wait to see what the other one does. This tanker is very fast, at least 11.5–13 knots, probably not faster. I set 11.5 knots in the calculator and sight in on the bridge, the forward structure of the ship. The advantage of this is that the eel will hit further aft if the tanker is going faster than estimated. I fire and miss. At 2,000 meters, distance is too great. I underestimated her speed. Now I must give chase. I run on the surface at full speed for one and a half hours. This puts me in front of the tanker again. It is a relatively clear and bright night, even without the moon. The sea is calm, even with an offshore wind of 13 knots. A strong marine phosphorescence makes me act very cautiously. The luminescence of our wake is quite noticeable. The second tanker drops behind to the south and is not in sight. I know its exact course because these ships sail along the offshore buoys.

0152 Qu. DB6177. I turn and fire an ATO [compressed air torpedo] from tube 1 at a distance of 500 meters. I lie almost stopped with one engine running dead slow. After 22 seconds, a hit in the tanker's engine room. Her stern sinks immediately to the bottom. She doesn't radio. The tanker is an Esso Balboa type, about 9,500 GRT. A modern motor-tanker that can make 13 knots. Since it didn't burn, the second tanker might not have noticed anything.

0207 I turn south in the direction of the second ship and see a shadow in front of the Brunswick buoy. It's closer to the coast now so they did notice something. I must go even closer to the coast. The moon now is rising, and I want to attack out of the west with the dark background of the wooded coastline. Because of the shallow water, the tanker must and does change course to 25 degrees to get into deeper water. I am again at the latitude of the previous sinking. I can see many reflections of the moon dancing on the water. Everyone on this tanker probably is looking to starboard at the wreck of my other victim and is happy I didn't get them; they don't look at their port side where we are passing.

0244 Now this tanker lies directly in the bright moonlight, a clear, pretty silhouette. I fire an ETO, an electric eel from tube 2, range 800 meters. After 60 seconds a direct hit in the engine room. We are beginning to specialize in tankers. This is my tenth sunk with this boat. A fierce detonation this time, with flames and smoke. It, too, radios nothing. It seems bigger than the first, and I estimate 10,000 GRT. Now back to the first wreck only four miles away and easy to see. Stern lies on the bottom; smokestack, bow, and bridge can be seen out of the water.

0300 A few shots in the bridge and bow so that air can escape from the front so it will sink further. . . . Total loss!

0333 Now back to the other tanker. Artillery fire would be a waste because at 13 meters water depth, it is already completely on the bottom. Smokestack, bridge, bow, and some ventilators can still be seen, but the upper deck or main deck is underwater.

0400 We leave on course 150 degrees.

0640 Qu. DB6446. Submerge. Boat on bottom at 28 meters.

1958 Surface. Move toward lightship at St. Johns River.

At some time during the period that U-123 was on the bottom, *Evelyn* passed the U-boat close at hand on her way to the rendezvous with the U.S. Coast Guard off St. Johns lightship. The maneuvering of U-123 during these two attacks clearly illustrates the extraordinary calmness and tactical competence of its commander. Conditions were not all favorable: The boat was close to shore off St. Johns River breakwater, in relatively shallow water, near an airfield, and probably with small patrol craft nearby. To Hardegen's advantage were the well-lighted coastline, a moonless yet bright night, and the superior speed of his boat. A simplified chronology and the maneuvers of U-123 are shown on the map on page 144.

The two American tankers that KL Hardegen attacked on 7–8 April 1942 between Jacksonville Beach, Florida, and Brunswick, Georgia, were salvaged. Both tankers, according to Ensign Powers's reports, were fully

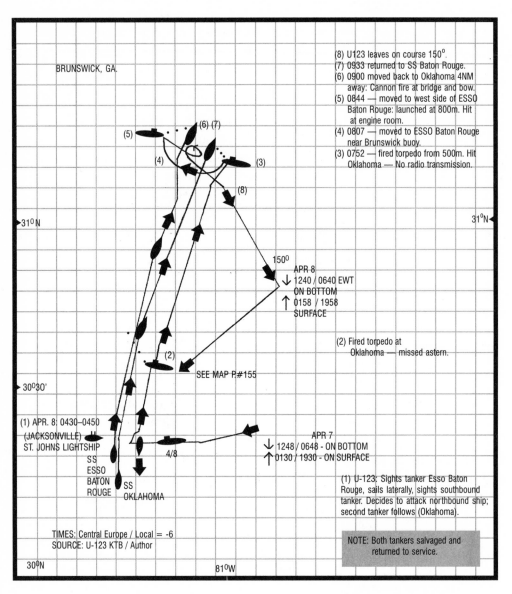

BRUNSWICK, GA.

(8) U123 leaves on course 150°.
(7) 0933 returned to SS Baton Rouge.
(6) 0900 moved back to Oklahoma 4NM
    away: Cannon fire at bridge and bow.
(5) 0844 — moved to west side of ESSO
    Baton Rouge: launched at 800m. Hit
    at engine room.
(4) 0807 — moved to ESSO Baton Rouge
    near Brunswick buoy.
(3) 0752 — fired torpedo from 500m. Hit
    Oklahoma — No radio transmission.

(5)
(6) (7)
(4)
(3)
(8)

31°N   31°N

150°
APR 8
↓ 1240 / 0640 EWT
ON BOTTOM
↑ 0158 / 1958
SURFACE

(2) Fired torpedo at
    Oklahoma — missed astern.

(2)
SEE MAP P.#155

30°30'

(1) APR. 8: 0430–0450
(JACKSONVILLE)
ST. JOHNS LIGHTSHIP

SS
ESSO
BATON
ROUGE   SS
        OKLAHOMA

4/8

APR 7
↓ 1248 / 0648 - ON BOTTOM
↑ 0130 / 1930 - ON SURFACE

(1) U-123: Sights tanker Esso Baton
    Rouge, sails laterally, sights southbound
    tanker. Decides to attack northbound ship;
    second tanker follows (Oklahoma).

TIMES: Central Europe / Local = -6
SOURCE: U-123 KTB / Author

NOTE: Both tankers salvaged and
returned to service.

30°N   81°W

7–8 April 1942: U-123 attacks on SS *Oklahoma* and SS *Esso Baton Rouge* loaded with a hundred thousand barrels of petroleum products. Neither ship burned, although SS *Oklahoma*'s cargo included thirty thousand barrels of gasoline. Both ships were lost later in the war: *Esso Baton Rouge* was sunk by KL Günter Poser (U-202) on 23 February 1943 in the eastern Atlantic, south of the Azores. *Oklahoma* was sunk by Fregattenkapitän Ottoheinrich Junker (U-532), very late in the war, on 28 March 1945, north of Brazil. While this concluded the saga of KL Hardegen and the two tankers, it was by no means the end of Reinhard Hardegen's adventures in U.S. waters.[5]

In the late evening of 8 April, U-123 was once again at St. Johns River lightship. As twilight ended, Hardegen was both annoyed and amazed by the lights he saw. He was irritated because from his position offshore he could not easily distinguish the automobile lights on land from the moving lights on ships sailing along the coast. He was amazed because America's coastline still was not blacked out. But then he did not consider that Europe had been at war for several years and its people were conditioned to the wartime discipline placed on civilian and military personnel alike. Americans, he would learn later, were capable of such discipline.

At twenty minutes before midnight, von Schroeter observed a north-bound shadow. Hardegen saw it also. It was a fast-traveling freighter, about twelve knots. It was too close and at too broad an angle for a successful attack. Hardegen turned north, ran well ahead of the target, then maneuvered to set up his attack position. It took time. Not until 0116 was U-123 set for a surface attack. At a range of six hundred meters, von Schroeter launched a torpedo from tube 1. It struck the ship on the starboard side under the main or after mast. The victim radioed the attack: "SSS SOS SSS. SS *Esparta*, United Fruit Company, torpedoed." The 3,365-GRT *Esparta* carried a refrigerated cargo of bananas. She was en route from Honduras to New York. Normally, Hardegen would not have attacked such a small ship, especially a freighter. He wanted tankers with his remaining eels. But he said, "we had overestimated its size. Even though it was small, it was a valuable cold storage vessel." The U-boat commander's rationalization was correct. *Esparta* sank approximately fifteen miles off St. Mary's Entrance, Georgia, and twenty-three miles northeast of St.

Johns lightship. She was a total loss. A more enterprising U-boat commander might have retrieved a ration or two of green bananas for his crew. But this commander would not risk his boat and crew for green bananas.[6]

At 0400, 9 April, U-123 came upon another northbound steamer, a bulk carrier. Hardegen noted six hatches and a forest of king-posts (vertical members of a derrick or hoist) forward of the bridge. "She is big," he exclaimed. Hastily, he fired a torpedo from tube 2. It missed. He recorded the action:

> I am forced to attack with the moon directly behind us, but I must attempt it. My data are precise, and the deck watch on the steamer probably are paying no attention. I'm almost stopped with one engine running dead slow. I let the target come into my line of fire. Fire tube 2 from a distance of 400 meters. I have to fire from an acute angle because the distance is getting smaller. Unfortunately, the torpedo doesn't make it. Just before reaching the steamer's bow it jumps out of the water, angles steeply downward, and apparently buries its nose in the ocean's bottom. Another attempt is not possible due to the moonlight. Too bad! I steer southeast to deeper water.[7]

At 0724, with the sun breaking through the horizon, Hardegen put U-123 on the bottom in twenty-eight meters of water. There he rested his boat and crew until sundown. While Hardegen would rest his body, his mind found no comfort. He was upset with himself. He had expended his fourteenth torpedo, only to waste it on the bottom of the Atlantic. He had only three eels left. He admonished himself for being too eager. He had deviated from his normal well-planned and well-disciplined tactics and he had paid the price by gaining nothing. This was the thirty-eighth day of his current patrol; eighteen days since his first attack, *Muskogee*; thirteen days since his encounter with the U-boat trap *Carolyn*; and he had directed a total of ten attacks. Was the strain on the human body and mind beginning to take its toll? If so, Kapitänleutnant Reinhard Hardegen would be the last to admit it, even to himself.

At 1747, as darkness fell, Hardegen took U-123 to periscope depth and cruised underwater on course 230 degrees toward the lighthouse at St. Augustine, south of Jacksonville Beach. After two hours, he surfaced and continued his approach toward the coast. At 2320, only three miles off the coastline, U-123 changed course to 165 degrees and ran southward, parallel to the beach. At 0058, now into a new day, 10 April 1942, Hardegen met a 5,000-GRT freighter on a reciprocal course. Her speed was estimated at 12.5 knots. U-123 was brought about and gave chase to the now invisible target, lost in the haze and darkness. At full speed, Hardegen followed the freighter's wake. After two hours he caught up with his prize, moved ahead, and established his attack position. His log entry at 0309 local time reads as follows:

> She approaches, and the distance is getting very close. I must turn because in my present position it could ram us. Now I fire at an angle of thirty-two degrees. I see that we are considerably closer and have trouble moving away from its oncoming hull. It races by at about 10 knots. They see us, and they must be just as startled as we were, for they suddenly turn on their bridge and navigation lights. They must be really surprised and terrified. When we launched, the distance to target was less than 100 meters. We could have been damaged if the torpedo had hit and detonated. We were too close. It could have rammed us if its lookouts had been more alert. This time the miss is entirely our fault. We badly overestimated the distance due to the bad visibility. But the torpedo still detonates after 48.4 seconds. If it had kept its set depth of 2.5 meters, it could not have hit bottom. The water depth was 17 meters. It must have passed below the target in a wave trough. We see a glare of fire and a black detonation cloud. Maybe it hit a wreck or something else. I change course and continue southeast.[8]

At 0603 U-123 came upon a stopped freighter. Its two white range lights and the red and green running lights shone brightly, and it was smoking heavily. Hardegen was suspicious and watched it from a distance of three thousand meters. He did not want to be "trapped" again. He did not want to try his luck again, but he was tempted by the challenge. He waited patiently. After thirty minutes it moved northward. He did not take the bait. The sky to the east began to brighten; it was dawn. He would not have the benefit of darkness. With a U-boat-trap, he needed all the advantages. Prudence prevailed. After a fruitless and frustrating twenty-four hours during which he had run more than 105 nautical miles, using his limited diesel fuel at a higher than normal rate and expending his third to last torpedo on an apparently submerged wreck, the commander put U-123 on the bottom for the remainder of daylight hours. Maybe a banana from *Esparta* would have lifted his spirits and that of the crew.[9]

SS *Evelyn*, at 1600, on course 156 degrees, had Cape Canaveral broad on the starboard beam. Legwen had been alerted thirty minutes earlier by Dutch Schwaner, the underway watch officer, that Canaveral was coming into sight. Dutch knew the captain planned to reverse course at the Cape.[10] At about the time Dutch sent the messenger to the captain's cabin, a fast northbound tanker passed close by on *Evelyn's* starboard hand. The painted-over Gulf Oil Company logo on the funnel could be clearly seen. Her speed was estimated at fourteen to fifteen knots. Lieutenant Neville and I arrived on the bridge at 1545 and relieved Schwaner of the watch. Legwen appeared shortly afterward. By this time the Gulf Oil tanker was hull down, and a second oiler was in sight approaching from the south. As we brought *Evelyn* about to the reverse course, 336 degrees, we positioned ourselves outboard and approximately one-half mile ahead of this second tanker. We maintained this relative position, on the same course and, with the help of the Gulf Stream, the same speed over the ground at ten knots. Our next landmark, as we sailed northward some ten to thirteen miles off the coast, would be Ponce de Leon Inlet light. We should sight it between 1930 and 2000. Our next course change would be around 2245, south of St. Augustine Inlet.

The early evening of Friday, 10 April, was clear, with scattered cumulus clouds and a gentle northwest, offshore wind. The temperature was a balmy seventy-three degrees Fahrenheit, twenty-three degrees centigrade. The wind chill made it feel cooler. Legwen remained on the bridge for a short period observing Quartermaster Roger Metz taking bearings on the oiler that was following us off our port quarter. The bearings remained constant, indicating we were maintaining the same relative position. Before leaving the bridge, Legwen remarked that there had been no reports of attacks this far south, and he was glad we had turned. He was particularly pleased that we were in company with a tanker. "She's good bait," he commented. The captain went on to express his displeasure with Eastern Sea Frontier for not communicating U-boat actions along the coast. He felt he should have been getting coded messages reporting each submarine attack or sighting.

Like Hardegen, Legwen was restless, but for different reasons. He wanted his first kill, a white cap to put in Eastern Sea Frontier's trophy cabinet; one less menacing U-boat; one less enemy. Hardegen wanted his last kill on this patrol, an American tanker, 10,000 tons to add to his tally at U-boat headquarters; one less logistics ship carrying fuel to the enemy. Legwen was eager for a fight and a successful patrol, eager to expend his physical and intellectual energy in a deadly contest. Hardegen was eager to end his already successful patrol and take his boat and his crew home safely. But Herr Kaleu would continue his hunt so long as he had fuel, food, and ammunition. And Legwen would continue his deception until ordered otherwise. Both naval officers, as lawful belligerents, were willing and impersonal participants in this deadly game of war. They would play the game by their own rules. But fate would deal the hands.

The sun was about to set, and Neville and I anticipated a typically beautiful semitropical sunset. I asked Neville if the sunsets were equally as beautiful in the Orient. He said they were when his ship was far enough off the coast of the mainland and far enough from the haze and smells of the fishing villages. He particularly liked the sunsets observed from the east of Formosa. On a clear evening the sun would sink behind the island, outlining the silhouette of the irregular mountain range and reflecting the various colors from yellow to orange to magenta, all against a background of scattered clouds and cerulean sky. I told him I had never been to the Western Pacific but we would probably both get there before the war was over.

Larry Neville was in a talkative mood. We shared mixed feelings about being among unseen U-boats as we steamed along the coast from Virginia to Florida and then northward again without being attacked. Our purpose in being out there was to be attacked or to attack. We wanted the excitement of an engagement and, if successful, the satisfaction of knowing we could do what was expected, or at least hoped for, against incalculable odds. But realistically, there was the other side of the coin. There is usually a winner and a loser in antisubmarine warfare. Seldom is it a draw. We would not dwell on this matter. We had accepted the assignment, and we would take our chances. Legwen's tactical games kept us alert and prepared. We each had an optimistic view and felt a high degree of self-confidence. We felt we would know what to do while under attack, reacting either as part of a team or individually.

Lieutenant Neville and I could converse, even while scanning the ocean surface with our binoculars, or checking the tanker off our port quarter, or inspecting our wake to ensure the helmsman was not zig-zagging unintentionally, or observing the compass heading to make certain we were on course, or checking the bridge and fantail lookouts, or performing many other tasks for which the bridge watch officers were responsible while under way. After so many days at sea and standing the four-hour watch twice each day, the task becomes automatic, but never routine. The brief discussion Neville and I had about sunsets must have triggered a bit of nostalgia in the exec. He started a monologue on China Station and his duty in the coastal gunboat USS *Asheville* during the period 1937 to 1940. I assumed I was going to get a lecture on his exploits in China during the Sino-Japanese war. But instead I was entertained by a story I shall never forget.

> Ken, the captain's complaint about communications reminds me of an incident in *Asheville*. A visiting admiral had been invited to an official affair in Canton. He left his flagship, a cruiser, in Hong Kong and, with his young aide, embarked in *Asheville* to go up the Pearl River to Canton. He had dispatched his flag lieutenant ahead by train. The flag lieutenant would coordinate the admiral's visit with the American Legation in Canton. It was a very hot and humid trip up river and, in the opinion of the admiral, neither set of dress white uniforms he had on board was appropriate for the official occasion. There was no laundry facility aboard *Asheville*.
>
> The admiral told his aide to send off a radio message to the flag lieutenant, care of the American Mission in Canton, to have a washerwoman on the dock upon arrival of *Asheville*. Without delay the aide drafted and released the message as he had been directed. When a copy of the transmitted communiqué reached the admiral some minutes later, he screamed so loudly for his young aide that everyone on the ship and in southern China could hear his bellows. It seems as though in his haste to file the plain-language, priority message, which would be routinely copied by all navy commands in the western Pacific, a painful error was made. The word "washer" was inadvertently omitted from the text so

Q-SHIPS VERSUS U-BOATS

that the message read in part: "Have admiral's woman on dock immediately upon arrival of *Asheville* in Canton." Inadvertent was a word never recognized by the admiral. "Get a correction to that message out immediately," he demanded. The completely mortified aide, in an effort to redeem himself, took great care in drafting a succinct correction and released the second message without any further delay. The aide carried a copy of the transmitted correction to the admiral who, after reading it, exploded into a stream of expletives that defy translation into any of the many dialects of the Chinese language. The message read: "Refer my last transmission, insert washer between admiral and woman."[11]

Larry Neville's yarn was a pleasant diversion. It relieved at least temporarily the mental tension that had been building since leaving Norfolk on April fourth. Also, being in company with the friendly oiler gave us another object, other than the image of a surfaced U-boat, to dwell on from time to time. At 1900, at about the time of our Florida sunset, we went to General Quarters. This was an everyday routine since we knew the first hour of darkness was a prime time for submarine attacks. At 2030 we stood down from fully manned battle stations to readiness condition 2, whereby approximately one-third of the crew could secure. We had passed Ponce de Leon light, and we were making for a point south of St. Augustine Inlet. There a course adjustment would take us once again to St. Johns lightship on the north end of Jacksonville Beach.

With the setting of condition 2, Neville and I were duly relieved by Guy Brown Ray. Neville advised him that, except for the occasional cluster of lights on the beach, the darkened tanker off our stern was our only known companion; we were on course 336 degrees true; at about 2300 we would make a course change to steer for St. Johns lightship; and because we had lost some effect of the Gulf Stream, we were making eight knots good over the ground. With a long look at the tanker that was following us, Guy-Brown took the conn.

Friday, 10 April 1942, was a day much like 26 March when several opposing forces were moving from different directions toward a specific geographical point. On that day in March, Lt. Cdr. Harry Hicks in *Atik/ Carolyn*, Korvettenkapitän Heinrich Schuch in U-105, and Kapitänleutnant Reinhard Hardegen in U-123 were all converging on that place in the Atlantic Ocean identified both as 36-00 degrees north latitude 70-00 degrees west longitude and marine quadrant CA9578. At that location mortal combat took place. Now on the evening of 10 April, the stage was being set for another combative encounter.

USS *Dahlgren* (DD187), a 1918-vintage flush deck, four-stack destroyer and sister ship to USS *Reuben James* (DD245), on 10 April was commanded by Lt. Cdr. R. W. Cavenagh, USN. Cavenagh was relatively new to the ship, having taken command on Friday, 27 February. *Dahlgren* was attached to Service Squadron Nine, U.S. Atlantic Fleet. She was home based at Key West, Florida. Her primary mission was to operate on daily assignments with the Navy Sound School. Occasionally she would be detailed to make antisubmarine patrols along the Florida Keys and the coast as far north as Jacksonville. On Thursday, 9 April 1942, at 1316 *Dahlgren* had gotten under way from Key West for a patrol. She made her way up the coast. By midnight on Friday her position was approximately twenty miles south-southeast of St. Augustine light. At 0055 Saturday, 11 April, Ensign E. J. Dougherty Jr., the 0000–0400 watch officer, reported to the captain a darkened ship bearing 20 degrees true. At 0101 Cavenagh sounded General Quarters, brought the destroyer to readiness condition 1, battle stations, and proceeded to investigate the unidentified ship. The darkened *Evelyn* was at that location at that time. The apparently satisfied officers of *Dahlgren* secured from General Quarters at 0138 and left the scene on a southeasterly course of 150 degrees.[12]

At 2009 on Friday, five and a half hours before *Dahlgren's* investigation of the unidentified freighter, KL Hardegen had U-123 on the surface thirty-five miles south of St. Johns lightship. He was within sight of the lighthouse at St. Augustine, bearing 292 degrees. Hardegen and his IWO, Horst von Schroeter, were on the bridge. As always when prowling at night in the shipping lanes along the Atlantic Coast, he had his team in place: Oberleutnant Heinz Schulz, his engineer, or LI, at the controls; Wolf-Harold Schüler, his IIWO, in the conning tower at the Siemens torpedo deflection calculator; Walter Kaeding, the navigator, at the chart table in the control room; and Fritz Rafalski at the radio and the hydrophone. Hardegen and von Schroeter were still amazed by the lack of any visible defense effort on the part of the Americans.

U-123 was less than four miles off the beach. The boat was so close to the shoreline that the trees, the houses, and the radio towers with their red beacon lights were all easily discernible by the two officers on the bridge. Now they saw off to the south what appeared to be northbound ship traffic. They thought there were two ships because the deck houses were so far apart. Soon they could see it was a single tanker with a considerable space between the forward and after superstructures. Hardegen turned U-123 northward to establish an attack position well in front of the large tanker. It was not yet completely dark, and the U-boat commander waited so as not to reveal his presence. His target was none other than SS *Gulf America*, the Gulf Oil Company ship that had passed *Evelyn* earlier in the afternoon.

The tanker was fast, and U-123 raced at fourteen knots in an attempt to maintain its relative position. According to Hardegen, the "strong marine phosphorescence" caused by his high-speed wake was easily detectable from the air, so he decided to slow down and attack from behind the target. It would appear that the commander and his surface attack officer miscalculated the tanker's unusually fast speed, fourteen knots, and had to be content with a high-risk shot from a position off the port quarter of the target. With such a prize in his sights, Hardegen would take the calculated risk. This maneuver took time. Two hours and thirteen minutes after sighting his prize, he launched his second-to-last torpedo. At precisely 2222 local time, Friday, 10 April, he fired tube 1 at a range of two thousand meters. Hardegen had his attack officer set the cross-hairs of the surface target aiming binoculars well forward of the bridge. He gambled with a broad, obtuse angle of 121 degrees. Von Schroeter took great care in marking the angle and range. He reassured the commander of his accuracy. After almost three minutes the electric eel struck home, a hit below the after mast. Hardegen was jubilant.[13] He described the events that followed the attack in his KTB:

> The tanker becomes an enormous torch that illuminates everything as bright as day. A rare show for the Florida tourists who probably are having supper now. It is the biggest tanker we have ever seen. It is a type similar to the Shëhërazade class, 13,467 GRT, only that the after mast is located above the midsection tanks. Its length must be more than 160m

[488 feet], because it fills three-fourths of the UZO at an angle of ninety degrees at a range of 1,900m. [UZO (Uboot-Zieloptik): surface target-aiming binoculars mounted on the bridge.] It appears to have its back broken. Its stern might be on the bottom already. Now I want to finish the job quickly. We shoot many artillery shells at the bridge and the forward bunkers to set the rest of the ship on fire. We make many hits. She burns furiously and we have to hasten to get out of the bright glow of the flames. I am sure I estimated her size conservatively at 12,500 GRT. She was painted gray. At 0453 CET [2253 local time] we depart on course 165 degrees. But still, after one hour and twelve miles, our submarine is illuminated by the fire. A formation of large clouds reflects the red glow of the burning tanker. The oil spreads on the water from the tanker and is burning over a large area. It is so bright that a newspaper could be read on our bridge.[14]

Kapitänleutnant Reinhard Hardegen had added a big and valuable prize to his tally. He did not know her name. That did not matter. What did matter was that he had attacked her successfully and he was coming to the end of a very satisfactory patrol, by any standard. He had not forgotten his encounter with the U-boat trap, *Carolyn*, and the loss of his midshipman, Fähnrich zur See Rudy Holzer, but he was satisfied that, by his own estimate, he had attacked and destroyed on this patrol more than sixty thousand tons of enemy ships. And he still had one eel and many rounds of ammunition in his lockers. He had more hunting to do, more tonnage to tally and, he hoped, fewer aircraft and patrol vessels to encounter that might blemish his record or threaten his boat and crew this late in his patrol. He would do nothing to intentionally threaten his phenomenal luck. But as long as he had fuel and ordnance, he would continue his hunt.

Lt. H. A. Burch, USNR, in the Office of the Chief of Naval Operations, on 27 April 1942, wrote his memorandum for file, "Subject: Summary of Statements by Survivors, SS *Gulf America*, American Tanker, 8081 G.T., Gulf Oil Company." Pertinent excerpts from his six-page report stated:

The Gulf America was torpedoed and shelled without warning at 2220 EWT on April 10, 1942, at 30:10N-81:15W while en route from Port

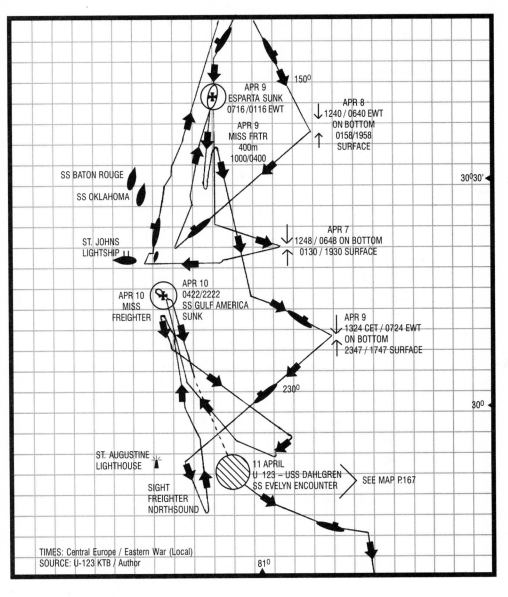

7–10 April 1942: U-123 attacks on SS *Esparta* and SS *Gulf America*

Arthur, Texas, to New York, with 90,000 bbls. fuel oil. The ship was down by the stern listing 40 degrees to starboard on April 11, and turned over and sank on April 16, 1942.

The tanker was on course 352 degrees true, speed 14 knots . . . all lights out but shore lights bright and may have silhouetted ship, radio silent, 4 lookouts—2 on top of pilot house, and 2 gun crew on poopdeck. The sea was smooth, wind NW force 2–3, visibility good, no ships in sight.

Two torpedoes were fired in quick succession at an angle of 35 degrees from stern to starboard, one struck the after bunker number 7 tank, second in engine room at after mast about 10 feet below water line. Explosions shattered after main mast and immediate fire resulted. The engines were stopped and the order given to abandon ship. About 5 minutes later, as radio distress calls were sent on 500 KCS, shell fire started from one-quarter to one-half mile distance at an angle from the port side astern. Approximately 10 or 12 shells were fired in addition to red tracer machine-gun bullets followed by machine-gun fire apparently to locate and destroy the mainmast and radio antenna. The 4" after gun was manned and loaded but no defensive fire offered.

Submarine not seen. Gun flashes clearly seen however. Subject vessel was under the command of Captain Oscar Anderson.

A Navy gun crew consisting of an Ensign and six apprentice seamen was on board.

There is a difference of opinion, though it appears that two torpedoes were fired in quick succession, coming at an angle of approximately 35 degrees from stern to starboard.

The shelling from the submarine was attended by machine-gun fire. No apparent attempt was made to use the machine gun on the survivors in lifeboats and in the water.

Eleven (11) of the crew, including the captain, left subject ship in approximately ten (10) minutes by the port side forward lifeboat number 1, this being the first to leave the ship.

There is some difference of opinion with respect to the conduct under stress of the Navy gun crew. According to Ensign J. H. Teach Jr., USNR, his 4-inch aft gun was loaded but no opportunity was afforded to use the gun; that they looked for the submarine but did not see it.

Captain Anderson expressed the opinion that a reasonable effort should have been made by the Navy gun crew to use the aft gun as the flashes from the gun of the submarine afforded a good opportunity for a target. . . . A more experienced gun crew might have handled matters differently. To the contrary, the Third Mate who had served seven years in the U.S. Navy stated he could not criticize the Ensign in any way.

According to William M. Meloney, radio operator, distress signals were sent on a frequency of 500 KCS approximately five (5) minutes after the ship was torpedoed. . . . Mr. Meloney stated that he used both main and emergency transmitters; that the reading on the main antenna indicated that his message was going out but apparently no one received or acknowledged it.[15]

Lieutenant Burch included in his report an interview with Capt. Sverre Peterson, master of the ship SS *Ohio*. Captain Peterson stated he witnessed the submarine attack on SS *Gulf America*. He was headed south in *Ohio* and was approximately three miles north of *Gulf America* when the torpedoing and shelling occurred. The captain's statement reads in part: "The first thing that I heard was a loud explosion and a flash with it. A big fire immediately flared up and the shelling which followed continued for twenty to thirty minutes. The flames were immense. It took about a minute or more for the sound of the guns to reach our ship. We were some distance away. It sounded like heavy guns. The shell firing started a little while after the loud explosion occurred." When Captain Peterson saw what was happening, he stopped his ship and waited until the shelling was over. He then turned to enter the St. Johns River and anchored off Mayport for the night. His observations served to substantiate the time and location of the attack, and that both artillery and torpedoes were employed to sink SS *Gulf America*.[16]

Transcripts of the *Gulf America* episode present some contradictions. From the standpoint of the historian or the behavioral scientist, these issues present a curious challenge. They are presented here to emphasize the differences in perception of individuals experiencing various levels of stress. Many in the crew of *Gulf America* were under the impression that two torpedoes struck the tanker. Seaman First Class Dandy, a member of the navy gun crew on watch on the stern of the ship saw only one torpedo. Captain Peterson of SS *Ohio* heard a loud explosion and saw a flash, indicating a single hit. KL Hardegen's KTB, no doubt the most reliable record, states only one torpedo was fired. Based on this information, it is reasonable to conclude that only one torpedo struck *Gulf America.* Two other matters are noteworthy. The apparent conduct of the navy gun crew was subject to review and evaluation. Captain Anderson's criticisms were not supported by his third mate, the officer fourth in command. It would appear that Anderson, instead of leaving his command in the first boat, might have gone aft, if possible, to encourage his gun crew to take action. The young ensign may well have lacked self-discipline and courage under fire, but there obviously was a lack of leadership on the part of the more mature and experienced ship's officers. The one exception is the radio officer. The deportment of William Meloney, the wireless operator, was laudatory. Despite the shelling from the U-boat and the probable damage to the antenna, he remained at his station long enough to key a comprehensive distress signal on both his main and emergency transmitters. Although his actions were in vain, he nonetheless did his duty. Notwithstanding these inconsistencies of data, the fact remains that the American oil tanker SS *Gulf America* was torpedoed and shelled by U-123 off the coast of Florida on Friday, 10 April 1942, at 2222 hours EWT.

The beacon presented by the burning SS *Gulf America* summoned the forces that would challenge the tactical skills and phenomenal luck of the highly regarded commander of U-123. Kapitänleutnant Hardegen had taken U-123 away from the inferno on a course to the south-southeast. At 2346, one hour and twenty-four minutes after he torpedoed *Gulf America* and left her burning, aircraft began dropping parachute flares and a patrol craft commenced shooting star shells in the vicinity of the tanker. "Now things really get started," Hardegen commented. "Three airplanes drop flares continuously and star shells are being fired from the sea side." But then the aircraft moved further south along the steamer route and closer to the still-surfaced U-boat. Hardegen stopped the boat in an attempt to stay unseen and to study the situation. At 0020 on 11 April 1942 a tanker and a freighter on a northerly course were sighted by the starboard lookout. The U-boat commander did the unpredictable. He maneuvered U-123 to a position between the two ships that were moving abreast of each other. Because of the aircraft and the flares, he dared not race northward to an advanced attack position. He waited patiently for the air to clear and hoped he would not be seen or heard nestled between the two steamers. His stratagem was sound, but only for the short term. At 0056 an aircraft dropped a flare directly in front of the U-boat. It turned and then made a run directly at U-123. Alarm! Crash dive! Hardegen laid the boat on the bottom at twenty meters and remained there for ten minutes.[17] He made the following entry in his log:

> While diving, we just catch a message on 600-meter wavelength that the steamer "Evelyn" is reporting a U-boat sighting with exact location. She must have seen us when the flare was dropped by the aircraft. Now it is about time we disappear from here, so I surface and move out to deeper water.
>
> (0145 EWT) We see a slow-moving freighter. She appears to be on a northerly course. She would be an easy target, but I don't want to attack because of those annoying flares.
>
> (0206 EWT) On port side a suspicious shadow. It doesn't look like a freighter. It's almost motionless or is going very slowly on a northerly course.[18]

KL Hardegen brought U-123 to the surface. He headed for deeper water and away from the "thick air" activity along the coast. He was twenty-seven miles from the burning *Gulf America*. He saw only a faint reddish glow on the horizon to the northeast. Outwardly Hardegen was calm, but his mind was not at ease.

Earlier, at midnight on Friday, 10 April 1942, *Evelyn* had been located approximately seven miles offshore and twelve miles southeast of St. Augustine, steering course 342 degrees true. This heading would take the Q-ship to St. Johns lightship. The accompanying oil tanker was now on the port beam, on the same course, and making the same speed. She was about fifteen hundred meters inboard, or on the land side of *Evelyn*. At 0032, now Saturday morning, Lt. Dutch Schwaner noted the red glow of a large fire ahead on the horizon. He summoned the captain and sounded General Quarters. Legwen relieved Schwaner of the conn, and Neville and I took our station on the bridge. At 0050 an aircraft at about three thousand feet altitude dropped a parachute flare a short distance ahead of the ship. Darkness turned to daylight in the immediate area. The aircraft continued on a southerly course, appeared to descend several hundred feet and passed on our port side between the oil tanker and us. At that moment I moved my binoculars downward to study the characteristics of the oiler when I picked up the image of the surfaced submarine. I cleared my throat and said to Lieutenant Neville who was only a few feet away: "Mr. Neville, look in line with the oiler's stern and about two-thirds the distance, there is a surfaced submarine."

"Yes, I see it. Glenn, look over here, we've got your U-boat." Legwen reacted immediately. He directed the helmsman, Quartermaster Third Class Arthur Muscher, to come left 5 degrees. He then turned to Neville and said he was coming left toward the tanker so that Schwaner could get a clean shot without hitting the oiler. He then told me to take the sound-powered phone and tell Schwaner to lower the curtains on the port side, to train in on the submarine off the starboard beam of the oiler, but to hold fire until his line of sight was clear of the tanker. I took the phone from Yeoman First Class Carric Andrew and relayed the message verbatim to the gunnery officer. Lieutenant Schwaner acknowledged, and I reported his acknowledgment to the captain. By the time I returned to the wing of the bridge, the U-boat was submerging. Hurriedly, Quartermaster Second Class Roger Metz who had been assisting Chief Cook with the coastal navigation, took a compass bearing on the U-boat. Schwaner's gun crews never had a chance to shoot. Neville then told Legwen he would have the standard "submarine sighting" message transmitted. Andrew passed that word to Ensign Lukowich in the radio room.[19]

Legwen now had a worthy opponent and would spend the next several hours playing a deadly game of "Mystify, Mislead, Surprise!" He would attempt to be as shrewd and crafty as his idol Gen. Stonewall Jackson. He told Neville that he was committed to attack. He brought *Evelyn* around to starboard and slowed to four knots. The tanker was now clear on a northward course and would not be in the way of his maneuvering. He had Muscher steady the ship's heading up on the compass bearing where the U-boat had submerged. The captain then directed Andrew to call down to Ensign Ray in the engine room to stop the main engine and to come immediately to the bridge. Neville asked no questions for he knew Legwen's next move. This would be the captain's game—his rules, his stratagem, and his plays. Legwen would be the referee, the coach, and the quarterback; only the game was not football.

Legwen had his officers and his telephone talker, Andrew, huddled on the bridge. He outlined his intentions: "We have sighted a submarine moving northward off the stern of that tanker. It has now submerged. It can go in any direction. We have stopped our engine so we can listen. It most likely will go in either one of two directions: follow the tanker, or head for deep water. I suspect it will follow the tanker submerged until the aircraft stop dropping flares, then it will surface and commence its attack run. We must catch it before it surfaces or it will outrun us." He directed Ensign Lukowich to stand by the sonar operator and to commence a passive search. He told Schwaner to keep the camouflage down and the gun crews at the ready and to set the depth charges at fifty feet; they would be fired from the bridge. Legwen planned to fall in behind the tanker. If it was not there, he would circle back and look for it on an easterly course, heading for deep water. He told Guy-Brown to stand by the telephone in the engine room; he would want full power when called for. Finally, he turned to Neville and me and asked that we stay on the bridge.[20]

Legwen carried out his plan. For fifteen minutes he followed the tanker and listened for the slower screws of the submerged submarine. Nothing was heard other than the tanker's single propeller. Legwen brought *Evelyn* right on a wide sweeping reverse S curve, first to east then southwest then east and then north again. He completed this maneuver at about 0145. He stopped and listened. Aircraft still dropped flares from time to time, but further to the south. Legwen was certain that this kept the U-boat submerged. Luke reported two sets of propeller noises to the southeast. Legwen turned and approached at half speed. It was 0215 on Saturday. An aircraft dropped a flare to the south-southeast, in the direction of one reported propeller sound. Legwen charged forward. Neville and I saw a grayish, ghostlike object that appeared on the fringe of the illuminated area. We said in unison, "it's a four-piper," meaning a flush deck, four-smokestack destroyer. Legwen turned left to a northeast heading to pursue the other noise. It was regained faintly on a bearing of 95 degrees true. At 0225 an aircraft dropped a flare precisely on that bearing at a distance of approximately two miles. There appeared to be several aircraft in the area, but no bombs were dropped. Legwen had his target, changed course to 95 degrees, and prepared for action. Neville asked, "Glenn, what about that destroyer?" Legwen replied, "He can play his own game. I shall ignore him unless he interferes."

The destroyer did intrude on Legwen's playing field. There was an exchange of indistinguishable blinker light signals between the destroyer and the aircraft in the area to the south. Then the four-piper commenced echo-ranging, no doubt investigating this suspicious, blacked-out mystery ship that appeared to be making "unusual" maneuvers. The destroyer, on a northerly course, overtook *Evelyn*, made a wide sweep to the east, and picked up a sound target on an approximate bearing of 150 degrees true. Her "pings" and echoes were clearly discernible on *Evelyn's* sonar. She apparently lost interest in *Evelyn* and concentrated on her new contact, Legwen's opponent. "Crap!" said Legwen. To ease the tension, the resourceful Neville responded, "Hell, Glenn, I bet you are senior to that destroyer's commanding officer. Pull rank. Signal him you are SOPA [senior officer present] and taking over tactical command for the attack." Legwen replied, "Hell of a good idea, Larry. But in this situation, it wouldn't work. He and I would be arguing here toe to toe, nose to nose, signal number to signal number, and that German would sink us both. Let him have his fun. We'll clean up the mess afterward. I just hope he doesn't waste his time challenging us."

Reinhard Hardegen must have been near mental and physical exhaustion this late in his patrol, although he would never admit it nor would he show it. He wanted deeper water and a respite, yet he still had work to do. The U-123 commander was puzzled by this "slow-moving freighter." Suspicion made him wary. He had been seen and reported by this steamer *Evelyn*. He had had a flare dropped overhead by an aircraft; he must have been seen by the pilot. He was running surfaced for the sanctuary of deeper water. He had this elusive, haunting feeling of being pursued. He anticipated more flares and possibly an attack from the surface or from the air. He must reach deeper water before daybreak. How long would they keep him on the bottom? His mind raced on.

Kapitänleutnant Hardegen had an extraordinarily keen mind, analytical, quick, perceptive; solving riddles was a game he thoroughly enjoyed. But exhaustion makes stress a malady, an unwholesome condition, rather than a challenge. Hardegen did not associate the steamer *Evelyn* with the U-boat-trap *Carolyn*. Gröner's merchant fleet handbook would highlight the similarities of the two old merchant ships. Since *Carolyn* had been converted into a Q-ship, would it not be reasonable to suspect that her sister ship, *Evelyn*, could also be a U-boat trap? Would not the visual similarities of the ships' characteristics raise suspicions? Neither Hardegen nor Kaeding nor Rafalski nor von Schroeter made the connection. Certainly the near-disastrous battle with *Carolyn* only a few weeks earlier must have left an indelible impression and image in the minds of both Hardegen and von Schroeter. Yet twice in the past two hours both Hardegen and von Schroeter had had the slow-moving, suspicious shadow in their sights without recognizing it as a trap.

At 0215, Hardegen, on the bridge with von Schroeter and the lookouts, saw a shadow moving south. It was coming up from aft on his starboard quarter. It was the "suspicious shadow" he had seen nine minutes earlier. It was a small, slow-moving ship, but in the darkness it was impossible to identify. Hardegen's mind raced forward with no consideration for the size of the target. He decided to attack. He turned U-123 to starboard to wait for the approaching vessel to lessen the angle and to close the range from two thousand meters to five hundred meters. He did not want to miss with his last eel. He would have preferred a larger target, a tanker, perhaps, but this was a positive addition of three to four thousand tons with such little effort. He waited patiently. All was in order. Apparently, on the surface, he did not hear the echo-ranging.[21]

Suddenly the tranquility was broken. As if from nowhere, the sound of its approach masked by the U-boat's diesels, an aircraft appeared in the darkness from behind the surfaced U-boat and dropped a flare directly overhead. The immediate area was brightly illuminated. Another aircraft was signaling to the "suspicious shadow." Hardegen and von Schroeter could now see clearly, at a range of fifteen hundred meters, that this second ship was a flush deck destroyer. Hardegen sent his two lookouts below in anticipation of another crash dive. Von Schroeter, without success, tried to read the messages being flashed between the destroyer and the aircraft. Hardegen noticed another plane approaching from the stern on his starboard side. The commander stopped both diesel engines hoping the pilot would not see the submarine's wake. It was too late, the aircraft banked steeply to port and came straight at the U-boat. Hardegen called down, "alarm!" Von Schroeter instinctively jumped down the hatch. Hardegen recalled, "We never had a faster crash dive. When I fell through the hatch, the aircraft was almost on top of me. It was a single engine, low wing aircraft, similar to our He70. I am sure he saw us." The time was 0225. U-123 hit the mud at twenty meters. Hardegen had braced himself for the expected bomb, but apparently none was dropped.[22]

Fritz Rafalski on the *Horchgerat* [hydrophone], the underwater sound detector, reported fast propeller noise and echo-ranging. The bearing was in the direction of the shadow, the destroyer. Now the concerned U-boat commander "restored creeping speed," heading for deeper water on course 120 degrees. At 0310, Rafalski reported: "Propeller noise is exactly aft and is becoming louder. Distinctly destroyer propellers." Hardegen was in the *Kommandoturm*, or conning tower, with von Schroeter at the *Vorhaltrechner*, the deflection calculator. He commented to his IWO: "This fellow is passing exactly overhead. It does not sound very melodious." At 0317 six depth charges detonated in rapid succession. The U-boat was shaken violently. Those who were standing were flung off their feet. Men and equipment were thrown about the boat. In the relatively shallow water the boat was heaved and rocked. The bow was lifted and then fell to the hard floor of the Atlantic. Most mechanical systems failed, and hissing and generally confusing noises could be heard throughout the boat. Back-up lighting only increased the confusion.[23]

The destroyer turned and again charged directly toward U-123. Hardegen wanted the E-motors checked. U-123 might have to move to take evasive action or even attack the patrol vessel. Hardegen had the boat on the bottom at twenty-two meters with all machinery turned off. The only sound now was the swishing of the fast propellers of the attacking destroyer and the incessant "pinging" of her sonar. The ominous, rhythmic beat of the propellers could be heard by all hands in the now-vulnerable U-boat. Schulz, the engineering super-achiever, must have been overwhelmed by the size and complexity of the task at hand. The main battery banks were partially discharged. It was not known if the batteries had the power to move the boat. The safety fuses on the batteries had to be reconnected. The pressure of the compressed air to blow tanks had to be checked. The rudders and diving planes had to be checked. Hardegen ordered the crew to stand by their escape lungs. He thought of the possibility of abandoning and scuttling the boat. If so, classified material would have to be destroyed.[24]

At this point KL Hardegen seriously contemplated abandoning U-123 because he felt another depth charge run was imminent and he could not take evasive action. Furthermore, he feared his boat was damaged so severely that he could not again transit the Atlantic. Hardegen moved toward the escape hatch where he would be able to see his officers and men dispatched to the surface. But his mind continued to seek alternatives and evaluate all possibilities. He would use every available moment before making an irreversible decision. His quick mind and sense of command, even under these extremely stressful conditions, permitted him to systematically consider his next move in terms of probabilities and to maintain his composure. He loved games of chance, and he would gamble. But like an astute gambler he would insist on favorable odds. Hardegen's thoughts raced on: If this destroyer makes only one depth charge run, all may not be lost. If the boat was abandoned now and the crew was in the water, they would be killed if the attacker made another run without seeing the men in the dark. Alternatively, if he stayed with the boat, he just might survive another attack. He considered all alternatives and then concluded that the boat would not be abandoned.

Little did Hardegen suspect that another adversary waited for him some ten fathoms above and two thousand meters away. Legwen was on the scene, also dealing in probabilities in this deadly game. The destroyer passed overhead again, but this time no depth charges were dropped. For twenty minutes more the enemy passed close by U-123, but in a passive sonar mode—no impulses. Schulz and Hardegen checked the boat: It appeared tight; no inrushing sea water threatened their iron quarters. Hardegen said a short and silent prayer of thanksgiving; he had time to lick his wounded pride. But how much time? On that day, Saturday, 11 April 1942, U-123 had suffered her second serious attack in U.S. waters.

And the day was not over. Hardegen was still in enemy waters with a wounded U-boat, a wounded command, and 3,800 miles from home base.

The American destroyer that had intruded in Legwen's game, it was later learned, was USS *Dahlgren*. Entries in the log book of USS *Dahlgren* for the 0000–0400 watch on Saturday, 11 April 1942, read as follows:

> 0055 Sighted darkened ship bearing 020 degrees true. 0101 Went to General Quarters, steered various courses investigating unidentified ship. 0135 Came to base course 150 degrees pgc (per gyro compass). 0135 Secured from General Quarters. 0200 Sighted St. Augustine light bearing 292 degrees, 12 miles. 0215 Aeroplane dropped flares. Challenged plane but plane did not answer. 0235 Aeroplane dropped several flares around ship. 0252 General Quarters. 0312 Made sound contact bearing 150 degrees true and distance 1,900 yards. Changed course to 150 degrees pgc and 148 degrees T, and made attack at 0316. No evidence that an underwater depth charge contact was made. 0333 Changed course to 340 degrees pgc, 338 degrees T, and resumed zigzagging. Speed 18 knots. 0358 Secured from G.Q. /s/ E. J. Dougherty Jr., Ensign, USNR 0–4 Watch /s/ R. W. Cavenagh LCdr. USN Commanding Officer USS *Dahlgren* (DD187)[25]

Insofar as Lieutenant Commander Cavenagh was concerned, that episode was of little substance. However, there was no doubt that he missed an opportunity to obtain a U-boat commander's white cap. The reasons for his lack of success are a matter of conjecture. Little substantive evidence is available in the archives. Cavenagh and his naval reserve ensign may not have had sufficient training in antisubmarine warfare to competently carry out the secondary mission of the ship. Although that would appear incongruous since *Dahlgren* was attached to the Atlantic Fleet Sonar School at Key West and operated with friendly submarines. The brevity of the log entries, considering the events that did take place during the period 0000 to 0400 on 11 April 1942, is indicative of ineffectiveness somewhere in the command. It would seem that a more detailed evaluation of the target based on the quality and characteristics of the sonar contact would be a more appropriate log entry than the overly simplistic

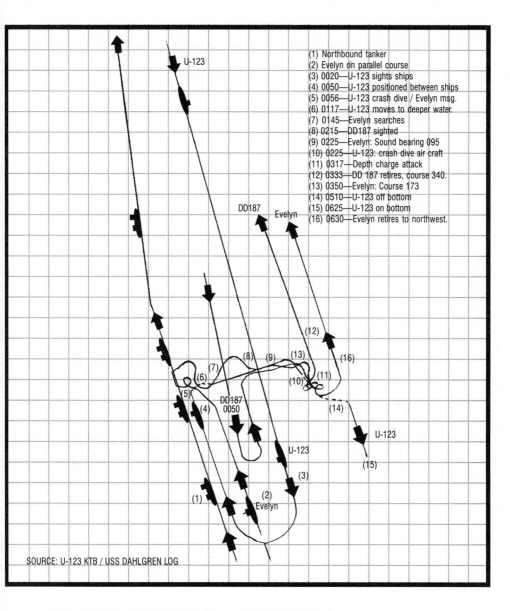

11 April 1942: U-123/USS *Dahlgren* (DD187)/SS *Evelyn*

statement: "No evidence that an underwater depth charge contact was made." Inexplicable as well is why a succinct statement such as "six depth charges were expended" was not recorded in the log. One final observation: No log entry was made referring to *Evelyn's* submarine sighting message.

Commander, Gulf Sea Frontier, based in Key West, Florida, recorded the *Evelyn/Dahlgren* incident in his daily war diary as follows:

> April 11, 1942. At 0133 EWT, a submarine surfaced near the SS *Evelyn* in Lat. 29-40 N and Long. 80-56 W, southeast of St. Augustine, but attack was evaded. Three planes arrived at this location at 0230 EWT searching area. Flares were dropped at two points and the USS *Dahlgren* being near by proceeded to area making one questionable contact. The *Dahlgren* continued searching this area until 1237 EWT, when she was ordered to proceed to area of the SS *Gulf America* sinking to search for submarine which sank that vessel.[26]

The perfunctory content of this entry is obvious. Apparent, too, is the absence of any analytical review and evaluation that might have provided a basis for improving the effectiveness of the defense forces. Although the purpose of most logs is to record events in a summary fashion, better judgment might have been exercised in defining the parameters of succinctness so as to provide pertinent and, where possible and practicable, conclusive detail. Otherwise, omissions, errors, misinformation, incompetence, and poor judgment are neither identified nor corrected. In this regard, the commander in chief U-boats, Admiral Dönitz, made it standard procedure to review with each U-boat commander his war diary at the conclusion of each patrol.

At 0345 all was not well aboard U-123. Some thirty-eight minutes after the destroyer's attack, Hardegen and Schulz, his LI, had checked the boat out for lethal damage. It seemed that both crew and U-boat had withstood the violent impacts of the six charges. U-123 was in no immediate danger of foundering. Full internal lighting had been restored. The tower hatch that had partially popped open because it had not been griped down tightly when it was closed had been secured, and sea water no longer cascaded down the ladder. Most, but not all, of the air leaks from the head valves had been stopped and the valves resealed. However, Hardegen would not be satisfied that all was well until he had checked out his propulsion plant, both on batteries and with diesels. The check and repair activity kept the crew busy and their minds off the destroyer that had been circling above. Hardegen wrote in his KTB: "When considering the behavior of the destroyer, I can say only, 'It's your own fault!' It is proof to me how inexperienced these defense patrols are. The destroyer captain probably thought we were finished when he noticed the air bubbles and didn't hear anything. To be on the safe side, he passed over us for an hour and took the intensive flow of air bubbles as evidence of our sinking."[27]

Evelyn, like a seahorse at King Neptune's starting gate, and Legwen, holding firmly to the reins, were eager to enter the fray. All hands were still at their battle stations. Carric "Andy" Andrew, the bridge talker, was broadcasting the destroyer's attack on the sound-powered telephone circuit to keep the crew informed: Lt. Dutch Schwaner with his gun crews; Ensign Guy Brown Ray in the engine room; "Doc" Fignar, Larry Flanagan, and Chief Percy Barton with the damage control parties on the mess deck below; and Gunner Harry Lamb at the depth charge station. Seaman Frank Clifton was operating the sonar console and Gil Ciucevich was maintaining a log of Clifton's reports of bearings and ranges. Ensign Lukowich was in the radio room monitoring the radio traffic and the sonar reports and passing pertinent information to Legwen on the bridge. Quartermaster Second Class Roger Metz was recording the ship's position, course changes, and activities. Quartermaster James Pearson was the helmsman and Quartermaster Arthur Muscher was at the engine room telegraph. Chief Quartermaster Lionel Cook was the bridge supervisor. Every five minutes he would take a compass bearing on the 161-foot lighthouse at St. Augustine. All four quartermasters were in the wheelhouse, the enclosed area of the bridge. The two bridge lookouts, Seaman First Class Harry Bowman and Seaman Second Class George Walters, were stationed in each wing of the bridge.

Lieutenant Neville and I maintained our vigil on the bridge in close proximity to Legwen. We kept occupied with frequent visual searches of the surface and sky around us and, of course, the maneuvers and attack by the destroyer. We were conscious of Legwen's presence as he alternated between pacing the deck and studying the movements of the "four-piper." He had little to say. At 0333 the destroyer completed a final pass over the place where it had laid its depth charge pattern and left the area on a course to the northwest. Legwen turned to Neville: "What do you think happened there, Larry?" Neville was prepared. He anticipated the question and was eager for a dialogue. He knew Legwen's aggressive and impetuous nature, and he wanted to be a restraining influence, if necessary, without being impertinent or disrespectful. Neville excelled in this role and relationship.

As for me, a junior staff officer, I relished my unique position on the bridge and my physical closeness to these two naval officers. I protected my incomparable status by speaking only when spoken to and reporting all matters that I deemed significant to the tactical situation. I felt comfortable, purposeful, and responsible in my station. It was reminiscent of the days as a teenager that I had stood on the bridge with my father as he piloted his United Fruit Company ship into the many ports served by this great organization: New York, Havana, Nassau, Miami, New Orleans, the Panama Canal, San Francisco, Acapulco, the numerous Central and South American banana plantation and loading ports, and other places, including this coast of Florida. Indeed, I felt a sense of belonging during these critical and dangerous periods. I was eager to hear Lieutenant Neville's evaluation: "Glenn, I know there is a submerged object out there. I have good reason to suspect it's a U-boat. I know the destroyer dropped only one pattern of DCs [depth charges]. I don't know why he made more passes without further attacks or stopping. He did not stop to examine wreckage or to pick up survivors if there were any, so I assume he was unsure of his contact. Why? I have no idea."

Legwen listened carefully: "I agree with your observations, Larry. I must follow up with an attack. I don't want to wait. If you disagree, say so now. Otherwise, let's start the attack run. Have the sonarman start echoranging and give me the bearing and ranges of the target." Neville was in complete agreement with Legwen, and he called for sonar bearings and ranges. Legwen continued: "If that guy is down there, I will sink him or keep him submerged. I can't let him come up. He can outrun us on the surface. If he chooses to surface and shoot it out, we are the bigger target and easier to see at night. I can't let him surface. We will make as many DC attacks as necessary and then stay on top of him till daylight."

Seaman Frank Clifton, who had completed Fleet Sound School in Key West, picked up intermittent "mushy" echoes on compass bearing 173 degrees true. Legwen called out for new course 173 and to ring up full ahead. Pearson called out "Aye, aye, sir; new course 173 degrees." Muscher, at the engine room telegraph, pushed the double arms forward to full and acknowledged, "Ahead, full." Neville asked for water depth. Metz turned to the fathometer and responded, "10 fathoms, sir." Legwen called out to double-check settings on the depth charges for fifty feet. Andrew passed the word to Lieutenant Schwaner. Trigger setting at fifty feet was acknowledged. Sonar reported bearing on target remained at 173 degrees, range twenty-three hundred yards. The time was 0349.

Legwen then turned to me: "Ken, I want you to concentrate on looking for anything in the water, big or small, dead ahead of us. Yell out if you see anything. Try to identify it if you can. It could be the sub, the conning tower, a periscope, wreckage, or even survivors. As we pass over the target area, report anything you see. If there are people in the water, I will not depth charge. If it's light wreckage, I will fire. If it's a partially submerged U-boat, I'll probably ram. Keep a sharp lookout, Ken." My mind raced along with his, and even though he didn't mention it, I thought of the U-boat commander's white cap. What a trophy it would be. At the time I was thinking about material things rather than the human implications of a successful attack. His words "people in the water" jolted my sense of compassion for the victims, but that thought was quickly replaced with more utilitarian subject matter. The sea was smooth except for a gentle ocean swell. The wind was light from the northwest, offshore. Although it was a moonless night, visibility was excellent as was my night vision with the aid of my constant companion, my 7 x 50 binoculars. I moved to the extreme end of the port wing of the bridge so I could have an unobstructed view beyond the forecastle. Since the wind, light as it was, was from right to left of the ship's course, the port side position gave me a clear picture of anything floating on the surface downwind. At eight knots it would not take long for *Evelyn* to transit the two thousand yards to reach point zero, although to me it seemed like an eternity.

Legwen, as if he could see through the dark water of the Atlantic, had envisaged the black hull of the U-boat dead ahead and vulnerable to *Evelyn*'s lethal charge. He moved into the bridgehouse, or pilothouse, where he could better hear the ranges being sung out by the sonarman. He had to use his best judgment as to when to fire the depth charge pattern after passing over the target, since the Y-guns were on the stern and would fire out on both sides of the ship, angled about ten degrees aft. *Evelyn* had no instruments to calculate the precise time to fire. The other variable, of course, was the accuracy of the range obtained by the sonar and the recording instrumentation, neither of which had been calibrated. Legwen realized how ill prepared *Evelyn* was for attacking a submerged submarine.

Legwen had taken *Evelyn/Asterion*, with battle ensign flying from the gaff, within a thousand yards of point zero, his imaginary target. Lionel Cook sighted St. Augustine light bearing 283 degrees, 30 minutes, distance eleven miles. Metz made the log entry. I remained in the port wing of the bridge with my glasses fixed near where the water had been disturbed by the destroyer's depth charges. I saw nothing on the surface and so reported. Legwen called for sonar reports. Ensign Lukowich responded that the retractable sonar was malfunctioning. Perhaps the nearness of the destroyer's depth charge blasts had affected the instruments extended below the hull of the ship. There was apparent damage to the transducer and circuitry. The passive listening components could receive signals, but the head would not rotate. The active subsystem had also failed and echoranging was impossible. Legwen was perturbed, to say the least. Before Legwen could contemplate his next move, he sensed the absence of the main engine vibration and felt the ship losing headway. Guy-Brown in the engine room called the bridge with a most untimely report. He stated that a bad leak in the propeller shaft alley could not withstand a depth charge shock. The stern tube seal, bushing, and stuffing box were leaking badly. This rupture, where the propeller shaft exits the hull, could not be repaired at sea. Guy-Brown further reported that he could make a temporary fix but it would take time and that prolonged steaming would not be possible. Then the chief engineer reported he had to stop the main engine. Legwen turned to Neville, dismissing Guy-Brown's calamitous words, "Larry, I want to make this depth charge run on this German." Neville made no response. As the gravity of Guy-Brown's report sank in, Legwen called his chief engineer to the bridge.

Elsewhere in the ship, preparations were being made for the attack. Schwaner reported that depth charges had been rechecked on the K-guns and were ready to fire. Gun captains reported all guns manned and ready. Guy-Brown arrived on the bridge: "Captain, I was on my way up here. Bad news. The main engine probably has shifted on its foundation. I have an alignment problem—" Legwen cut in with an angry retort: "What in the hell does that mean, Chief?" Guy-Brown continued: "Specifically, Captain, it means two things. One, if I run the main engine as she is, I will wipe bearings and she will bind up, burn up, or tear up. Two, if we make a depth charge run, the engine could jump off its pedestal and fall through the bottom of the damn ship. If the boilers collapse, we could have one hell of a fire down there. I can't guarantee anything, but, by God, if you want to make a run, we will hold on and hope for the best."

Legwen had no reason to doubt his chief engineer's assessment. Neville, always the arbitrator, was ready to enter the conversation, but he hoped the captain would let off steam for a moment and then settle down to reasonableness. "Christ," Legwen exclaimed, "now I know why Washington expected my command to last only thirty days. If the Germans didn't sink me, I would self-destruct. I would like to take this so-called man-o-war and run it up their. . . ." "Constitution Avenue?" Neville injected. I almost laughed out loud. Even Legwen was amused with Neville's selection of words. But the seriousness of the situation could not be dismissed. A more composed Legwen brought his attack to a halt, but he continued to vent his frustration.

It was 0418, about two hours before dawn. Legwen wanted to get as close to this submarine as he could and stay there; keep him submerged until daylight. If the U-boat moved or stuck up its periscope, Legwen would attack with depth charges regardless of the self-inflicted damage. If it surfaced, Legwen would take it under gunfire or ram it. He much preferred a surface artillery duel. Legwen seemed determined not to let this U-boat get away. He thought too that the boat might be so damaged that it could not move or was already doomed. He would wait and listen.

Legwen, though disappointed and terribly frustrated, welcomed the brief interlude. He had to collect his thoughts, rethink his options, assign degrees of probability, weigh the odds, and give the orders. Meanwhile, there was much ship repair work to be done.

Officers and crewmen went off in all directions. Ensign Lukowich and Chief Electricians Mate Earl Bowling went below to the sonar well to trouble-shoot, find the problem, and hopefully, repair the damaged circuitry. They determined the damage was outside the hull and inaccessible. Quartermaster Second Class Roger Metz took it upon himself, as a thoughtful and well-intentioned act, to send the bridge messenger, Seaman Mercury "Fleet-feet" Brown, to the wardroom for hot coffee for the three officers on the bridge.

Fleet-feet Mercury Brown graciously complied and returned to the darkened bridge with a tray and three cups atop three saucers. He collided head-on with the stone-hearted, "old-navy" Chief Quartermaster Lionel M. Cook, the self-anointed scourge of all "nonregulation" seamen. Hot coffee cascaded from cups to saucers, to tray, to Cook's midsection. Cook roared as only an old salt can roar, using adjectives and adverbs long since censored out of the Naval Terms and Usage Handbook. Fleet-feet would rather have been on the German submarine than in the pool of coffee and humiliation. The pilothouse was promptly swabbed with you-know-whose T-shirt. Roger Metz, the unintentional perpetrator of the incident, salvaged the coffee and offered partially filled cups to Legwen, Neville, and me. We accepted the still-warm brew.

Ensign Guy Brown Ray was busy in the engine room. Chief Machinist Mate Matt Jansen and Machinist Mate First Class Raymond Dunn hastily repacked the stern tube seal as a temporary measure. Resecuring the main engine to the bedplate was another matter. Cracks had formed at the base of two of the cast-iron legs. Previous welds had failed. Undue stress on the cast-iron housing could cause further damage and render the engine useless, a chance Guy-Brown did not want to take. He did agree in an emergency he could run the engine at slow speed. Legwen retained his composure and turned to Neville: "Larry, we are in a situation I never even dreamed of. It's a damned disaster." "No, Glenn," was Neville's quick response. "It could be worse. So far we have had no personnel casualties." Legwen conceded: "Thank God for that, Larry. But I could accept casualties if it served a worthwhile purpose. I will do what I have to do without being reckless. Maybe he is finished down there and we are worrying needlessly. However, I cannot let our guard down. I must know. I must have some tangible evidence that he is finished." As Legwen was speaking, Clifton at the sonar console detected strange noises close by the ship. He reported he could not identify the sound, but it appeared to be moving away. He could not determine the direction. The time was 0515.

By 0510 Leutnant Heinz Schulz had half of U-123's batteries repaired. The other half became operable after reconnecting the safety fuses. Hardegen wanted to surface before daylight to recharge his batteries and to reinvigorate his crew. He was still oblivious to the Q-ship above and unsure of the location of the destroyer. He used his supply of compressed air to blow out tanks sufficiently to lift the boat off the bottom. His diving planes and rudders were operable, but the stuffing boxes were leaking sea water. As U-123 rose off the mud, Schulz engaged the E-motors to a creeping speed. As Hardegen described it, "Both shafts are out of line and knocking, and at this speed they make a hell of a noise."

Evelyn was stopped on a heading of 188 degrees. Chief Quartermaster Cook reported he could no longer see St. Augustine light because of a large rain squall to the northwest. Neville listened at the sonar console. He detected slow propeller noises with a resonating background sound of varying wave lengths. He visualized a propeller turning on a bent shaft or on one out of alignment. He reported to Legwen that the target was moving and that it sounded as if it had a problem in its power train. Legwen, without the aid of a directional fix, assumed the German was making for deeper water. Accordingly, he brought *Evelyn* around slowly to the left in a moderate circle and then to the right to complete a figure eight maneuver. Neville called out each time when the underwater sound was the loudest. Metz marked the spot and the ship's compass heading on the maneuvering board. Legwen repeated the circles, moving each time further to the east. Metz's plots indicated a movement on a compass heading of 123 degrees. Legwen brought *Evelyn* around to the left one more time. Clifton, now at the sonar console, called out as the sound began to increase in volume, and Legwen, using only his own good judgment, told the helmsman to steady up on course 123 degrees.

Neville stood at Legwen's side wondering what the captain was going to do. He finally asked: "Glenn, what do you have in mind?" Legwen was as determined as ever to continue the attack. "Larry, if I can pass directly over this guy I will fire depth charges and take the consequences. Have Luke stand by to transmit another submarine sighting report. Eastern Sea and Gulf Sea Frontiers should know this U-boat is still with us. We will not report our attack until we know the outcome."

Hardegen had raised U-123 off the bottom and was moving ahead at slow speed on his electric motors with both bent shafts protesting loudly. Rafalski, at the sonar, reported a slow, single propeller noise in the area, definitely not a destroyer. The ever-cautious commander decided to make an evasive move: "LI, stop the E-motors; give me half power astern, both motors. Hard left rudder." After thirty seconds, the commander continued his maneuver: "Stop. Move rudder amidships. Ahead both motors, full." Hardegen took U-123 away from the confusing surface noises above. He would surface when possible, charge his batteries, test out his boat, and strike later if the opportunity presented itself.

Neville had some reservations about a depth charge attack, considering the probable major and uncontrollable damage to the ship. Also, he knew that the probability of "passing directly over the sub," with Legwen's desperation maneuvers, was very low indeed. He deferred comment. Clifton reported that the strange propeller noises indicated an increase in revolutions and that the volume was decreasing, suggesting that the U-boat had turned abruptly off the 123 degrees heading and that the range to target was increasing. *Evelyn* was now engulfed in a heavy downpour of rain as the squall line passed overhead. Visibility was reduced to zero. Guy-Brown called the bridge. He must stop the main engine because two bearings had badly overheated.

The distraught Legwen moved to the wing of the bridge for a few moments of solitude. He asked himself, What hope of success do I have? He did not want to retreat from this U-boat, but he could not find and destroy it if it remained submerged. He would wait for this squall to pass and hope he would find it on the surface. Legwen believed the German would surface and attack with his deck guns at close range. By 0630 the weather had cleared and the dawn revealed no surfaced U-boat. There were no intelligible sounds from below. Legwen accepted the fact that it would be imprudent to search further when *Evelyn*'s seaworthiness was questionable and any overt actions would compromise the ship's disguise. Furthermore, he concluded that if the U-boat intended to attack, it would have done so before daylight. Legwen would capture no white cap this day.[28]

10

The Game Is Over

I WOULD BY NO MEANS RETREAT WHILE
ANY HOPE OF SUCCESS REMAINED.

John Paul Jones, Paris, France, 1778

HARDEGEN'S DECISION to stay with the boat proved to be a wise one. After half an hour, U-123 was brought to the surface. It was still dark. One of the MAN (Maschinenfabrik Augsburg-Nürnberg AG) diesels failed while trying to blow air out of the diving tanks. Welding solved this problem. Schulz had trouble blowing some tanks because the head valves were twisted shut and were opened only with great difficulty. Somehow the bent shafts turned and the unwelcome noise subsided. The boat was reasonably stable but was not "crash-divable." Hardegen remained on the surface even though aircraft were again dropping parachute flares behind him to the north. He moved south. He must recharge his batteries and run clear of his attacker before dawn revealed his location.[1]

Kapitänleutnant Reinhard Hardegen's harrowing experience is summarized in these excerpts from his log:

Somehow we were losing air. We found later that all head valves had been sprung open and air was escaping through them. . . . The tower hatch had also cracked open, but it could be closed again. It is surpris-

178

ing to me that the enemy was not tougher, using depth charges in these shallow waters in both cases. All he had to do was place another pattern in the same spot that had been marked by the rising air bubbles and we would have had to abandon the boat—climb out. We had already begun preparations to destroy all classified material. Also, it is hard to believe that he didn't want to see the white cap of the commanding officer as proof of his kill. If it [had been] daylight hours, he would have been able to locate the boat. I am sure we were dealing with people inexperienced in defense against submarines. In all probability they thought we were finished when they saw the escaping air bubbles and especially when they could not hear the strange noises below.

The experience had made an indelible impression on this courageous officer. Outwardly Hardegen displayed no emotion as he reflected on the frightening experience and the damage to his boat. He and his crew were still alive; now he must focus his attention on the future. While he was not totally satisfied with retreating from this adversary, he knew it was prudent to escape so as to evaluate U-123's damage and determine its ability to seek another opportunity for attack under more favorable conditions. So far as he was concerned, the episode was over. He expressed his feelings in his war diary: "When we again breathed the freshness of the night air, our hour of trial had already been forgotten. Now I had only one thought: 1 torpedo and 90 rounds of ammunition still available to do their duty." The cautious and calculating Hardegen stayed close to the Florida coast. That was where the tonnage was; it was also where he could test the seaworthiness of his damaged boat before undertaking the thirty-seven-hundred-mile transit of the Atlantic.[2]

On 12 April U-123 moved south and *Evelyn* steamed north. Both had damage to repair. *Evelyn*'s wounds restricted her speed, and with only passive sonar, Legwen was unable to launch a meaningful attack. Further, aircraft continued to drop flares that illuminated the decoy, making it an easy target for a torpedo attack by a submerged submarine. Indeed, with dawn approaching and no U-boat in sight, it was best for *Evelyn* to move away. Legwen concluded that no hope of success remained. Apparently, Hardegen was oblivious to the nearby presence of the crippled *Evelyn* with her lethal weaponry. Had he suspected another U-boat trap

eager to play cat and mouse, it would have added another dimension to
his puzzle.

> True luck consists not in holding the best of
> the cards at the table: Luckiest is he who knows
> just when to rise and go home.
>
> *John Milton Hay, Distichs, 15*

U-123 made its way slowly on the surface toward Cape Canaveral. At
0625, as daylight approached, Hardegen settled his boat on the bottom
at one hundred meters. The forty-five minutes on the surface had given
Schulz time to check the various essential systems, make temporary
repairs and adjustments where needed, and be assured that U-123 was
ready to begin the long transit homeward. Hardegen was pleased and
turned his full attention not homeward but to the remaining "1 torpedo
and 90 rounds of ammunition."

Legwen, in the meantime, transmitted a coded radio message to
Eastern Sea Frontier Operations that *Evelyn/Asterion* was in need of dry-
docking to repair the sonar and main engine. Operations responded
clearing *Evelyn* to proceed to New York, the Atlantic Basin Iron Works in
Brooklyn, where the services had been arranged. Legwen acknowledged,
"if *Evelyn* can make it to New York." Guy-Brown assured the commanding officer that with flattened tin cans for shims in the bearings and jacks
and braces for the main engine, he could coax the "old girl" around the
world—but not at a fast pace.

At 1800, Hardegen, refreshed from a six-hour rest in his bunk and a
hot meal from the galley, took U-123 at periscope depth toward Cape
Canaveral. The eleven hours and thirty-five minutes on the bottom at
100-meters and with no air bubbles had provided all hands except the
cook and messmen time to make repairs, titivate the boat, and get some
much needed rest and relaxation. Hardegen, after his rest, took time to
record the attack in rough draft form and then to carefully state the significant details in his KTB. He shuddered as he revisited the attack and
thought how close he had come to scuttling his 123. He was satisfied with

the final outcome. He would not dwell on seeking answers to all his questions, especially why the enemy had not dropped a second round of depth charges. He was thankful for his good fortune and recalled with a degree of self-satisfaction the maxim of the nineteenth-century Prussian field marshall Count Helmuth von Moltke, "Luck in the long run is given only to the efficient." It would appear that this U-boat commander had earned by his sound judgment, his cleverness, and his attention to details the long string of good luck he continued to enjoy.

At 2009, well after the sun had set beyond the Florida coast, IIWO Wolf-Harold Schüler on the bridge sighted a northbound vessel. Hardegen was called to the bridge. Starlight and the reflection from the land enhanced visibility. He studied the potential target for several minutes. She appeared to be a slow-moving combination passenger-freighter of approximately 5,500 GRT, larger than *Esparta*. The sky was cloudless. The wind was gentle from the northwest, and the sea was calm except for a moderate swell that gently moved the boat up and down. There were no aircraft in the area. It would be an easy kill.

Hardegen enjoyed the comfortable spring weather off the Florida coast. The fresh, balmy air put him in a relaxed, philosophical state of mind. He enjoyed a feeling of self-satisfaction as he approached the end of a very successful war patrol in enemy waters. His last torpedo, his fiftieth as a U-boat commander, rested below, subject to his command. Another tanker would provide an added sense of exhilaration. But this was not a tanker. He hesitated. Capriciousness replaced hard, technical judgment. He was caught up momentarily in the fanciful. He decided to attack the freighter and not wait for a tanker. Why? "I am provided with this opportunity and cannot allow it to escape, otherwise fate will punish me." Hardegen gave von Schroeter permission to commence a surface attack. The target was on a due north course at a speed of six knots. She was radio silent and with no lights. The target approached too close and von Schroeter had to take the boat to a new attack position off the starboard bow of the freighter. At 2311 and at a range of six hundred meters, tube 4 was fired. The torpedo hit the midsection of the ship after forty seconds. The cargo hold absorbed much of the explosion, but a dark, high detonation column of water could be observed. U-123 remained in the immediate area long enough only to see the stricken ship turn over and sink. She then moved south, cruising on the surface in the darkness.[3]

Lt. H. A. Burch, USNR, from the Office of the Chief of Naval Operations, summarized survivors' statements in his report dated 29 April 1942. He identified the ship as the SS *Leslie*, a U.S. freighter under charter to the Grace Steamship Company. She was torpedoed without warning at 2320 EWT. *Leslie* was loaded with raw sugar and was en route from Havana to New York. She was 2,609 GRT, considerably smaller than Hardegen had estimated. Survivors reported that approximately one hour after the attack they heard cannon fire and could see gun flashes four miles to the southward. Lieutenant Burch's report included the statement: "The following morning, upon coming ashore, the 'Leslie' survivors ascertained that the vessel attacked by gunfire was the Swedish Motor Vessel 'Korsholm.'"[4]

After sinking SS *Leslie*, the self-satisfied Hardegen recorded: "This torpedoing will not be noticed immediately, and since it is still early, I will continue southward to find cannon fodder. I have ample fuel. While I can still shoot, I have no reason to begin passage home, even though I have expended my torpedoes in this fertile area. I have not yet exploited all attack possibilities." At 0030 on 13 April 1942, Hardegen was again rewarded. The port bridge lookout reported sighting a northbound shadow. U-123 was fourteen miles south of the position where *Leslie* had been attacked. The 137-foot high lighthouse at Cape Canaveral, displaying its three flashes every sixty seconds, could be seen plainly to the northwest. Again, the U-boat commander was called to the bridge. The jubilant Hardegen scrutinized his target. It was fully loaded and to him it appeared to be in the 8,000 GRT class. He called out: Auf Artilleriegefechtsstationen! [to artillery battle stations!] Schüler and his gun crew manned the forward 10.5-centimeter cannon. Horst von Schroeter stood beside Hardegen on the bridge and looked at Schüler busily checking the details of his gun crew, the 10.5, and the ammunition handlers. He recalled clearly that on the last patrol that was his station. Like most "boys," he enjoyed the artillery shoots—he often wished he could be the pointer, or trainer, actually aiming and firing the cannon. His objective was to sink ships, not kill humans. Now, in his new, exalted position as IWO, he must be content to stand by his commanding officer and watch.[5]

Schüler called up to the bridge where Hardegen, only a few meters away and conspicuous in the dark with his white cap, continued to study the target with his binoculars: "Ready to fire, Herr Kaleu." The range was one thousand meters. Hardegen directed his lieutenant to fire first at the bridge structure and wireless, and then to concentrate on the water line. He gave the command: "Commence firing." The time was 0145. The "exceptionally large bridge" was hit repeatedly. Hardegen and von Schroeter shielded their eyes from the muzzle flashes to avoid the temporary blindness. They saw the detonating shells tear apart the bridge house. Somehow, whether the freighter's helmsman was able to do it before the artillery barrage began or the captain had already given the order to ram, his only defense, the target turned to starboard in the direction of U-123. Schüler's gun crew pumped shells into the waterline of the approaching ship. Hardegen called for a temporary cease fire. He turned U-123 away, passed astern of the wounded freighter, and made a new approach from its port side at close range. The gunnery officer again opened fire, this time "methodically" along the waterline, perforating first below the funnel into the engine room and then into the bunkers. The cargo was ignited and "burned intensely." Hardegen considered the target destroyed.

The lookout reported another shadow appearing from the south. Hardegen looked at his watch. He noted there were still several hours before daylight. For a moment he considered investigating the new shadow. Von Schroeter, anticipating his intent, advised him that the only heavy-caliber shells remaining were in the upper deck ready-ammunition stock and not easily accessible. To von Schroeter's surprise, Hardegen laughed out loud, then gave the order to secure from battle stations and to make ready for the long Atlantic crossing. Hardegen called down to the control room: "Set course 045 degrees and make turns for ten knots." Both officers were facing aft elbow to elbow, observing the burning tanker and the steamer moving northward. Neither was a threat, and at ten knots, U-123 would soon outrun the shadow. The curious von Schroeter asked, "Herr Kaleu, why the loud laugh?" In one of his rare moments of informality,

Hardegen replied: "I was amused, Horst, when you mentioned upper deck ready-ammunition stock. It is named 'ready-ammunition' because it is never ready. It is stowed two decks below in the ammo room, yet it is called upper deck. As you know, it must be brought up from the lower deck to the main deck locker. Only then is it 'ready.' Moving those rounds one at a time is a laborious process that requires the use of special tongs. We will have that done during the next few days." Von Schroeter did not need the full explanation. As the former gunnery officer, he knew the details as well as if not better than his commander. Before going below, Hardegen took a close look at the horizon. Flames from the motor vessel *Korsholm* were clearly visible seventeen miles to the south. As the commander left the bridge, he told his IWO to set course zero degrees, due north, and to make turns for six knots. U-123 would ride the Gulf Stream for a while.[6]

Hardegen returned to his stateroom. He wanted to record the events of the day before he forgot the details. He was too energized to relax. He sat at his little desk and made notes. He was in a fanciful, romantic, poetic mood. He wished to translate reality into fantasy; he wanted others to read his words and experience his joy. But he could not concentrate. He went topside again for fresh air.

Korsholm was a Swedish freighter of 2,647 gross tons. She was attacked and sunk by gunfire, according to the 5 May 1942 confidential report of Ensign A. J. Powers, USNR, of the Navy Department. Her position was less than fifteen miles off Cape Canaveral Lighthouse. Her cargo was 4,593 tons of phosphate. She was on a northerly course, en route from Tampa, Florida, to Liverpool, England, via Halifax, Nova Scotia.[7]

Fuel conservation became Hardegen's next challenge. The boat was making "turns" for a conservative six knots and was being carried an additional four knots while nestled in the warm bosom of the Gulf Stream. Hardegen kept her there until she reached that point near Cape Hatteras where he would intersect a predetermined line that he called "a modified great circle route." If not diverted by BdU, he would cross the Atlantic and arrive at the Bay of Biscay and Lorient, France. Once more in his private compartment, he sat down to compose his report to BdU. Hannes greeted him with a cup of freshly brewed hot tea. The soothing effect of the aromatic beverage drained the tension from him. Hardegen reviewed his notes. His mind was clear and refreshed and still poetic. He had added another ship and eight thousand tons to his tally. He was eager to report: "Thus, we have sunk or destroyed 10 ships with 74,815 GRT on this patrol, and therefore, we have broken the record of our last voyage. With 300,141 GRT, U-123 is the second German submarine to pass 300,000 tons during this war."[8]

Hardegen claimed 74,815 tons on this patrol, based in part on visual estimates made during darkness. Since he did not know the name of the ship attacked in some instances, he could not get actual tonnage from Gröner's handbook. The correct tonnage was 59,394, a delta of 15,421, or 20.6 percent. Accordingly, U-123 was far short of the 300,000 tons claimed. The tendency to overestimate was characteristic among U-boat commanders, understandably so. Also, commanders at times used a poetic style for composing messages. Hardegen was no exception. He summarized his current exploits in this transmission to BdU:

> For BdU. From U-123—Hardegen.
> For seven tankers the last hour had come.
> The U-trap sank slower.
> Two freighters also lie on the ground,
> Each one sunk by the Kettledrum beater![9]

This brief message was followed on the night of 13 April by a lengthy situation report giving the list of ships attacked and considered lost. Where names were not known, type of ship and estimated tonnage data were used. At 2100 13 April, U-123 received the following radio message: "For Hardegen. Bravo. This, too, was a kettledrum beat. Commander in Chief [Dönitz]"[10]

Lt. Cdr. Glenn Legwen took *Evelyn* up the coast toward Cape Lookout. He stayed outside the shipping lanes, but close enough to receive quick assistance should Guy-Brown's calculations regarding *Evelyn's* seaworthiness be flawed. At 0628 on 14 April, as *Evelyn* was making Diamond Shoals lightship off Cape Hatteras, some twenty-four miles to the northeast, a freighter of approximately six thousand tons passed close by on the

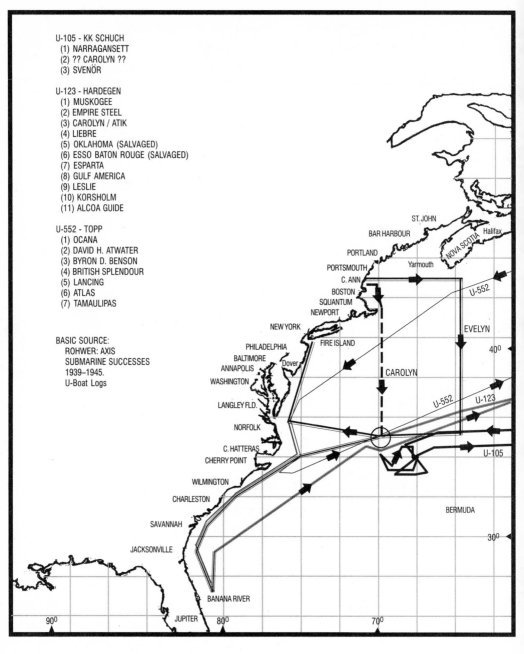

March–April 1942: Selected U-boat activities. U-105, U-123, U-552 vs.
SS *Carolyn* and SS *Evelyn* (attacks in western Atlantic waters)

port side on a parallel course. She was proudly flying the British ensign at her gaff. Lieutenant Neville and I had the bridge watch. The sky was clear and the sea calm. Although it was daylight, the sun had not yet tipped the horizon. The freighter was still in sight in the distance when Guy-Brown arrived at 0745 to relieve the officer of the deck. I made the report to Guy-Brown giving him the bearings on the freighter and the lightship, both within one degree of each other to the northeast. Neville advised Legwen that the Diamond Shoals light was in sight, knowing that we would go to General Quarters for the two- to three-hour transit around the Cape.

At 0800 Legwen was on the bridge, and Neville sounded the General Quarters alarm. We were still south of the lightship by approximately fourteen miles. At 0926, with the lightship only two miles ahead and the freighter beyond and on the port bow, a high column of black smoke suddenly appeared at the location of the distant vessel. As the smoke rose and dissipated, it was replaced by a geyser of white water. The torpedoed ship remained upright and settled on the bottom in approximately sixty feet of water. Its masts, bridge, funnel, and gaff with the British flag still flying were all above the ocean surface. *Evelyn* rounded the lightship and approached the sunken freighter. We could see clearly three lifeboats in the water, each with a red sail hoisted to the mast. As we got closer, a motor lifeboat could also be seen. Legwen stopped and picked up the captain and crew, and the captain's dog. Legwen invited the captain to the bridge. The other officers and the crew were taken to the mess deck. "Doc" Fignar and "Tiny" Law provided first-aid and food, mostly hot tea, to the very unsettled guests. As anyone on board *Evelyn* would know she was not an ordinary merchantman, Legwen briefed the British captain on *Evelyn*'s mission; he then addressed the assembled group, admonishing them to say nothing about the ship except that she was a small freighter.[11]

The stricken vessel was the 6,160-ton British freighter *Empire Thrush*, operated by the Canadian Pacific Steamship Company. She had been built in Kearney, New Jersey, in 1919 as the SS *Lorain*. *Empire Thrush* was en route from Tampa, Florida, to Halifax, Nova Scotia, to join a convoy for Great Britain. She was fully loaded with a cargo of rock phosphate, citrus pulp, citrus concentrate, and 745 tons of TNT and gunpowder.

The ship was armed with a 4-inch cannon on the poop deck. The gun was manned, but the attacking submarine did not surface. The captain, concerned that a second torpedo hit might detonate the TNT, ordered the crew to abandon ship. There were no personnel casualties. *Evelyn* proceeded to Hampton Roads where the survivors were transferred to a U.S. Navy craft. *Evelyn* then continued on to New York. Kapitänleutnant Rolf Mützelburg in U-203 claimed credit for attacking *Empire Thrush*.[12]

At six o'clock on the morning of 16 April, U-123 was approximately 335 miles east of Cape Lookout, North Carolina. Radioman Heinz Barth copied the following message: "For U-123, commander and crew, I express to you on your new great success my special appreciation. From Supreme Naval Commander [Raeder]." In late afternoon of that same day, U-123's lookout reported a smoke cloud at 80 degrees compass bearing. Then, seven minutes later, two masts and a smokestack were reported at 350 degrees. Hardegen was aware that this area was a junction for the shipping routes from the Windward Passage, between Cuba and Haiti to Canada, and from the northeast ports of the U.S. to the eastern Caribbean and West Indies. He was not surprised by the ship traffic. He selected the steamer bearing 350 as his target. It was on a course of 160 degrees and was heading in the direction of the surfaced U-123. It was 1844 local time, about half an hour before dusk. The cautious Hardegen took the boat down to periscope depth and waited for his target to come closer: "I want to have a good look at it through the periscope while it is still light."[13]

The commander let the freighter pass within three hundred meters. He estimated the size at 5,000 GRT. He saw machine guns, but no heavy weapons. Cargo booms were secured to the masts. Many huge, yellow-painted boilerlike tanks and uncrated trucks were loaded on the main deck between the masts. "A worthwhile target," said Hardegen to von Schroeter. "I have to fire very economically to sink it with so little ammunition." U-123 fell in behind the steamer. At 2011 U-123 was brought to the surface. For an hour and forty minutes, in the darkness, the U-boat made a broad sweep around the right side of the target to a position well in front. The time was used to bring Schüler and his crews on deck to prepare the artillery pieces and to break out the now "ready" ammunition. At 2150 Hardegen and von Schroeter had the boat running slow-ahead forward of and off the starboard bow of the freighter. They waited for it to approach within range at four hundred meters. At 2155 Hardegen gave the command to open fire. The first several 10.5-centimeter projectiles hit the bridge structure. After ten hits, Schüler's forward gun put eight rounds into the waterline at the engine room. As the target moved ahead, U-123 was brought around its stern and up the port side. The upper decks were then raked with the 3.7-centimeter rapid fire guns.

The ship transmitted its call letters, but did not state its name or location, only "en route from Norfolk to Guadeloupe. Captain injured, crew in lifeboats." The ship's call letters were located in the international call letters listing and identified as the SS *Point Brava*, 4,834 GRT. Hardegen permitted its crew to leave the ship in lifeboats. He then resumed firing. The ship was abandoned with the rudder hard right and the engine at full speed ahead. Fire swept through the upper decks. After two hours, 27 rounds of 10.5-centimeter, 86 rounds of 3.7-centimeter, and 120 rounds of 2-centimeter had been fired at and into the target; it settled stern first into Davy Jones's locker. Hardegen added the eleventh ship to his tally with an increase of tonnage, by his count, from 74,815 to 79,649. The "very satisfied" U-boat commander resumed his homeward voyage on course 60 degrees. Hardegen's target was correctly identified by its original name, *Point Brava*. But the name had been changed to SS *Alcoa Guide*, and it was owned by the Alcoa Steamship Company, a U.S. firm. The captain and one seaman died of wounds from the intense gunfire. Five crew members were missing. Twenty-seven survivors were rescued on 19 April by the destroyer USS *Broome* (DD210).[14]

On 23 April, in the mid-Atlantic, U-123 vibrated with new excitement. A radio message was received from the Führer awarding Hardegen the Oak Leaf Cluster to his Knight's Cross of the Iron Cross. On 2 May 1942, with the customary band, the girls with flowers, and the usual array of military personnel and civilian workmen, U-123 glided slowly toward the Keroman bunkers at Lorient. To Hardegen's great surprise, standing next to Admiral Dönitz was Grossadmiral Raeder. Hardegen was pleased to see the two admirals; he was also thankful that, as he brought U-123 coasting toward the dock, his approach and seamanship were flawless. He could be heard giving the fewest of possible maneuvering commands to his LI and helmsman as his boat settled gently against the wooden fenders, with the bridge precisely in line with where Raeder and Dönitz were standing. Somewhat unkempt and grimy, all U-123's officers and men not involved in ship's work stood in ranks on deck. The homemade tonnage pennant flew proudly from the periscope.[15]

U-123 was made fast alongside the Keroman dock and the gangplank was moved into place and secured. The first to come aboard was Raeder, followed closely by Dönitz. The Grossadmiral announced to the assembled crew his pleasure with U-123's patrol to American waters and the tonnage sunk. He further stated that he would personally inspect the crew on the next day and would award Iron Cross decorations, as appropriate. Raeder told Hardegen that he would be awarded the Oak Leaf Cluster to his Knight's Cross of the Iron Cross directly from the hands of the Führer. He then invited U-123's commander to lunch, where they were joined by other U-boat commanders including KL Erich Topp.[16]

The formal inspection of the officers and crew by the Grossadmiral took place as scheduled. Key enlisted personnel as recommended by Hardegen were awarded Iron Crosses by "Onkel Karl." Von Schroeter and Mertens were promoted to the next higher rank. Following the inspection, Herr Kaleu flew to Paris, the location of Dönitz's new headquarters. There der Löwe, the Lion, reviewed Hardegen's carefully prepared KTB. He was pleased that U-123 had traveled 9,228 nautical miles, exceeding the design range of the IXB boat by some 695 miles. The fact that Herr Kaleu brought the boat into Keroman on E-motors (batteries) with no diesel fuel in the tanks was a matter noted but not discussed. The Lion's endorsement of the written report was replete with complimentary phrases: outstanding success; unique achievement; superbly executed; exemplary spirit. In response to the admiral's request, Hardegen provided a brief written commentary on his two patrols. Dönitz would use this "lessons learned" treatise as a primer and cautionary reminder for the U-boat commanders departing on their first western Atlantic patrol.[17]

Hardegen returned to Lorient for a brief period. Then he and Erich Topp were flown to eastern Germany for an audience with the Führer. The meeting was intended to boost morale by recognizing outstanding service by military commanders. The award of the coveted Oak Leaf Cluster was an honor for any recipient. To receive it from the hands of the Führer was a double honor for most; it was more a curiosity for others. For Raeder and Dönitz the ceremony was an opportunity to parade the naval uniform in the eyes of Hitler, who was not an ardent supporter of the sea service.

Once again we have the opportunity to examine the conduct of the two U-boat commanders, Hardegen and Topp. This time the comparison relates to personalities rather than their tactical competence as U-boat commanders. The loyalty of both to their fatherland is unquestioned as are their honor and dignity. Neither officer was flamboyant, but Topp was more reserved than Hardegen. Topp's restraint is evident in his concise entries in his KTB. His verbal statements were equally terse and restrained. Unlike Hardegen, Schepke, Lüth, and a few other U-boat commanders, Topp, like "Silent Otto" Kretschmer, preferred not to participate in propaganda speeches or writing articles based on his patrols and successes. He did appear, however, in some wartime newsreels and news accounts. As a U-boat ace in the "Red Devil" boat, he could do no less. In 1946 he supported Admiral Dönitz at Nürnberg. His personal conduct no doubt contributed to his success in the Bundesmarine, where he achieved the rank of vice admiral. He later published his memoir, *Flares over the Atlantic*.[18]

Reinhard Hardegen, on the other hand, was more expressive and professorial, no doubt a trait inherited from his father. He adhered to the generally accepted code that maintained the dignity of command: Don't fraternize with the crew. He made detailed and extensive entries in his KTB, acutely aware that this was a form of direct monologue to be read by his superiors at headquarters and especially the admiral. He recognized the importance of recording his observations, analyses, insights, and conclusions for the good of the U-boat service. Admiral Dönitz appreciated the contributions of this capable Kapitänleutnant.

The ceremonial meeting with the Führer was followed by dinner with Hitler and several senior general officers. It provided the U-123 commander a once-in-a-lifetime audience before which he could express his views —if given the opportunity. He responded to what might be considered an unintended opportunity from Hitler himself. According to Hardegen's own recollection, Hitler noted the Luftwaffe winged insignia he wore on his naval uniform and asked about its source. Hardegen responded that he had been a pilot in the naval arm of the air force. As the Führer and his distinguished guests, including Topp, dined on the carefully prepared food, the young U-boat ace delivered a tutorial on strategy and tactics that included the lack of wisdom on the part of the general staff in eliminating the naval air arm, the loss of *Bismarck*, the need for air support of U-boat operations, lessons to be learned from the Italians and the Japanese, and so forth and so on. Hitler's controlled rage and "fist on the table" concluded both lunch and Hardegen's discourse. Apparently there were no adverse repercussions. Admiral Dönitz had already decided that Kapitänleutnant Hardegen would be transferred to the Training Flotilla located on the Gulf of Danzig, at what is now Gdynia, Poland. Horst von Schroeter was given command of U-123. Admiral Dönitz agreed to the assignment of this relatively junior officer based on the strong recommendation of Hardegen.[19]

On 18 April 1942, some thirty-six hours after the sinking of the freighter SS *Alcoa Guide* and almost two weeks before U-123 arrived at Lorient, Legwen brought *Evelyn* past Ambrose light and entered the channel to New York harbor. Hardegen, too, had seen this light and the view of Coney Island just sixty days before. As we entered the Narrows, I could see the apartment building and windows at 9701 Shore Road, my home. It was a warm feeling, indeed. After the Narrows, we entered Gowanus Bay by Red Bank, Brooklyn, and the Atlantic Basin Iron Works. We were about to conclude our first patrol. We had no broom at our foremast, nor tonnage pennant at our main, but we were home. In a short time, we would be ready to sail again.

Any war patrol that ends with a bit of humor can be said to enjoy some degree of success. This one was no exception. Shipyard management at the Iron Works had been advised of our requirements and the need to expedite repairs. Accordingly, we were directed to place *Evelyn* in the dry dock rather than at a wharf or pier. Schwaner was on the poopdeck aft so as to direct the handling of stern lines and to keep an eye on the concealed ordnance. Chief Quartermaster Lionel Cook was on the forecastle in charge of forward line handlers and the anchor detail. There was no sound-powered telephone circuit on the forecastle, so all orders had to be passed by voice from the bridge. It was not a far distance. *Evelyn* was assisted only by a small yard-pusher boat for entering the old, narrow, wooden, floating dry dock. It had been flooded down to receive the ship between its two side panels. The wind was not helpful in attempting to ease the ship between the two sidewalls, so a considerable amount of line handling was required: "Hold the port bow spring line; slack off the starboard after breast line; take up the slack in the starboard forward breast line," and so forth. Chief Quartermaster Cook knew shiphandling as well as anyone and, for the most part, could anticipate orders from the bridge and give directions to his line handling crew.

Roger Metz on the bridge was aware, of course, of Cook's deaf ear but was not unduly concerned. That is, until a gust of wind from the reverse direction pushed the ship toward what had been the windward side, the starboard side. "Take in the slack and hold on to the port breast line," came the order from Legwen. "What did he say?" asked Cook of the person standing beside him. "Let go the port anchor" was the reply—from no one other than Mercury "Fleet-feet" Brown, who was standing at Cook's elbow. "Let go the port anchor," commanded Cook. No sailor in his right mind dared challenge the command of Chief Quartermaster Cook. The sledge hammer hit the pelican hook with a clang, and the anchor and chain rattled down the hawse pipe in a cloud of rust and the roar of a thousand thundering kettledrums. Into the water and through the wooden flooring of the dry dock went the anchor and a considerable length of chain.

Legwen's arms flew in all directions castigating the actions of the forecastle crew and yelling about both the line and the anchor. Boatswain's Mate Second Class Ulis Stansbury, also on the forecastle, had the presence of mind to correctly carry out Legwen's order regarding the breast line. But Cook was still engrossed in aural communications with the bridge, neither hearing nor understanding the commands. "What did he say?" asked Cook once more. "Let go the starboard anchor," said "Fleet-feet" with authority and conviction. "Let go the starboard anchor," demanded Cook before Stansbury could get his attention. The chief had spoken and clang went the pelican hook, up came the rust dust, and down went the starboard anchor into the water and through the wooden deck of the dry dock. It was anchors "away" all right, but not the traditional words or sounds of the U.S. Naval Academy marching band. A payment of four thousand dollars from the account of the Asterion Shipping Company to the Atlantic Basin Iron Works for miscellaneous services restored the wooden dry dock. The former Seaman First Class Mercury "Fleetfeet" Brown of Norfolk, Virginia, became Seaman Second Class Brown and the hero of the mess deck. The "three cups of coffee" incident had been avenged.

The second cruise of USS *Asterion*/SS *Evelyn* began on 4 May 1942. She had all items on the "fix" list repaired, but in the minds of many on board, she was still of marginal seaworthiness and very expendable. *Evelyn* completed six patrols, which took her to all corners of the Atlantic Coast, Gulf of Mexico, and the Caribbean Sea in search of U-boats. She witnessed many sinkings but was never offered the opportunity to attack, probably because of her small size. There is no evidence that any U-boat commander ever recognized her as a Q-ship.

On 10 January 1943 *Evelyn* arrived in New York from Trinidad. Her condition was such that the damage section of the Navy Department confirmed the opinion of Legwen that she could not successfully withstand even one torpedo hit and remain an effective fighting unit. By the time she was upgraded, 14 October 1943, the Tenth Fleet was organized and operating. The convoy system and the navy "hunter-killer" task groups, employing escort carriers and improved antisubmarine warfare destroyers and escorts, were becoming highly successful against the German U-boats. The worst was over and the services of *Evelyn*/*Asterion* were no longer required. She was transferred to the U.S. Coast Guard, served as a weather ship, was declared unseaworthy and scrapped. Her tasks greatly exceeded her abilities. The gallant old ship endured the abuses until she could function no more. For those who sailed in USS *Asterion* during her employment as a U-boat decoy, she will always be thought of as a proud and noble lady.

USS *Asterion* operated during the very deadly period of the battle of the shallows of the Atlantic coast. By Dönitz's own data, the rate of sinkings in North American waters for the period of January 1942 to 14 March 1942 was 1.2 ships per day. For the period 15 March 1942 to 20 April 1942, 2.2 ships per day. Then came the dramatic decline in successful attacks. From 21 April to 19 July 1942, the daily rate did not exceed 0.7. It was during this last period that the total number of U-boats operating at one time in the North American Zone, Cape Sable to Key West, reached its peak of sixteen to eighteen.[20] And during this period U.S. forces accounted for six U-boat kills:

U-352, KL Helmuth Rathke, by USCGC *Icarus*
U-157, KK Wolf Henne, by USCGC *Thetis*
U-158, KL Erich Rostin, by Patrol Squadron 74
U-701, KL Horst Degen, by U.S. Army Bomber Squadron 396
U-153, KK Wilfried Reichmann, by U.S. Army Bomber Squadron 59 and USS *Lansdowne*
U-576, KL Dieter Heinicke, by U.S. Navy Squadron VS9 and Armed Guard Unit on SS *Unicoi*[21]

Before 15 April, three U-boats were sunk by U.S. forces:

U-656, KL Kröning, by U.S. Navy Squadron VP82
U-503, KL Gericke, by U.S. Navy Squadron VP82
U-85, OL Eberhard Greger, by USS *Roper* (DD147)

Indeed, the U-boat blitz on the American coast was over. While some sinkings continued, especially in the far reaches of the Caribbean around Trinidad, Aruba, and the Panama Canal, made possible by the introduction of U-tankers, the cost to Dönitz in terms of U-boat losses began to mount. By the end of 1942, after losing fifteen boats to U.S. forces, Dönitz redeployed his U-boats to the North Atlantic convoy area and to the southeast Atlantic. In 1942 sixty-one U-boats were lost in the Atlantic and eighty-five worldwide.

For Dönitz, the situation never did improve. In May 1943 he lost thirty-eight U-boats, or 32.2 percent of his operating force. It is true that November 1942 was a disastrous month for Allied shipping in the Atlantic with 603,000 tons sunk, an average of about three ships per day. But by May 1943 this figure was reduced to 212,000 tons, one ship per day. Also, by now the Allied shipbuilding industry was beginning to launch ships far in excess of the losses. Dönitz's strategy in the short term may have been successful, but the achievement of his primary goal is questionable. From the viewpoint of the total war and its outcome, Paukenschlag and the subsequent operations in America's coastal waters were inconsequential. War is a game of strategy and tactics, but the outcome is often determined by chance. For Dönitz, Paukenschlag was a bold move, a deviation from the strategy of attacking convoys. The calculated risk was whether the change in tactics would produce the overwhelming or "tremendous blow" to Allied shipping in American coastal waters the admiral anticipated. The Lion's future unequivocally was linked to the success of this bold venture.

It is important to understand the German U-boat strategy from their point of view as it applied to the western Atlantic from late 1941 to June 1942. The U-boat offensive in American coastal waters was analyzed and recorded by Frigattenkapitän Günter Hessler, a son-in-law of Admiral Dönitz, a former U-boat commander (U-107), and the operations officer to Flag Office U-boats. Hessler's findings were translated and published by Her Majesty's Stationery Office under the title *German Naval History: The U-Boat War in the Atlantic, 1939–1945*. The work was done after the war at the request of the British admiralty. The report provided some interesting insights into the thinking of Dönitz and the U-boat staff during that period. A summary of the principal points is provided in the following paragraphs.[22]

As early as September 1941, the German naval staff concluded that "action should be taken against American vessels carrying supplies to Britain." Dönitz was party to this proposal and, as cited by Hessler, so stated in his war diary on 15 May 1942: "What counts in the long run is the preponderance of sinkings over new construction. Shipbuilding and arms production are centered in the American zone. . . . By attacking the supply traffic . . . in the American zone, I am striking at the root of the evil." According to Hessler, Dönitz made the commitment that "if only he could have his boats ready off the U.S. coast at the outbreak of war, he would be able to deliver a tremendous and sudden blow—*einen kräftigen Paukenschlag.*" The September proposal was rejected by Hitler "on political grounds." He did not want to provoke America into entering the war.

However, the Pearl Harbor attack precipitated Germany's declaration of war and the lifting of the restrictions on offensive actions against U.S. naval units and merchant ships. Dönitz had his Paukenschlag.

The German naval staff, according to Hessler, planned on the basis that American antisubmarine forces lacked experience and U-boats could operate near U.S. ports where the local defenses would be ineffective. Hardegen in U-123 confirmed the inadequacy of the United States' initial defenses. In the time frame of 1939 to early 1942, Hessler's assessment that "American antisubmarine forces lacked experience" was indeed a correct observation. The fact is the U.S. Navy had no organized antisubmarine capability. This was documented in late 1944 or early 1945 when Admiral King directed his staff at headquarters of the commander in chief (COMINCH), U.S. Fleet, to undertake a review of "antisubmarine operations against the German U-Boats in World War II." In response, a detailed summary, classified Top Secret (now declassified), including eight references and twelve enclosures, provided COMINCH with the data necessary to lay the foundation for the plan for the postwar peacetime navy. The report stated the obvious:

> Like most other U.S. naval activities, A/S [antisubmarine] developments between World Wars I and II suffered from lack of a continuing program. It is probable that A/S matters suffered more than the average because there was no agency of any importance, or having any real weight of authority, to push developments and tactics.
>
> Except for improvements in echo-ranging equipment, there were practically no advancements made in A/S equipment between World War I and II. . . .
>
> Suffice it to say that . . . until the spring of 1943, we were not doing as well as we should have liked in the antisubmarine war . . . largely because of lack of forces, inability to train forces we did have available, owing to their continued operational employment, and the use of outmoded tactics and equipment. All sorts of miscellaneous surface craft had been put into service.[23]

Considering the United States' state of unpreparedness, it is no wonder that Roosevelt and King, in January 1942, resorted to the expendable Q-ships as an expedient tactic to fill the temporary antisubmarine void.

Not until April–May 1942 did Allied forces begin to make their presence along the American coast felt. Hessler observed that from April onward it was unsafe for U-boats to attack except at night and during moonless periods. The boats were vulnerable to the increased number of patrol vessels and aircraft. The first kill along the coast was made on 14 April when U-85 was sunk near Cape Hatteras. U-576 and U-701 were lost on 15 June and 7 July, respectively, also in the Hatteras area. In May, Hessler noted, sinkings of Allied vessels along the coast began to decline, and it was necessary to reconsider the U.S. coastal battle. He concluded, "On 19th July the two boats still operating near Cape Hatteras were ordered to evacuate the coastal area. Thus the increasing ascendancy of the American A/S forces drove us from the coast, and henceforth it was our intention to send only single boats there occasionally, and perhaps to lay mines off the ports."[24]

Dönitz considered his Paukenschlag operation and American coastal battle a success. This conclusion is subject to challenge. For political reasons within the German high command, that is to appease Hitler and curry his favor, it was in the admiral's best interest to emphasize individual U-boat successes, such as U-123 (Hardegen) and U-552 (Topp), rather than the somewhat disappointing reports of average tonnage sunk per boat. Reporting apparent shortfalls from his expected goal of crippling the Allied supply line would only jeopardize the position of the Kriegsmarine, which was in competition with the Luftwaffe and Wehrmacht for Germany's limited resources. Some historians identified the Paukenschlag operation as the "Pearl Harbor of the Atlantic." Considering the lives lost and the ships and material destroyed, there can be no argument that the uncontested attacks on Allied merchant shipping were serious. However, it is difficult to make an objective judgment as to the overall results, the precise level of achievement or failure. One approach would be to evaluate the operation in terms of whether it accomplished Dönitz's intended objective. Another would be to measure the impacts of the attacks on the political attitude and military-industrial responsiveness of the United States.

Paukenschlag was a decisive strike, but it could hardly be termed a "tremendous blow," as Dönitz intended. It would seem reasonable for Dönitz to expect his five boats to destroy seven or eight targets each for a total of thirty-five to forty to meet his goal. They attacked only twenty-four, or 60 to 69 percent of expectations. While Dönitz might consider the extended coastal battle a tactical success, there is ample evidence that, strategically, it was a failure or at best had minimal impact on the flow of supplies to Europe. For a short period the coastal offensive did threaten the lifeline to the British Isles and to Murmansk and Archangle. But a thorough study of the U-boat operations in American waters can only conclude that in the overall evaluation of the Battle of the Atlantic, the threat was more significant than the losses actually suffered.

Pearl Harbor, Germany's declaration of war, and the U-boat attacks along the coast all gave credence to the efforts made by Roosevelt to prepare the United States for war. Industrial mobilization planning and implementation had already begun. The president had formed the War Production Board, and annual goals were set for the building of guns, tanks, aircraft, and merchant ships. The target for merchant ship production was set at 8 million deadweight tons for 1942 and 10 million for 1943. Construction of the DE (destroyer escort) type ship had already begun. Congress willingly appropriated the necessary funds to support this "incredible program."

To counter the loss of ships and material, the navy placed added emphasis on an antisubmarine program. Admiral King established an antisubmarine analysis unit, a convoy and routing section within his office, and special schools and training courses for antisubmarine warfare. He focused on the North Atlantic and the interface with the British and Russians. King relegated to the newly established Sea Frontiers the responsibility for operations in coastal waters. The Sea Frontiers pressed into service a variety of Coast Guard cutters and patrol craft, converted yachts, and some twenty-two armed trawlers on loan from the British, manned with experienced officers and crew. By 1 July 1942 these efforts caused Dönitz to retreat from the American coastal campaign. While Samuel Morison thought the Paukenschlag Operation a "merry massacre" and "humiliating" to the United States, there is little if any evidence of humiliation on the part of the president, the Congress, or the no-longer apathetic American public.[25]

Dönitz's self-proclaimed Paukenschlag success, without doubt, was attributed in no small part to Hardegen. The admiral gave his Kapitän-leutnant an appropriate reward: Sea command for the ace concluded with his return from his second patrol to American waters. Kals, Zapp, Mohr, and Topp also achieved their individual tonnage goals and received their awards. But other U-boat commanders did not sink the tonnage the admiral had expected. While Dönitz deserves much credit for the concept of Paukenschlag, the totality of the operation must be considered in evaluating and determining its degree of success. The deficit was in the implementation of the plan.

Horst von Schroeter took command of U-123 and made several more war patrols but none to the Western Atlantic. Von Schroeter survived the war, remained in the German peacetime navy, the Bundesmarine, and rose to the rank of vice admiral. U-123 was located in Lorient at the end of hostilities and eventually was scrapped by the French government.

In early 1945 Reinhard Hardegen, with the rank of Korvettenkapitän, served on Grand Admiral Dönitz's staff at Flensburg-Mürwick. There, with other staff members, he surrendered to the British who imprisoned him based on a mistaken identity with a member of the Waffen SS also named Hardegen. After eighteen months in prison, the matter was cleared up mainly through the efforts of Barbara Hardegen who provided proof of his name and his U-boat service. Hardegen returned to his home in Bremen to raise his family; serve his city in Parliament; form and manage a marine oil distribution company; and retire. He travels the world from pole to pole and continent to continent, mostly on the surface.

While *Evelyn* was retired from Q-ship service in 1943, the officers and men of the former U.S. mystery ship still had fighting to do at sea in both the Atlantic and the Pacific. Advances in technology would replace basic electrical and manually controlled machinery. Warships, for the most part, would be of "modern" design, rather than World War I– or 1920-vintage. And most important, tactics would no longer dictate a passive mode. *Evelyn/Asterion* had been expendable; she was expected to absorb the first hit and then lure the U-boat to the surface. Hopefully, this desperate measure has been removed from the books of naval strategy and

200   Q-SHIPS VERSUS U-BOATS

tactics. *Asterion*'s officers and men welcomed the change of duty and the return to the "regular and modern" U.S. Navy.

Glenn Walker Legwen was promoted to the rank of commander while in *Asterion*. In early 1944 he took command of Escort Division 47. For heroic service in operations against the enemy during the amphibious invasion of southern France, he was awarded the Bronze Star. Later, on the staff of commander, Amphibious Group 8, he participated in the assault and capture of Mindanao in the Philippines and Balikpapan, Borneo, and then the occupation of Nagoya, Japan. Legwen was promoted to the rank of captain in 1945. He retired from active duty in 1957 and died 12 December 1981.

Lawrence (Larry) Robert Neville was promoted to commander in 1944 and captain in 1952. In 1944 he joined the staff of commander, Seventh Fleet in the Western Pacific. While serving as fleet operations officer, he was awarded the Legion of Merit with combat V for "exceptionally meritorious conduct during operations against enemy Japanese forces." After the war Captain Neville served in command and staff positions, including assistant attaché at the American Embassy in Rome. Neville retired on 1 November 1959 with the rank of rear admiral. He died 9 January 1986.

Henry C. (Dutch) Schwaner Jr., while on board *Asterion*, was advanced to the rank of lieutenant commander. In 1944 he was promoted to commander and saw duty in the cruiser USS *Chester*. There he was engaged in enemy action during raids on the Japanese-held islands of Palau, Yap, Ulithi, and Woleai. This was followed by bombardments of Marcus Island and operations in the Kurile Islands, at Leyte in the Philippines, Iwo Jima, Okinawa Gunto, and the Japanese homeland. After hostilities ended he served in various offices and commands, including the Office of the Chief of Naval Operations and as commander, Escort Division 42, where he was promoted to the rank of captain. Later he was given command of Destroyer Squadron 36. Captain Schwaner died 8 December 1965 of cardiac arrest while on active duty.

Guy Brown Ray retired from the navy in October 1946 with the rank of lieutenant commander. He died in Seattle, Washington, on 3 January 1969.

Lionel M. Cook, who came aboard *Asterion* as a chief quartermaster, was later commissioned ensign and then lieutenant. He retired in 1946 and is deceased.

Roger C. Metz, the assistant quartermaster to Chief Cook, was commissioned ensign while in *Asterion*. Metz advanced through the ranks after the war. During the Korean conflict, he was commanding officer, USS LSM355, and LSM Division 32 commander. As a lieutenant commander, he was commanding officer, USS *Basset* (APD73). After promotion to commander, he saw duty as executive officer, USS *Taconic* (AGC17). Roger Metz retired in 1960 and lived in Westerville, Ohio. He died in August 1996.

John Lukowich changed his surname to Luke and apparently resigned from the naval service. His postwar record could not be located.

As for me, I left *Asterion* on 9 October 1943, for a ten-month tour of shore duty. During this time I married my Barbara. Most of 1945 was spent aboard a service force ship providing logistics support to the fleets in the Western Pacific: Eniwetok Atoll, Ulithi Atoll, Leyte Gulf, and Okinawa. After the war I transferred to the regular navy with the rank of lieutenant commander and remained in the supply corps. During the next five years I served in various billets ashore, including the nuclear weapons program, and was promoted to the rank of commander. After completing the master's program at Harvard Business School, I was assigned to the attack carrier USS *Bennington* (CVA20), then to Washington, D.C., first to the Naval Supply Systems Command, later to the new Bureau of Naval Weapons. In 1959 I advanced to the rank of captain and was transferred to the staff of commander, Task Force Seventy-three (Mobile Logistics Support Force, Seventh Fleet), embarked in USS *Ajax* (AR6), and based in Sasebo, Japan. In 1963 I returned to the United States to duty at the Electronics Supply Office as executive officer and then commanding officer. My final tour was with the Department of Defense on special assignment to the assistant secretary, Installations and Logistics. The navy saw fit to award me the Legion of Merit. I retired from active duty in 1968 and for seventeen years found a second career in management with Ingalls Shipbuilding Division, Litton Systems. This, to my great satisfaction, I found to be an agreeable addendum to my naval service, for it placed me in the midst of several of the navy's most advanced ship design and construction programs: the *Spruance*-class destroyers, the *Tarawa*-class amphibious assault ships, the *Ticonderoga*-class Aegis cruiser, and the beginning of the *Arleigh Burke*–class Aegis destroyers. After a total of twenty years in private industry, I again retired to concentrate on being a novice author to tell this story.

One final word on Project LQ. The veil of secrecy hung like a shroud over the project long after the *Atik* affair and the transfer of *Asterion* to the U.S. Coast Guard. Only a few officers at Eastern Sea Frontier, who sponsored the Q-ship USS *Big Horn*, a tanker hull, and those who sailed in her maintained an interest in decoy-ship operations. *Big Horn* was no more successful than *Asterion*. Roosevelt, King, Nimitz, and Horne had other much more important things to do: fighting a war on a global scale. Furthermore, because of U.S. technology and industrial might, better weapons were now available to use against the U-boats. Indeed, by late 1943 Dönitz's "happy times" were over and his desperate times began. At the end of the war Project LQ was fragmented in secret files entombed in security vaults in a few offices in the Navy Department. Surviving officers and men who had sailed in *Asterion* and *Big Horn* looked back through the haze and smoke of the North Africa landing, the southern Europe invasion, D-day, and the Western Pacific campaigns and recalled those exciting yet frustrating days of setting the U-boat trap as just another tour of duty.

According to the last roster filed with the Navy Department, 133 enlisted personnel and 6 officers were lost in *Atik*. The next of kin of each officer and man was notified on 7 May 1942 that his or her relative "was missing following action in the performance of his duty and in the service of his Country. He was officially reported missing in action as of 27 March 1942 when the ship in which he was serving was long overdue and presumed lost in the North Atlantic area." No further official correspondence was provided for two years, until 5 May 1944 when the Bureau of Naval Personnel advised that in accordance with public law, the missing servicemen were presumed dead on 5 April 1944. Under the date of 5 April 1944, President Franklin D. Roosevelt signed and forwarded a certificate in memory of each of the deceased servicemen. In a letter dated

8 May 1944, the acting secretary of the navy, James Forrestal, offered his personal condolences. On 7 July 1944, the secretary of the navy awarded the Purple Heart, posthumously, to each person serving and lost in *Atik*.

Understandably, there was considerable anxiety and grave concern on the part of the families. They had little or no information during the period 7 May 1942 to 5 May 1944 as to the status of their relatives. The Navy Department knew no better way to proceed with this personally sensitive and highly classified matter. There was no better way. *Atik's* war, like *Asterion's*, was a secret war, and the few facts known to the Navy Department could not be revealed. The families of USS *Atik's* officers and men endured uncertainty, skepticism, and suspicion regarding the status of their missing relatives. The frustration and mental anguish suffered by the families left in a state of vagueness—"missing in action"—must be recognized and addressed here. The newlywed Mrs. Joyce, the dissenting Mrs. Deckelman, the acquiescent Mrs. Beckett, the family of the bachelor Armand "Frenchy" Ouellette, the wife and children of Chief Yeoman Daniel Kosmider, the parents of the young ensign Edwin Leonard, and the many others who had loved ones serving in *Atik* all must have experienced the day-to-day pain of this perplexing silence, not for a week or three, but for almost two years.

Most families apparently waited in silence; a few did not. Mrs. Deckelman, Mrs. Beckett, and Mrs. Joyce, together, visited Eastern Sea Frontier headquarters in New York and learned nothing. Ethel Deckelman, later Ethel Delston, expressed her grief in her novel *Of Love Remembered* published in 1972. Mrs. Paul H. Leonard of Columbia, South Carolina, mother of Ensign Leonard, on 12 January 1946, wrote to the secretary of the navy, James Forrestal, with a copy to Sen. Burnet Maybank, asking many questions and reviewing her unsuccessful efforts to obtain information regarding her son. Her near despair was evident in her statement: "I am deeply hurt that the Navy has overlooked those of us whose hearts have been so torn and hurt for almost four years by failing to give us facts it evidently had and withheld." No copy of or reference to a reply to Mrs. Leonard was found in the archives, although there is on file at the Naval Historical Center a marked-up copy of an unclassified memorandum from Admiral Horne to the secretary of the navy, dated

18 March 1946. This suggests that a draft letter might have been prepared and an unclassified response made. Without doubt, the absence of a meaningful response to the families before the end of the war was based on the need for the utmost secrecy of Project LQ.

On 15 June 1946 Captain Legwen forwarded to the chief of Naval Operations a recommendation for appropriate commendations for officers and men of *Asterion* and *Atik*. Legwen's nine-page letter detailed the unusual nature of the mission and the hazards involved in that "neither ship was expected to last longer than a month after commencement of assigned duty." (This proved to be true for *Atik*.) He outlined accomplishments and praised his officers and men. There is no record to be found of action taken or a reply made to Legwen's letter. It has been stated by some authors that Cdr. Harry Hicks, as commanding officer of *Atik*, had been awarded the Navy Cross posthumously. The Office of the Secretary of the Navy has no record of such an award.

Across the Kieler Förde from Kiel, Germany, is the U-Boot-Ehrenmal, the U-Boat Memorial. Cast in bronze is the name of each German officer and man lost in the submarine service. For the period 1914 to 1918, 5,249 names are listed. For World War II, 1939–45, the names of 33,003 men and 739 boats are cast in the bronze plates that fill both sides of the open U-shaped corridor that forms that channel of honor. One of the names under U-123 is Fähnrich z. S. Rudy Holzer. Although Midshipman Holzer is buried alone at sea not far from where *Atik* rests, his memorial stands proudly among those of his comrades for all to see. He, too, is a part of the story of Project LQ and the American coastal campaign of World War II.

For those who died aboard *Atik* in her secret and lonely war, there is no special remembrance except in the hearts of their families and friends. They were expended and almost forgotten. Hopefully the telling of this story will serve as a reminder if not a recognition of their heroism. They were among the valiant in what would become the greatest navy the world has ever known.

The recognized intelligence expert, researcher, and author Ladislas Farago, in his book *The Tenth Fleet*, gives a succinct and objective evaluation of the U.S. Navy's Q-ship project:

Despite its futility, and even though it claimed the lives of one hundred and forty-one officers and men in an unproductive adventure, the project stands out as one of the sagas of the anti-U-boat campaign. It was mounted when we had nothing better to throw into the breach—when it was our sole aggressive effort to harm the marauders. The mystery ships demanded the utmost in seamanship and courage from their officers and men. If nothing else, they created an offensive spirit when the defensive was trump and defeatism was still rampant on the East Coast.[26]

With those thoughts I conclude my story. I am pleased to have served.

Audentes Deus ipse iuvat [God himself helps the brave].

Appendix 1:
Ship's Roster (Enlisted Men),
USS *Atik*/SS *Carolyn*

(Names alphabetically arranged without regard to ratings)

Appleate, Gilbert B.

Arledge, Kenneth U.

Bagley, Hollis F.

Bailey, Forrest A.

Barr, Jack F.

Bell, Robert E.

Barnard, Robert D.

Blaine, Robert E.

Blum, Carl H.

Bowen, Leroy M.

Boyd, Charles S.

Boykin, David S.

Brunet, Frank

Buck, Kenneth M.

Burgess, Roy E.

Burton, John W.

Cahalan, Frank R.

Cash, Lester M.

Cerveny, Bert M.

Cinowalt, William J.

Clem, Fred E.

Clinkinbeard, Willis

Collins, James P.

Cornwell, Irving G.

Czinky, William J.

Dalton, John F.

Dana, Edwin L.

Darrah, Henry C.

Davenport, Joseph M.

De Witt, Charles F.

Deatrick, Ralph M.

Dibble, Harold V.

Dykeman, Harold E.

Eiseman, Irving

Embrogno, Joseph

Finnegan, John J., Jr.

Freeland, Owen W.

Galusha, Lawrence A.

Garcia, Manuel, Jr.

Gayde, Peter A.

Goddard, John D.

Goebel, Henry J.

Golden, Walter S., Jr.

Goodman, Robert C.

Guest, Vernon W.

Haas, Walter J.

Hall, Raymond A.

Hall, William F., Jr.

Haynes, John D.

Heath, Fred T.

Hedrick, Charles E.

Holcomb, Byron E.

Hoyle, Carl E.

Huber, Lowell H.

Irvin, Stuart

James, Edward F.

Jared, Benjamin E.

Jarvis, William H.

Johannes, Charles J.

Johnson, Elbert M.

Jordan, Joseph F.

Kaiser, George J.

Kilsby, Thomas B.

Kinder, Murhl F.

Kosmider, Daniel

Kowalewski, Charles S.

Kutz, William I.

Lane, William G.

Langeliers, Terrance H.

Lanham, Richard N.

Little, James N.

Low, Donald Banks

Lucas, Myrton A.

Mantel, Julius A.

Maple, Chester A.

Mathis, Jewell Asa

May, Robert Elias

McArther, Ernest K.

McCall, Herbert H.

Michelswirth, Anthony G.

Miller, Charles Alva

Nichols, Edward
Ouellette, Armand R.
Pittman, Roy Lee
Quatrara, Anthony D.
Ray, Don Edison
Roberts, Raymond J.
Roth, Richard
Schow, Clifford W.
Smith, Clarence Edw.
Snow, William D.
Stevenson, Wilbur W.
Storer, Max C.
Sutton, Theodore R.
Temte, Robert
Vairetta, Stephen P.
White, Woodrow W.
Wool, Meyer T.
Zeringue, Philip J.

Noble, Wilson P.
Pamperin, Robert W.
Podres, Ladislaus
Raines, Horace F.
Rice, John, Jr.
Robertson, John A.
Sanko, Francis P.
Schultz, Leo F.
Smith, Clarence Eug.
Sparrow, Joseph P.
Stewart, Thomas A.
Stumpf, Bernard W.
Taylor, Donald C.
Theobald, Rudolf H.
Walker, Noel J.
Wilson, John G.
Young, Carroll

Olesnevich, George J.
Paredes, Manuel N.
Poppas, Edward
Rathsack, Walter C.
Rickard, Len Grundy
Robusto, Louis J.
Schmidt, Adam J.
Seely, William H.
Smith, George Blane
Stephenson, Lionel
Stinchcombe, Guy, Jr.
Surma, John
Templeton, Chester H.
Thompson, Jessie D.
Warner, Joe H.
Woodside, Joe L.
Zeiger, Joseph M.

Appendix 2:
Precommissioning Detail
(Key Petty Officers), USS *Atik* (AK101)

Lieutenant Duffy, executive officer and navigator; Chief Quartermaster John Dalton; Roy Burgess, quartermaster first class; Chief Yeoman Daniel Kosmider; Yeoman First Class Edwin Dana; Chief Pharmacist's Mate Richard Roth; and Forrest Bailey, pharmacist's mate first class.

Lieutenant Deckelman, gunnery officer and first lieutenant; Chief Boatswain's Mate Ken Arledge; Joseph Embrogno, boatswain's mate first class; Gunner's Mates First Class Donald Taylor, George Smith, and Raymond Roberts; Gunner's Mates Second Class George Kaiser, Willis Clinkinbeard, Charles De Witt, Don Ray, and John Rice.

Ensign Leonard, communications officer; Chief Radioman Max Storer; Radioman First Class Kenneth Buck; and Signalman First Class Horace Raines.

Lieutenant Beckett, engineering officer and damage control officer; Machinist Mates First Class Edward Poppas and Carl Blum; Chief Watertender Walter Golden; Boilermaker First Class Anthony Quatrara; Chief Shipfitters Joseph Sparrow and Elbert Johnson; Chief Electrician's Mates Anthony Michelswirth and Henry Goebel; Chief Metalsmith Herbert McCall; Chief Carpenter's Mate Manuel Paredes; Clarence Smith, carpenter's mate first class; and Armand Ouellette, carpenter's mate second class.

Lieutenant, junior grade, Ed Joyce, supply officer; Chief Storekeeper Peter Gayde; Lawrence Galusha, storekeeper first class; Chester Maple, storekeeper second class; Chief Commissary Steward Frank Cahalan; and Ship's Cook Joe Woodside.

Appendix 3:
Ship's Roster (Enlisted Men),
USS *Asterion*/SS *Evelyn*

(Names alphabetically arranged without regard to ratings)

Andrew, Caric A.	Ballinger, Marion W.	Bandlow, John H.
Barton, Percy	Becker, Robert L.	Bertner, Morris
Blackburn, Robert L.	Blasco, Vincent G.	Bowan, Harry
Bowling, Earl J.	Bradds, George R.	Brown, Mercury L.
Bunting, Jack M.	Campbell, Colin	Carroll, William T.
Casey, Roy A.	Champion, Leland C.	Chapel, Vernon C.
Chapman, Robert G.	Chapman, William	Churchill, Edw. F., Jr.
Ciucevich, Gilbert T.	Clark, Ralph H.	Clark, William L.
Clarke, Charles A.	Clifton, Frank W.	Collins, William A.
Cook, Lionel M.	Cowie, Adam Edw.	Custer, Lewis T.
Dabbs, Leland W.	Darling, Charles G.	Dimes, Frank
Downs, Stephen C.	Drew, John F., Jr.	Duffy, Thomas Edw.
Dunn, Raymond Don.	Earl, Julius R.	Eaton, William B.
Edson, Felipe O.	Evans, Clarence C.	Faber, Adam W.
Fenner, William E., Jr.	Fignar, Andrew	Flanagan, Lawrence A.
Flynn, James Edward	Frazia, Anthony	Gaffney, Joseph A.
Gaylord, Burner D.	Glowacki, Edward J.	Graham, Robert E.
Grennon, Joseph C.	Griffin, Charles A.	Heath, Earnest C.
Henigsman, William F.	Herren, Charlie S.	Hine, Maurice F.
Holloway, Malcolm	Hubbard, King B.	Jacks, Rudolph W., Jr.
Jansen, Matthias H.	Jenkins, Patrick A.	Jones, Franklin P., Jr.
Journey, Elmer N.	Kaiser, Joseph G.	Kalscheuer, Raymond B.
Klingensmith, Robt. T.	Lamb, Harry M.	Latour, Leslie S.
Law, Willard T. R.	Lehman, Ernest F.	Lenzo, Joseph M.
Lundgren, Oscar A.	Maguire, Francis H.	Mallane, Philip J.
McBride, Whitley	Metz, Roger C.	Meyer, Charles J.
Mieduch, Stanley A.	Miller, Reuel J.	Mirts, Marshall W.

Morgan, Harry G.
Mulvaney, William F.
Muscher, Arthur R.
Pearson, James H.
Peterson, Russell H.
Prothero, Harold B.
Rethmeier, Frederick
Ross, Robert C.
Seymour, George L.
Snyder, Paul W.
Spies, Henry S.
Swanson, Harry E.
Toce, Richard E.
Turja, Richard H.
Verret, Roy R.
Walters, George L.
Worthley, Alger G.

Morgan, Henry Edw.
Murphy, Everard G.
Nitkiewicz, Fred A.
Peterson, Raymond S.
Plaushak, John
Ragan, Edward
Richardson, Ben T.
Sampson, William R.
Siembieda, Theodore
Snyder, Samuel R., Jr.
Stansbury, Ulis W.
Temple, Marting C.
Towse, Avery W.
Valant, Joseph, Jr.
Walker, Robert B.
White, Robert M.
Young, Perry A.

Moseley, Ralph
Murphy, William
Ostrem, Robert S.
Peterson, Robert E.
Pridemore, William H.
Reeves, Forest R.
Riggs, Russell R.
Sanguin, Clyde E.
Smith, Charles J., Jr.
Sonak, Harry A.
Steffey, Melvin D. G.
Titsworth, Charles L.
Traughber, Charles W.
Vanhorn, John B., Jr.
Wallace, Thomas F., Jr.
Wise, James H.
Youst, Paul, Jr.

New and Replacement Crew Members as of 4 September 1943

Althouse, Robert V.
Barnes, James E.
Black, Malcolm M.
Bradley, Francis T.
Brown, Charles
Carr, Francis P.
Cristy, Alfred
De Mario, Anthony J.
Driscoll, Ralph L.
Greiser, C. B., Jr.
Hampovchan, John J.
Julien, Donald S.
Kestner, Frederick A.
McDole, John W.
Meyer, Carl W.
Myers, Franklin A.
Peterson, W. M., Jr.
Puig, Catlos
Rocco, Biagio

Applegate, Richard
Bauer, Gregory H.
Boruszewski, Frank E.
Bradley, Thomas K.
Buss, Maynard L.
Chapman, William
Davis, Byford D.
Dinsmoor, Lewis M.
Edman, Alexander E.
Gunn, Louis C.
Healey, William A.
Kaley, John F.
Kilijanski, Chester
Medefindt, Robert
Montgomery, Wilford I.
Newhouse, Howard "D"
Philbrick, Charles W.
Rambler, Joseph
Shepardson, D. W.

Ayala, Nery
Bernd, John D.
Bourdelaise, Robt. E.
Brady, Francis C.
Buss, Wilmer H.
Ciancio, Joseph M.
De Goff, John E.
Dixon, Charles "W"
Friedman, Melvin J.
Hall, Britton F.
Jenkins, John H. G.
Karasinski, Theo. A.
Lynch, V. J. A., Jr.
Metz, Donald W.
Mosher, Bertram F.
Perlman, Louis
Pogorzala, Harold A.
Resker, John R.
Shipp, Bernard

Appendix 3

Slater, James W. Smith, Sidney S. Snedeker, Raymond H.
Sprout, Richard B. Sutton, Arthur Thomas, John J.
Thompson, Philip J. Traughber, Charles W. Turk, Jerry V.
Ubaldi, Eugene T. Vanschoick, Raymond Walsh, Richard A.
Walton, Harry A. Waryasz, Chester E. Weaver, Bert J.
White, Robert M. Winikoff, Benjamin Wood, Fred O.
Yarbrough, Byron W.

New and Replacement Crew Members as of 20 September 1943

Allen, William O. Buchanan, John A. Cline, Robert L.
Cramer, Edward L. Cucola, Louis S. Czarkowski, Edward C.
Davidson, Thomas E. Dawson, Norman L. Dorn, James W.
Dowling, Francis G. Drabot, Walter J. Driscoll, Francis H.
Edwards, Roy Estes, James H. Kirk, Henry
McDyer, T. J., Jr. Moore, Willis J. Pimpinella, John J.
Starcher, Damon G.

Appendix 4:
Precommissioning Detail (Officers and Key Petty Officers), USS *Asterion* (AK100)

Chief Boatswain's Mate Charles Darling; Boatswain's Mate First Class Elmer Journey; Chief Gunner's Mates Maurice Hine and Oscar Lundgren; Gunner's Mates First Class Colin Campbell, Harry Lamb, and Clyde Sanguin; Gunner's Mate Second Class Marshall Mirts; Gunner's Mates Third Class Frank Dimes and Ernest Lehman; Chief Quartermaster Lionel Cook; Quartermaster Second Class Roger Metz; Chief Signalman Stephen Downs; Chief Electrician's Mate Earl Bowling; Electrician's Mate First Class Ralph Clark; Chief Radioman Richard Turja; Radioman First Class Leland Champion; Chief Carpenter's Mate Percy Barton; Carpenter's Mate First Class John Plaushak; Shipfitter First Class Lawrence Flanagan; Shipfitter Third Class King Hubbard; Machinist's Mates First Class Matthias Jansen and John Drew; Watertender First Class Henry Morgan; Boilermaker First Class William Chapman; Chief Metalsmith Julius Earl; Chief Yeoman Charles Clarke; Yeoman First Class Carric Andrew; Chief Storekeeper Joseph Kaiser; Storekeeper First Class Joe Grennon; Storekeepers Second Class Jack Bunting and William Murphy; Chief Pharmacist's Mate Andrew Fignar; Pharmacist's Mate First Class Reuel Miller; Chief Commissary Steward Edward Ragan; Ship's Cook First Class Willard Law.

Notes

Chapter 1. Looking toward the Unknown

1. Kimball, *Churchill and Roosevelt*, R-119, 16 March 1942, 1:406.

2. This and the paragraphs that follow are based on the author's participation in the events described.

3. Chief of the Bureau of Navigation to Ensign Kenneth M. Beyer, SC-M, USNR, USS *North Carolina*, via Commanding Officer, orders 19666, 2 February 1942, "Change of duty"; original in author's possession.

4. Naval Historical Center, Operational Archives, Navy Department, Washington, D.C., hereafter cited as NHC-OA, Miscellaneous File, Chief of Naval Operations to various addressees, Op-23N-1/31/42, Serial 018023, 31 January 1942, SS *Evelyn* and SS *Carolyn*—preliminary conversion to AK.

Chapter 2. America's Awakening: Project LQ

1. Dyer, *On the Treadmill to Pearl Harbor*, 373. McCrea had been executive officer of USS *Pennsylvania* (BB38), flagship, U.S. Fleet, to Charles Edson, secretary of the navy. Both Vice Adm. Adolphus Andrews, Commanding Scouting Force, U.S. Fleet, and Rear Adm. E. J. King, General Board, Navy Department, were in attendance. McCrea later was promoted to captain and flag rank. As captain, McCrea commanded USS *Iowa*.

Sherwood, *Roosevelt and Hopkins*, 767. Sherwood writes of Roosevelt's concern and Churchill's anxiety with the U-boat attacks, and states that Roosevelt cabled the prime minister on 6 February that the matter was being given urgent consideration by Stark, King, and him. Sherwood also relates that in November 1943, Roosevelt embarked in USS *Iowa* for transport to Oran, Algeria. The commanding officer of *Iowa* was Captain McCrea, Roosevelt's good friend and former naval aide.

2. Sherwood, *Roosevelt and Hopkins*, 365.

3. Ibid., 498–99.

4. Howarth, *Men of War*, 77; chapter on Admiral King contributed by Robert W. Love Jr; Kimball, *Churchill and Roosevelt*, 1:397.

5. Rohwer and Hummelchen, *Chronology of the War at Sea*, 113.

6. Howarth, *Men of War*, 82–83, 158–60.

7. Morison, *Battle of the Atlantic*, 281–82; Farago, *The Tenth Fleet*, 85. Farago states 19 January 1942 as the date of the meeting between Roosevelt and King at which the subject of Q-ships was discussed. He gives no specific attribution.

8. Van Der Vat, *Stealth at Sea*, 212–14.

9. Terraine, *U-Boat Wars*, 325.

10. Lewin, *Ultra Goes to War*, 119.

11. Roskill, *The Secret Capture*.

12. Terraine, *U-Boat Wars*, 318–27.

13. Van Der Vat, *Stealth at Sea*, 214.

14. Terraine, *U-Boat Wars*, 424–25, 456–59.

15. Rear Adm. W. W. Honaker, USN, conversation with the author, San Diego, California, October 1955. This terse discourse by Admiral King was repeated by Admiral Spear to Lt. Cdr. W. W. Honaker (later rear admiral), one of the action officers in the Bureau of Supplies and Accounts.

16. NHC-OA, Q-Ship File: Personal and privileged letter from Rear Adm. T. J. Ryan Jr., USN, Retired, to Vice Adm. W. S. Farber, USN, Navy Department, Washington, D.C., 12 February 1946 (declassified).

Chapter 3. Operation Drumbeat

1. Dönitz, *Memoirs*, 198, 202.

2. Ibid., 195–98.

3. National Archives and Records Administration, National Archives, Washington, D.C., hereafter cited as NARA, "German Navy/U-Boat Messages, Translations and Summaries," RC457, Box No. 7 (NSA) SRGN 5514-6196, 9 January 1942; NHC-OA, U-Boat File, "Headquarters U-Boats War Diary (KTB-BdU)," 9 January 1942.

4. Reche, *Die "Quadratur der Meere,"* 120–22.

5. Rohwer, *Axis Submarine Successes*, 73, 74.

6. Van Der Vat, *Stealth at Sea*, 158–73, 202; Hadley, *Count Not the Dead*, 80–82.

7. Rohwer, *Axis Submarine Successes*, 74. Rohwer identified the target as SS *San Jose*. The 4,000-ton freighter claimed by Hardegen has never been identified. The U.S. Coast Guard's "Ships' Casualty File, *San Jose*," states that the vessel was sunk as a result of a collision with SS *Santa Elisa*.

8. NARA, "German Navy/U-Boat Messages," 17 January 1942.

9. Dönitz, *Memoirs*, 203, 207.

10. Ibid., 203, 204.

11. NHC-OA, Q-Ship Miscellaneous File, Adm. H. R. Stark Memorandum to various addressees, file Op-23E-RSM, 23 January 1942.

12. NHC-OA, Bureau of Naval Personnel, Enlisted Detail Office, Letter to the Chief of Naval Personnel, Subject: Anti-Submarine Vessels—Information Regarding, 22 June 1942.

13. NHC-OA, Memorandum of Agreement between the Navy Department and the Office of the Maritime Commission regarding loan of steamers *Evelyn* and *Carolyn*; U.S. Department of the Navy, *Dictionary of American Naval Fighting Ships*, 1:435, 446–47.

14. Personnel Allowance of USS *Atik* (AK101) and USS *Asterion* (AK100), Form N. Nav. 331-A, approved 31 January 1942; copy in possession of the author.

15. NHC-OA, Q-Ship File, COMINCH message to Commander Eastern Sea Frontier, date-time group 201345JAN42.

16. U.S. Department of the Navy, *Dictionary of American Naval Fighting Ships*, 2:33.

17. F. J. Lawton, to the director, Bureau of the Budget, Washington, D.C., intraoffice memorandum, 17 February 1942; copy in possession of the author.

18. The details as described are based on a conversation between Rear Adm. W. W. Honaker, SC, USN, and the author, November 1955; NHC-OA, Q-Ship File, letter from Admiral Stark to Mr. Robert V. Fleming, 19 February 1942, Washington, D.C.; U.S. Government Public Voucher, 19 February 1942, transfers $500,000 from the Emergency Fund of the President to the U.S. Navy Department; copy in possession of the author.

19. NHC-OA, biographical file of U.S. Naval Officers.

20. The meetings between Ryan, Legwen, and Hicks have been reconstructed based on Legwen's recollection of the details as expressed to the author during a visit with the captain in 1951 in Norfolk, Virginia, and from conversations the author had with Legwen and Hicks during the period of ships' conversions, February and March 1942, at Portsmouth, N.H.

21. From conversations the author had with Legwen and Hicks during the period of ships' conversions, February and March 1942, at Portsmouth, N.H.

22. NHC-OA, Eastern Sea Frontier File, Commander North Atlantic Naval Coastal Frontier, Headquarters, Commander Eastern Sea Frontier to Commander in Chief, United States Fleet, "Queen Ships," 29 January 1942.

23. NARA, SRMN-038, "Functions of the Secret Room (F-21) of COMINCH Combat Intelligence, Atlantic Section Anti-Submarine Warfare, WWII

[undated]," Naval (Admiralty) message date-time group 121716, 12 January 1942 to COMINCH.

24. NHC-OA, Officer Personnel File, Glenn Walker Legwen Jr. and Harry Linwood Hicks.

Chapter 4. Carolyn and *Evelyn:* The Ships and the Men

1. Chief of the Bureau of Navigation to Ensign Kenneth M. Beyer, SC-M, USNR, Bureau of Supplies and Accounts, Washington, D.C., orders 20486, 7 February 1942, "Change of duty"; original in possession of the author.

The major portion of the narrative in this chapter is based on the author's recollection of activities, discussions, and associations. Memories were stimulated by visits to the shipyard during the preparation of the manuscript.

2. NHC-OA, Q-Ship File, Vice Chief of Naval Operations, Op-10 Hu, Washington, D.C., to Commander Eastern Sea Frontier, USS *Asterion* (AK100), USS *Atik* (AK101), and USS *Eagle* (AM132), 30 March 1942, Enclosure (A), Characteristics of three subject ships.

3. U.S. Department of the Navy, *Dictionary of American Naval Fighting Ships*, 6:233. The loss of *Squalus* is described briefly in the history of *Sailfish* (SS192).

4. Lt. Ed Joyce and the author met frequently to discuss both official subjects and personal matters. Most of the author's impressions of *Atik's* officers were gained from firsthand associations and comments offered by Joyce. The contrast between the leadership styles of Neville and Duffy was a topic of private discussions. Later during this period, opinions and subjective evaluations of Hicks, Legwen, Schwaner, and Deckelman were exchanged. In every case it was concluded that Ryan and McColl had made excellent selections.

5. The quotation is from U.S. Naval Academy, *Lucky Bag*, (Rochester, N.Y.: DuBois Press, 1929), 167.

6. U.S. Department of the Navy, *Dictionary of American Naval Fighting Ships*, 6:233.

7. NHC-OA, Q-Ship File, Commandant Navy Yard, Portsmouth, N.H., to OPNAV (Rear Adm. W. S. Farber, USN), MAILGRAM 061310, 6 March 1942, "Commissioning vessels."

8. NHC-OA, Q-Ship File, VCNO to Eastern Sea Frontier, Letter, 30 March 1942, USS *Asterion*, USS *Atik*, and USS *Eagle*.

Chapter 5. Getting Under Way

1. NHC-OA, Eastern Sea Frontier War Diary, chap. 2, "Queen Ships," October 1943, 6. A summary of the operations order is contained in this document.

2. Ibid.

3. NHC-OA, BdU [Headquarters, U-boats] War Log, translation of PG/30305a, 1–15 March 1942, 122; Rohwer, *Axis Submarine Successes*, 82.

4. NHC-OA, BdU War Log, translation of PG/30305a, 1–15 March 1942, 123.

5. Legwen assembled his officers periodically, usually in the evening, to discuss tactics. These sessions were used to train and evaluate his watch officers. The events described in this chapter, for the most part, are based on the author's involvement. Specific attribution is stated where applicable. NHC-OA, Eastern Sea Frontier War Diary, "Queen Ships," 6.

6. All accounting records, including vender invoices and canceled checks (Riggs National Bank) for the Q-ships are, at this writing, in the possession of the author. These documents would have been destroyed by a navy security officer had the author not been contacted to identify the contents, which were marked Secret. All documents were declassified. At an appropriate time, these original papers will be donated to the proper archive or museum.

7. Dolores M. Ouellette, letter to the author, 14 January 1991.

8. Delston, *Of Love Remembered*. The widow of Lt. Daniel Deckelman expressed her grief and near desperation in this novel. The narrative presented regarding Mrs. Deckelman, who later remarried, is based on that book and several conversations with Deckelman's son, a physician living in New York.

9. Anthony, *Down to the Sea in Ships*, 358.

10. NHC-OA, Eastern Sea Frontier War Diary, "Queen Ships," 8.

Chapter 6. Advancing toward Destiny

1. NARA, "U-123 War Diary—Kriegstagebuch (KTB)," 1 March 1942. Microfilm T 1022 2973. (Hereafter references to U-boat war diaries will state the boat number followed by the abbreviation "KTB." KTB translations from German to English were made by Fred N. Geils and the author.) The standard format for the U-boat KTB required at a minimum a recording every four hours of the boat's position (quadrant) and every noon the wind direction and force, the sea state, cloud cover, visibility, the total nautical miles traveled in the past twenty-four hours, the total miles from base, and the distance traveled each day while submerged. Each daily entry was signed by the U-boat commander.

2. NHC-OA, Eastern Sea Frontier War Diary, "Queen Ships," 8.

The author has reconstructed what he thinks happened on board *Atik/ Carolyn* based on (a) his association and discussions with Hicks and the other officers of *Atik* while in Portsmouth, (b) the Eastern Sea Frontier Operations Plan, (c) his knowledge of the ship's characteristics, (d) the training and readiness procedures followed by *Asterion/Evelyn*, and (e) a reasonable, practicable, and realistic assumption of activities leading to the events of 26–27 March 1942. (See also n. 2, chap. 7.)

3. U.S. Navy Department Ordnance Pamphlet No. 747 (first revision), "Depth Charges: MARK 6, MARK 6 MOD 1, MARK 7, MARK 7 MOD 1. Operating and Maintenance Instructions," reissued 22 December 1943. Depth charge safety setting procedures as stated are consistent with the original ordnance pamphlet.

4. NHC-OA, Q-Ship File, Commanding Officer, USS *Asterion* to Commander Eastern Sea Frontier, "Narrative of first cruise of USS *Asterion* (SS *Evelyn*)," 3 May 1942, hereafter cited as USS *Asterion* first cruise.

5. NHC-OA, Eastern Sea Frontier War Diary, "Queen Ships," 7–8. The second operating plan is summarized in this document.

6. NHC-OA, Q-Ship File, USS *Asterion* first cruise, 24 March 1942.

7. Ibid.

8. Rohwer, *Axis Submarine Successes*, 87.

9. U-123 KTB, 1, 3 March 1942.

10. Ibid., 6 March 1942. The events recounted in the remainder of this chapter, except where noted, are extracted from the U-123 KTB.

11. NARA, microfilm, T1022—Roll 3033–34, U-105 KTB, KK Heinrich Schuch, 24 March 1942.

12. Rohwer, *Axis Submarine Successes*, 85–87.

Chapter 7. The Mystery of the Mystery Ship

1. U-123 KTB, 25–26 March 1942.

2. The author at this point reemphasizes that except for two radio messages transmitted by *Carolyn* no documentation exists of the events aboard that U.S. Q-ship to portray the activities described in this chapter. The author has reconstructed what he thinks could have taken place based on his knowledge of the ship and the personnel involved, his analysis of the documented torpedo attacks, and his earnest attempt to provide a word picture so the reader can envisage a reasonable account of *Carolyn/Atik's* loss. The events described are compatible with data recorded in the patrol diaries (KTBs) of U-123 and U-105. The names

of personnel are actual (see appendix 1), and the assignment of individuals is consistent with their rank and ratings and the ship's organization.

3. U-123 KTB, 27 March 1942; *Bibliothek für Zeitgeschichte* hereafter cited as *BfZ*, U-123 *Schussmeldung* (torpedo shooting report) No. 5556, 27 March 1942, Library of Contemporary History, Stuttgart.

4. NHC-OA, Q-Ship File, SS *Carolyn* radio message, 0055 GMT 27 March 1942.

5. Ibid., SS *Carolyn* radio message, 0055 GMT 27 March 1942.

6. U-105 KTB, 27 March 1942; *BfZ*, U-105 *Schussmeldung* No. 5596, 27 March 1942.

7. Rohwer, *Axis Submarine Successes*, states, "U-105 heard one detonation and observed the target ship with a slight list. Possibly the torpedo hit but did not detonate," 87 n. 28.

8. NHC-OA, Q-Ship File, USS *Asterion* first cruise, 26 March 1942; NHC-OA, Eastern Sea Frontier War Diary, "Queen Ships," 9.

9. *BfZ*, U-123 *Schussmeldung* No. 5556, 0430h (CET), 27 March 1942.

10. NHC-OA, Q-Ship File, USS *Asterion* first cruise, 26 March 1942.

11. Rohwer, *Axis Submarine Successes*, 87.

12. Hardegen, "Auf Gefechtsstationen!" 204.

13. NHC-OA, Q-Ship File, USS *Asterion* first cruise, 29 March 1942.

14. Ibid.

15. Before getting under way, Neville briefed the officers on the U-boat attacks as reported by Farley.

Chapter 8. The Search for the Unknown

1. Rohwer, *Axis Submarine Successes*, 88. Neville was referring to the attack by KL Johannes Oestermann (U-754) on the tugboat *Menominee* and the three barges in tow on 31 March 1942.

2. NHC-OA, Q-Ship File, USS *Asterion* first cruise, 4 April 1942.

3. Ibid.

4. Rohwer, *Axis Submarine Successes*, 87.

5. Dönitz, *Memoirs*, 193.

6. Sherwood, *Roosevelt and Hopkins*, 374, 382–83.

7. Ibid., 370.

8. Ibid., 380–81.

9. Ibid., 437.

10. NHC-OA, BdU War Log, translation of PG/30306a–30308b, 1 April–30 June 1942, 5.

11. NARA, U-552 KTB (KL Erich Topp), microfilm T-1022, roll 2981–82, 1–15 April 1942. Events related to U-552 recounted in the remainder of this chapter, except where noted, are extracted from the U-552 KTB.

12. NHC-OA, Q-Ship File, USS *Asterion* first cruise, 4 April 1942; NHC-OA, BdU War Log, translation of PG/30306a–30308b, 10 April 1942.

13. Rohwer, *Axis Submarine Successes*, 85–86.

14. NHC-OA, Eastern Sea Frontier War Diary, April 1942.

15. U-552 KTB, 7, 10 April 1942; Rohwer, *Axis Submarine Successes*, 89.

16. U-552 KTB, 11 April 1942.

17. Ibid., 11–12 April 1942.

18. Morison, *Battle of the Atlantic*, 154–55.

Chapter 9. Confrontation

1. This incident with the Coast Guard off the mouth of the St. Johns river is as clear in my mind at this writing as it was the day it happened. This was a foolhardy, almost ridiculous thing for Legwen to do. I still cannot offer a reason for this action other than frustration. It did, for a time, lower my esteem for this fine officer. My primary concern was the high probability that the ship would be mistaken for an enemy raider and attacked by aircraft with deadly results. It is interesting to note that there is no mention of this event in the commanding officer's narrative of the first cruise. Eastern Sea Frontier made only a general statement in its war diary, cloaked in the phrases "contact with friendly surface craft . . . awkward situations."

2. NHC-OA, Eastern Sea Frontier War Diary, October 1943, chap. 2, 10–11.

3. NHC-OA, OPNAV File, Office of the Chief of Naval Operations, Memorandum for File, hereafter cited as OPNAV memo for file, 21 April 1942, "Summary of Statements of Survivors, SS *Oklahoma*, American Tanker, Standard Oil Company," A. J. Powers, Ensign, USNR.

4. NHC-OA, OPNAV memo for file, 21 April 1942, "Summary of Statements of Survivors, SS *Esso Baton Rouge*, American Tanker, Standard Oil Company," A. J. Powers, Ensign, USNR.

5. Rohwer, *Axis Submarine Successes*, 151.

6. U-123 KTB, 9 April 1942; NHC-OA, OPNAV memo for file, 25 April 1942, "Summary of Statements of Survivors, SS *Esparta*," A. J. Powers, Ensign, USNR.

7. U-123 KTB, 9 April 1942.

8. Ibid., 10 April 1942.

9. Ibid.

10. NHC-OA, Q-Ship File, USS *Asterion* first cruise, 10 April 1942.

11. During the review of the draft manuscript by a well-informed naval historian, the author was told that this yarn had been around in navy circles for many years. The source is not known. At the time of Neville's recitation, there was no reason to doubt its authenticity. With due apology to its creditable source, the yarn was retained for the enjoyment, hopefully, of the reader.

12. NARA, Log of USS *Dahlgren* (DD187), 9 April 1942.

13. U-123 KTB, 10 April 1942.

14. Ibid.

15. NHC-OA, OPNAV memo for file, 27 April 1942, "Summary of Statements by Survivors, SS *Gulf America*," H. A. Burch, Lieutenant, USNR.

16. Ibid.

17. U-123 KTB, 11 April 1942.

18. Ibid.

19. NHC-OA, Q-Ship File, USS *Asterion* first cruise, 11 April 1942.

20. This narrative is reconstructed from the author's memory. It recounts in substance, if not verbatim, Legwen's statement and the events that took place immediately thereafter. In 1951 the author visited Legwen in Norfolk, Virginia, when he was commanding officer of USS *Calvert* (APA32). While discussion included many topics related to *Asterion*, Legwen's focus was on the missed chance to engage the U-boat off the Florida coast. This conversation brought into focus the events of that day in mid-April 1942. Some of the times of day and locations were taken from the U-123 KTB and the log of USS *Dahlgren*.

21. U-123 KTB, 11 April 1942.

22. Ibid.

23. Ibid.

24. Ibid.

25. NARA, Log of USS *Dahlgren* (DD187), 11 April 1942.

26. NHC-OA, Gulf Sea Frontier File War Diary, 11 April 1942.

27. U-123 KTB, 12 April 1942.

28. It is the understanding of the author, based on conversations with Neville, that Legwen preferred to make a verbal rather than a written report of the U-boat incident to Eastern Sea Frontier. It is not known what report was made. A written account could not be found in files at the Naval Historical Center, nor could the official log of USS *Asterion* (AK100/AK63) be located at the National Archives.

Chapter 10. The Game Is Over

1. U-123 KTB, 11–12 April 1942.

2. Ibid.

3. Ibid., 12 April 1942.

4. NHC-OA, OPNAV memo for file, 29 April 1942, "Summary of Statements of Survivors, SS *Leslie*," H. A. Burch, Lieutenant, USNR.

5. U-123 KTB, 13 April 1942.

6. Ibid.

7. NHC-OA, OPNAV memo for file, 5 May 1942, "Summary of Statements of Survivors, MV *Korsholm*," A. J. Powers, Ensign, USNR.

8. U-123, 13 April 1942.

9. Ibid.

10. Ibid., 14 April 1942.

11. NHC-OA, Q-Ship File, USS *Asterion* first cruise, 14 April 1942.

12. NHC-OA, OPNAV memo for file, 23 April 1942, "Summary of Statements of Survivors, SS *Empire Thrush*," A. J. Powers, Ensign, USNR; Rohwer, *Axis Submarine Successes*, 90.

13. U-123 KTB, 16 April 1942.

14. Ibid., 17 April 1942; NHC-OA, OPNAV memo for file, 29 April 1942, "Summary of Statements of Survivors, SS *Alcoa Guide*," A. J. Powers, Ensign, USNR.

15. U-123 KTB, 23 April 1942.

16. Gannon, *Operation Drumbeat*, 406–7; also conversation with Reinhard Hardegen at Cuxhaven (Altenbruch), Germany, July 1992. Mr. and Mrs. Hardegen were guests of Mrs. Beyer and the author at dinner at the Hotel Deutsches Haus in Altenbruch. Reinhard Hardegen had received from me a written list of questions regarding the attack on *Carolyn/Atik*. Answers to those questions, as well as other subjects, were discussed freely during and after dinner.

17. U-123 KTB, 10 February–2 May 1942, "Besondere Erfahrungen [special experiences]," 36–37.

18. Hadley, *Count Not the Dead*, 97–101, 180–81.

19. Gannon, *Operation Drumbeat*, 406–7; conversation with Reinhard Hardegen.

20. Dönitz, *Memoirs*, 219.

21. Tarrant, *U-Boat Offensive*, 107.

22. United Kingdom Ministry of Defense, *German Naval History*, chap. 4, 1–6, 10–11, 15. This work was written after the war by Frigattenkapitän Günter Hessler at the request of the British admiralty.

23. NHC-OA, OPNAV File, U.S. Fleet, Headquarters of the Commander in Chief, Navy Department, Washington, D.C., Declassified Memorandum (formerly Top Secret), Subject: Résumé of Anti-Submarine Operations against the German U-Boats in World War II (undated).

24. United Kingdom Ministry of Defense, *German Naval History*, 20.

25. Morison, *Battle of the Atlantic*, 126, 128.

26. Farago, *The Tenth Fleet*, 89. According to official navy records, 139 lives were lost when *Atik* was sunk.

Bibliography

Anthony, Irvin. *Down to the Sea in Ships*. Philadelphia: Penn Publishing, 1925.

Beyer, Edward F., and Kenneth M. Beyer, "U.S. Navy Mystery Ships," ed. John W. Klar and C. C. Wright. *Warship International* 28, no. 4 (1991): 322–43.

Blair, Clay. *Hitler's U-Boat War: The Hunters, 1939–1942*. New York: Random House, 1996.

Chatterton, E. Keble. *Q Ships and Their Story*. Annapolis, Md.: Naval Institute Press, 1972.

Delston, Ethel D. *Of Love Remembered*. New York: Delacorte Press, 1972.

Dönitz, Karl. *Memoirs: Ten Years and Twenty Days*. Trans. George Weidenfeld and R. H. Stevens. Annapolis, Md.: Naval Institute Press, 1990.

Dyer, George C. *On the Treadmill to Pearl Harbor: The Memoirs of Admiral James O. Richardson, USN (Retired)*. Washington, D.C.: Naval History Division, Department of the Navy, 1973.

Farago, Ladislas. *The Tenth Fleet*. New York: Ivan Obolensky, 1962.

Friedman, Norman. *U.S. Naval Weapons*. Annapolis, Md.: Naval Institute Press, 1988.

Gannon, Michael. *Operation Drumbeat*. New York: Harper and Row, 1990.

Hadley, Michael L. *Count Not the Dead: The Popular Image of the German Submarine*. Annapolis, Md.: Naval Institute Press, 1945; n.p.: McGill-Queens University Press, 1995.

Hardegen, Reinhard. "Auf Gefechtsstationen!" Leipzig: Boreas-Verlag, 1943.

Howarth, Stephen, ed. *Men of War: Great Naval Leaders of World War II*. New York: St. Martin's Press, 1993.

Kimball, Warren F., ed. *Churchill and Roosevelt: The Complete Correspondence*. 3 vols. Princeton, N.J.: Princeton University Press, 1984.

Lewin, Ronald. *Ultra Goes to War: The First Account of World War II's Greatest Secret*. New York: McGraw-Hill, 1982.

Morison, Samuel Eliot. *The Battle of the Atlantic, 1939–1943*. Vol. 1 of *History of United States Naval Operations in World War II*. Boston: Little, Brown, 1988.

Reche, Reinhard. *Die "Quadratur der Meere"—zur Umrechnung der Marine-Quadratkarte, 1939–1945* (The quadrature of the oceans—for the conversion of the naval quadrants chart, 1939–1945). N.p.: Marine-Rundschau, 1948.

Rohwer, Jürgen. *Axis Submarine Successes, 1939–1945.* Introductory material trans. John A. Broadwin. Annapolis, Md.: Naval Institute Press, 1983.

Rohwer, Jürgen, and Gerhard Hümmelchen. *Chronology of the War at Sea, 1939–1945.* Library of Contemporary History: Stuttgart, 1972; Annapolis, Md.: Naval Institute Press (expanded edition), 1992.

Roscoe, Theodore. *United States Submarine Operations in World War II.* Annapolis, Md.: Naval Institute Press, 1949.

Roskill, Stephen W. *The Secret Capture.* London: Collins, 1959.

Rössler, Eberhard, *The U-Boat: The Evaluation and Technical History of German Submarines.* Trans. Harold Erenberg. Annapolis, Md.: Naval Institute Press, 1981.

Scheina, Robert L. *U.S. Coast Guard Cutters and Craft of World War II.* Annapolis, Md.: Naval Institute Press, 1982.

Sherwood, Robert E. *Roosevelt and Hopkins: An Intimate History.* New York: Harper and Brothers, 1948.

Shirer, William S. *The Rise and Fall of the Third Reich.* New York: Simon and Schuster, 1960.

Syrett, David. *The Defeat of the German U-Boats; The Battle of the Atlantic.* Columbia: University of South Carolina Press, 1994.

Tarrant, V. E. *The U-Boat Offensive, 1914–1945.* Annapolis, Md.: Naval Institute Press, 1989.

Terraine, John. *The U-Boat Wars, 1916–1945.* New York: G. P. Putnam's Sons, 1989.

"U-Boot-Kameradschaft Kiel" (pamphlet). *Das U-Boot-Ehrenmal Möltenort an der Kieler Förde* in 2305 Heikendorf/Möltenort.

United Kingdom Ministry of Defense. *German Naval History: The U-Boat War in the Atlantic, 1939–1945.* London: Her Majesty's Stationery Office, 1989.

U.S. Department of the Navy. *Dictionary of American Naval Fighting Ships.* 8 vols. Ed. James L. Mooney. Washington, D.C.: Naval Historical Center, 1991.

U.S. Strategic Bombing Survey (Pacific). OPNAV P-03-100, Naval Analysis Division. *Interrogations of Japanese Officials.* Vols. 1 and 2. Washington, D.C.: U.S. Government Printing Office, 1946.

Van der Vat, Dan. *The Atlantic Campaign, World War II's Great Struggle at Sea.* New York: Harper and Row, 1988.

——. *Stealth at Sea: The History of the Submarine*. Boston: Houghton Mifflin, 1995.

Vause, Jordan. *U-Boat Ace: The Story of Wolfgang Lüth*. Annapolis, Md.: Naval Institute Press, 1990.

Index

Allied ships, attacks on: *Alcoa Guide*
  (Point Brava), 188–89; *Byron D. Benson*, 118, 121, 128; *David H. Atwater*,
  118, 121; *Empire Thrush*, 187–88;
  Esparta, 145–46, 155; *Esso Baton
  Rouge*, 138–45; *Gulf America*,
  152–58; *Korsholm*, 182–84; *Leslie*,
  181–82; *Narragansett*, 83, 94–95;
  Norness, 16, 20–21; *Oklahoma*,
  138–45; *Svenör*, 94–95, 107–9. *See
  also Atik (Carolyn)*; destroyers,
  attacks on, before U.S. at war
Anderson, Oscar *(Gulf American)*,
  156–58
Andrews, Adolphus, involvement of, in
  Project LQ, 35–36
antisubmarine resources: British, 13–17;
  U.S., 12–13, 35–36, 124–25, 131,
  194–200. *See also* Project LQ;
  Q-ships
armament: on Q-ships, 52–53, 71–72; on
  U-boats, 183–84
Asheville, anecdote about, 150–51
Asterion (Evelyn), 5, 194–95, 200–201;
  Atik's messages intercepted by,
  98–99, 105; BdU's report on, 121;
  officers of, meet, 44–48; repairs to,
  needed, 109–10, 172–77, 180; and
  search for *Atik*, 105–10; training exercises, 73; and U-boat encounters, 75,
  116–18, 128–29, 187–88 *(see also*
  U-123). *See also* Q-ships
Asterion Shipping Company, 28, 194
Atik (Carolyn), 5; attack on, analyzed by
  Legwen, 111–12; —, by Hardegen,
  83–90, 93, 98–104; —, response to,
  aboard ship, 85–90, 93, 96–98,

100–101; —, by Schuch, 85, 92–95,
  102–4; correspondence concerning
  loss of, 112–13, 203–5; departure of,
  from Portsmouth, 67–69; messages
  from, 98–99, 105; officers of, meet,
  47–50; training exercises, 70–73. *See
  also* Q-ships
Atik Shipping Company, 28

Bailey, Forrest, during attack on *Atik*,
  88–89
B-Dienst (radio observation service),
  121–22
BdU (U-boat headquarters), 77; comments from, concerning Q-ships, 61,
  121–22; Hardegen returns to, 189–92
Beckett, Harold James, background on,
  32, 49–50
Beckett, Irene Swann, 66–67, 204
Bell, Robert E., during attack on *Atik*,
  85–86
Beyer, Kenneth M., 149–50; arrival of, at
  Portsmouth Navy Yard, 37–44; assignment accepted by, 5–9; background
  on, 8, 35; during encounter with
  U-123, 160–62, 169–76; as lookout
  for U-boats, 116–18, 159–60, 169–72;
  orders for Project LQ received by,
  1–5; during search for *Atik*, 105–10;
  after the war, 202–3
Big Horn (Q-ship), 203
Bleichrodt, Heinrich (U-109), in Group
  Paukenschlag, 20–23
British admiralty, anti-U-boat strategy of,
  13–17
Brown, Mercury "Fleet-feet," 174,
  192–94

233

Bunting, Sydney, and Coast Guard incident, 136–37

Carolyn. See *Atik (Carolyn)*
Carter, W. J. "Nick," involvement of, in Project LQ, 4–7, 27–28, 35
Cavenagh, R. W. *(Dahlgren)*, 152, 166–68
Clark, A. B., 1–2
Coast Guard, *Asterion*'s encounter with, 134–38
Cook, Lionel M., 110–11, 174, 192–94; after the war, 202

Dahlgren, 152; U-123 attacked by, 162–69
Deckelman, Daniel Bernard: during attack on *Atik*, 85–90, 93, 96–98; background on, 31, 48–49
Deckelman, Ethel Schoenberg, 66–67, 204
Delston, Ethel (Ethel Schoenberg Deckelman), 204
destroyers, attacks on, before U.S. at war, 118–20
Dönitz, Karl, 131, 185, 189–92; Operation Drumbeat directed by, 18–23; strategy of, summarized, 196–200
Duffy, Leonard Vincent: during attack on *Atik*, 85–86; background on, 31, 47–48

Eagle Fishing Company, 28
Eagle (Q-ship), 26, 28, 32
Enigma, 14–17
Evelyn. See *Asterion (Evelyn)*

Farago, Ladislas, quoted, 205–6
Fignar, Andy "Doc," 107–8
Folkers, Ulrich (U-125), in Group Paukenschlag, 20–23
Forrestal, James, 204
Fraatz, Georg-Werner (U-652), attack by, on *Greer*, 119
Funk-Beobachtung-Dienst (B-Dienst), 121–22

Greer, attack on, before U.S. at war, 119
Group Paukenschlag, 20–23

Hamilton, Sir Ian Standish, quoted, 54
Hardegen, Barbara, 200
Hardegen, Reinhard (U-123), 75–76; attacks by, 123–24, 145–48, 181–86, 188–89; —, on *Atik*, 83–90, 93, 98–104; —, on *Empire Steel*, 78–80; —, on *Gulf America*, 152–58; —, on *Muskogee*, 77; compared with Topp, 124–26, 130, 191; in Group Paukenschlag, 20–23; KTB excerpts of, 90–91, 141–43, 146–47, 153–54, 159, 178–79; reaction of, to *Atik*'s counterattack, 90–92, 104–5, 108–9; return of, to BdU, 189–92; after the war, 200. *See also* U-123
Hicks, Harry L., 205; arrival of, at Portsmouth, 50–52; assignment accepted by, 34–36; during attack on *Atik*, 85–89; background on, 30–31
Hitler, Adolf, 23, 131, 189–92, 196–97
Holzer, Rudolf, 76, 80, 91, 104, 205
Honaker, W. W. "Walt," involvement of, in Project LQ, 6–7
Horne, Frederick J., involvement of, in Project LQ, 17–18
Hydra, 14–17

investigations, official, of U-boat attacks, 139–41, 143–45, 154–58, 182, 184

Joyce, Cora May, 66, 204
Joyce, Edgar Thomas: assignment accepted by, 5–7; background on, 35, 50; during attack on *Atik*, 89–90, 93, 101; orders for Project LQ received by, 3–5

Kals, Ernst (U-130), in Group Paukenschlag, 20–23, 200
Kearny, attack on, before U.S. at war, 119
King, E. J., involvement of, in Project LQ, 10–13, 16–18, 25–26, 29
Kipling, Rudyard, *My Boy Jack*, 113
KTB excerpts: Hardegen's, 90–91, 141–43, 146–47, 153–54, 159, 178–79; Schuch's, 92, 95; Topp's, 125–26

Legwen, Glenn Walker, 114–16; arrival of, at Portsmouth, 50–52; assignment accepted by, 33–36; background on,

30–31; and Coast Guard incident, 134–38; during search for *Atik*, 105–10; after the war, 201, 205. *See also Asterion (Evelyn)*; Q-ships, tactics of; U-123

Lemp, Fritz-Julius (U-110), Enigma captured from, 15

Leonard, Edwin Madison, 204–5; background on, 32, 50

log entries, ship's. *See* KTB excerpts; war diary excerpts

Longfellow, Henry Wadsworth, quoted, 68

Lukowich, John R. "Luke": background on, 32, 46; after the war, 202

Mahan, Alfred Thayer, quoted, 42

McCall, Herb, during attack on *Atik*, 97–98

McCrea, John L., involvement of, in Project LQ, 27

Meloney, William M., aboard *Gulf America*, 157–58

Metz, Roger C., 110–11; after the war, 202

Mohr, Johann (U-124), 81, 200

Mützelburg, Rolf (U-203), 188

My Boy Jack (Kipling), 113

Neutrality Act of 1935, 119–20

Neville, Lawrence "Larry" Robert, 114–16, 138–39; *Asheville* anecdote told by, 149–51; background on, 31; Beyer meets, at navy yard, 38–44; and Coast Guard incident, 134–38; during encounter with U-123, 160–62, 169–76; during search for *Atik*, 105–10; after the war, 201

North Carolina, 1–2, 12

Of Love Remembered (Delston), 204

Operation Drumbeat (Paukenschlag), 18–23, 196–200

op-orders, Q-ship. *See* Q-ships, op-orders for

Ouellette, Armand R. "Frenchy," on leave, 65–66

Ouellette, Dolores M., memoir of, 65–66

Paukenschlag (Operation Drumbeat), 18–23, 196–200

Peterson, Sverre, attack on *Gulf America* witnessed by, 157

Piening, Adolf (U-155), submarine decoy reported by, 61

Portsmouth Navy Yard: Beyer arrives at, 37–44; Q-ships commissioned at, 55–57; Q-ships converted at, 26–28, 52–55, 60

Preuss, Joachim (U-568), attack by, on *Kearny*, 119

Project LQ: beginnings of, 10–13, 16–18; described, 4–5; finances of, 5–7, 25–29. *See also Asterion (Evelyn)*; *Atik (Carolyn)*; Q-ships

Q-ships, 203, 205–6; acquisition of, 23–26; armament on, 52–53, 71–72; BdU's comments concerning, 61, 121–22; characteristics of, 33–34, 39–43; commissioning of, 55–57; conversion of, 26–28, 52–55, 60; officers for, selected, 1–5, 29–35 *(see also* names of individual officers); op-orders for, 59–60, 73–74, 111; precommissioning detail, 53–54; predeployment exercises, 61–63; stocking of, 63–65; tactics of, 51, 73, 112, 133–34, 138–39, 169–73, 176–77; —, if captured, 34–35, 74. *See also Asterion (Evelyn)*; *Atik (Carolyn)*; Project LQ

Raeder, Erich, 131, 188–91

Ray, Guy Brown: background on, 32, 46; during encounter with U-123, 172–76; after the war, 201

ready-ammunition stock (U-boats), 183–84

Rehwinkel, Ernst-August (U-578), submarine decoy reported by, 61

Reuben James, attack on, before U.S. at war, 118, 120

Riggs National Bank, 5–6, 27–29

Roosevelt, Franklin D., 10–13, 118–20

Roth, Richard, during attack on *Atik*, 88–89

Ryan, Thomas J.: commanding officers interviewed by, 33–35; Q-ships acquired by, 23–27; role of, in selecting officers, 29–33

Sailfish (Squalus), 52
Schuch, Heinrich (U-105): attacks by, 83, 107–9; —, on Atik, 85, 92–95, 102–4; difficulties of, 77–78, 82–83; KTB excerpts of, 92, 95
Schwaner, Henry Carl "Dutch," Jr.: background on, 31, 44; after the war, 201
Spear, Ray, involvement of, in Project LQ, 5–6
Squalus, 52
submarine decoy ships. See Q-ships
Submarine Tracking Room (England), 13–17

tactics, Q-ship. See Q-ships, tactics of
Tenth Fleet, The (Farago), 205–6
Topp, Erich (U-552): attacks by, 75, 121, 123–24, 126–30; —, on Reuben James, 118, 120; commendation of, 130–31, 200; compared with Hardegen, 124–26, 130, 191; KTB excerpts of, 125–26

U-boat attacks, 60–61, 81, 111–12, 114–18, 137–39; effectiveness of, 20–23, 123–25, 130–31, 185, 194–200; effect of, on Roosevelt's policy, 118–20; investigations of, 139–41, 143–45, 154–58, 182, 184. See also antisubmarine resources; names of individual U-boat commanders
U-boat decoys. See Q-ships
U-boat headquarters. See BdU (U-boat headquarters)
U-Boat Memorial (Germany), 205
U-Boot-Ehrenmal, 205
U-123, 158–60, 200; attack on, by Dahlgren, 162–69; escape of, from Asterion, 176–79; search for, by Asterion, 169–76; sighting of, by Asterion, 160–62. See also Hardegen, Reinhard (U-123)

von Schroeter, Horst, 76, 98–100, 182–84, 192; after the war, 200

Wainwright, John D., Q-ships commissioned by, 55–56
war diary excerpts: German, 61 (see also KTB excerpts); U.S., 69, 75, 138, 166, 168
Washington, 1, 12
Watts, William Parks, 2
Winn, Rodger, U-boat communications monitored by, 13–17

Zapp, Richard (U-66), in Group Paukenschlag, 20–23, 200

About the Author

Captain Kenneth M. Beyer is now retired after two successful careers, one in the U.S. Navy and one in industry. He was commissioned in June 1941 as an ensign in the supply corps, USNR. By the end of World War II, he had served on three ships, including USS *Asterion*, one of the two Q-ships featured in this book. At the end of the war, at age twenty-five, he transferred to the regular Navy in the rank of lieutenant commander. Shore duty followed, including organizing and serving as the officer in charge of the first special weapons supply depot in Norfolk, Virginia. He later held key positions in the Supply and Naval Weapons bureaus; as staff logistics officer, Mobile Logistics Support Force (CTF73), Seventh Fleet; and as commanding officer, Navy Electronics Supply Office. His final duty before retiring in 1968 was at the Defense Logistics Agency and on special assignment to the Office of Assistant Secretary of Defense, Installations and Logistics.

Civilian life began with Ingalls Shipbuilding Division, Litton Systems, in Pascagoula, Mississippi, and Los Angeles, California, as the director of integrated logistics systems, and later in Washington as Ingalls's director of liaison for the AEGIS cruiser and *Arleigh Burke* class destroyer programs. After he retired from Ingalls in 1985, he served for three years as the operations center executive for Halifax Engineering, Inc., in Alexandria, Virginia.

Captain Beyer is a graduate of Oregon State University (B.S.), the Harvard University Graduate School of Business Administration (M.B.A.), and the Industrial College of the Armed Forces. He and his wife, Barbara, live in Spotsylvania County, Virginia.